וירא שם כי בא ה שמ

וישם מראשתיו ויש

יהוה סלם מצב ארצ

והנה מלאכי אלהים

יהוה נצב עליו ויאמ

אליך ואלהי יצחק יהלך ה

עליה לך אתננה ולזר

הארץ ופרצת ימה וקד

ונברכו בך כל משפח

950

FOR THE LORD THY GOD BRINGETH THEE
INTO A GOOD LAND, A LAND OF BROOKS OF
WATER, OF FOUNTAINS AND DEPTHS THAT
SPRING OUT OF VALLEYS AND HILLS. (Deut. 8;7)

THIS BOOK IS DEDICATED TO THE LATE **ITZHAK BEN ZVI**, SECOND PRESIDENT OF THE STATE OF ISRAEL, WHO EMBRACED THE PRESENT WITH THE JEWISH SPIRITUAL HERITAGE, AND IN HIS ENDEAVORS TO FULFILL THE PROMISE OF THE PAST, SOUGHT FREEDOM, TRUTH AND KNOWLEDGE; THUS EMBODYING IN HIS PERSON THE RECENT CHAPTERS OF JEWISH HISTORY, HE HAS ENDOWED HIS SPIRITUAL GUIDANCE TO THIS WORK.

THE ILLUSTRATED

CHAIRMEN OF THE EDITORIAL BOARD

BENJAMIN MAZAR
MOSHE DAVIS

HISTORY OF THE

JEWS

FOREWORD

This book aims to give a concise description of Jewish history from its beginning to the present times, as told against the background of general history. The chapters, each devoted to a specific historical period, are arranged chronologically and are accompanied by authentic illustrations representing the various aspects of the life and culture of the nation.

Jewish history is essentially a strange phenomenon, covering a long period of time and extending over the four corners of the earth. It is unparalleled in the history of mankind.

For thousands of years its development did not follow a straight line of internal growth backed by secure tradition. Instead, it was shaped by specific conditions caused by stress and creating change, leaving a sharp imprint on the fate and character of the country and its various groups.

It passed through many stages of formation and crystallization, crises, dispersion and renewed consolidation, and changed its structure through complicated political, social, economic and spiritual processes.

The birth of the nation is shrouded in the mists of the Ancient East—the cradle of human civilization—and its adolescence and maturity in the heart of the Middle East, in Palestine which lies between the Mediterranean and the Arabian Desert on the borders of Egypt. Firm bonds were established with this small region on both sides of the Jordan. It was here that its fate was decided for nearly two thousand years, beginning at the time when Israelite tribes entered this area as an independent national entity. It was here that its remarkable vitality in the development of its political and social life and its creative spirit was revealed and given its most lofty and ancient expression in the Bible; that is, until the spread of Islam when Palestine ceased to be the political, demographical and spiritual land of the Jews.

The Jewish diaspora first appeared with the Judean exiles in Babylon and Egypt during Biblical times. It was during the Hellenistic and Roman periods that it became established and developed into important centers of Judaism along with that in Palestine. The Jewish diaspora covered an increasing periphery.

The continuation of the historical development constitutes the chronicles of Judaism according to its various branches in the lands of Islam and Christianity. It is the history of a nation without its own territory and its own state. Its centers in western Asia, North Africa and Europe underwent periods of adaptation, integration, suppression and uprooting. Political and cultural conditions, as the years passed, particularly in America, made possible renewed growth and the gain of new territories. Meanwhile, there was a transformation within Judaism and in its attitude toward the nations whose protection it sought. The vital force of the nation that held itself together in its dispersion expressed itself primarily in its constant struggle for a continued existence and preservation of its ancient heritage, as well as for its national and spiritual distinction and its eternal hope for the restoration of the nation's glory—a hope only realized in our time with the renascence of Jewish statehood in its historical land.

The historical concept given does not always reflect the general view held by many historians. Their analyses and conclusions about the contributing factors to the growth of Judaism are often divided and frequently opposed. The basic assumptions in the presentation of evidence and the sources and their fusion into a total picture reflecting a historical pattern often differ. Varying positions are taken on the cultural development, the determination of character of the Jewish nation and its subgroups, and its position in different countries during different periods. In a number of ways, however, the majority of scholars and various schools of historical thought arrived at a general consensus. They follow the general tendency to fuse political, social and economic aspects with the spiritual and religious tempos of the times. They follow the principle of not distinguishing between Jews and Judaism, just as one must not separate Jewish history in Palestine from that in the diaspora, and now consider Jewish history in its entirety related to the history of the world.

It becomes increasingly evident that the historian is obliged to consult the rich and varied literary sources handed down from past generations realizing their influence on the Jewish people and their culture. A multitude of discoveries are continuously unfolded and light is shed on the life of the nation. At the same time, the advance in the methods of historical, philological and archeological research open up new vistas in many areas. In our own time there is an inexhaustible supply of archeological and epigraphical evidence available. The findings in Palestine and its neighboring countries brings forth a wealth of data and revelations that demands a fresh consideration of already completed chapters in the cultural history of the Jewish people in the Biblical and post-Biblical periods.

On the other hand, the discovery and study of archives, forgotten literature and other sources that are uncovered are likely to illuminate what is already known about Jewish spiritual and material life in the different diasporas, in addition to finding completely new information. These developments demand a constant revision of Jewish historiography in order to arrive at a new synthesis of its evolution built on well established methods of research drawn from all sources available.

The comprehensive and concise historical survey presented here is the combined effort of a group of Israeli historians, the majority from the department of Jewish History at the Hebrew University in Jerusalem. Each has contributed one or more chapters and has used his own method to describe the historical process and those social and spiritual aspects he considered fundamental. Instead of one homogeneous and organic historical study, we have presented the reader with a collection expressing the modern historical approach by scholars steeped in Hebrew culture who enjoy the inspiration of living in the ancient, newly revived Jewish homeland. The illustrations accompanying the text serve as a living commentary to the history of the nation and its culture in its many vicissitudes and its contact with different civilizations.

B. Mazar

ACKNOWLEDGMENTS: The publication of a book of such vast scope demands, as a matter of course, the advice and assistance of numerous institutions, scholars and private individuals throughout the world. We are deeply grateful to the late President of Israel, Itzhak Ben Zvi, who not only gave graciously of his time and wisdom, but who also served as a fountain of inspiration in our work. We are also indebted to many individuals for their help. Among them are Dr. H. Lee, Miami; Mr. J. Makavy, Ramat-Gan; Mr. E. Pikovsky, Jerusalem; Mr. L. Robinson, Miami; and Mr. J. Vergara, Mr. Abraham Goodman and Mr. David Rose, all of New York.

Apart from the editors, members of the editorial board, the editorial advisory council, and the many assistants, we wish to express our sincere appreciation to those Israeli scholars with whom we consulted and who helped us in obtaining material. They are Dr. N. Aloni, Prof. D. Amiran, Prof. M. Avi-Yonah, Mrs. T. Dothan, Dr. K. Katz, Prof. I. Schattner, and Mrs. M. Tadmor.

Our thanks are also due to all photographers, collectors, archives, museums and individuals in Israel who helped to collect suitable photographs for a book as extensively illustrated as this. The photographers are Mrs. H. Biberkrout, Messrs. Allon, Bernheim, Gilai, Harris, Hirshbein, Merlin-Yaron, Meyrowitz, Oron (Oroshkes), Schlezinger, Soskin, Tal, Weiss, "Photo Alexander", "Photo Prior".

We wish to express our gratification for the use of the private collections of the late President Itzhak Ben Zvi, the late Prof. E. L. Sukenik, and the late J. Pinkerfeld. Those individuals who contributed photographs from their personal collections are Dr. J. Aharoni, Prof. D. Amiran, Prof. N. Avigad, Dr. H. Beinhart, Prof. M. Davis, Dr. A. Kindler, Prof. B. Mazar, Prof. H. Schirmann, Mr. S. J. Schweig, Dr. Z. Vilnai, Prof. Y. Yadin, and Prof. S. Yeivin—all of Israel; Mrs. D. Marcus, New York; Prof. Andre Parrot and M. René Oussaud, Paris.

We also acknowledge with gratitude the valuable contributions made by the many institutions and archives in Israel. They are the Bezalel National Museum, the Department of Antiquities of the Ministry of Education, the General Archives of the World Zionist Organization, the Hebrew University of Jerusalem, the Institute for Contemporary Jewish Studies of the Hebrew University, the Institute of Archeology of the Hebrew University, the International Publishing Company, Ltd., the Israel Exploration Society, the Israel Government Press Bureau, the Israel Government Tourist Corporation, the Israel Historical Society and Jewish Historical Archives, the Israel Army Publishing Division, the Jewish Agency, the Jewish National Fund, the Ma'arachot Publishing Company of the Israel Defense Forces, the National and University Library, the Ner-Tamid Publishing Company, Palphot Ltd., the Photogrametric Institute, the Rabbi Kook Foundation, the Tel Qasile Collection, and the United Israel Appeal.

We would also like to thank the many American and European museums, institutions and archives made available to us. Special acknowledgement is given to the American Jewish Archives, Cincinnati; the American Jewish Society, Cleveland; the Anglo-Jewish Historical Association, London; Augustine, New York; the Bollingen Foundation, New York; the British Museum, London; the Bund Archives, New York; the Cluny Museum, Paris; Congregation Shearith Israel, New York; Contact Collection, Amsterdam; Di Rossi Library, Padua; Europeische Verlagstadt, Frankfurt; Fotografía de Arte Moreno, Madrid; Hamburg Museum; the Institute of Archeology of the University of London; the Jewish Theological Seminary, New York; Marburg Photographic Institute; Municipal Library of Darmstadt; Municipal Library, Munich; Mt. Sinai Hospital, New York; Museo de Arqueología Nacional, Madrid; Museo del Prado, Madrid; Museo Nazionale di Napoli; Museum of Nuremberg; Nelson Publishers, London; Oxford University Press; the Pacific Theological Seminary, Berkeley; Palestine Exploration Fund, London; Photo L. Arrivas, Toledo; Photo Cavallero, Madrid; Princeton University; the Oriental Institute of the University of Chicago; Rijks Institute, Amsterdam; Royal Library, Amsterdam; Schocken Publishers, New York; the Shani Collection, Teheran; University of Tubingen; Welcome Marstone Expedition of the University of London; Wurzburg Museum; and the Yeshiva University, New York.

The Editors

The Editors	PROF. BENJAMIN MAZAR
	PROF. MOSHE DAVIS
	DR. CHAIM H. BEN SASSON
Associate Editor	DR. CHAIM BEINART
Art Editor	ITZHAK EFRONI

Contributing Editors

PROF. SHMUEL YEIVIN *(From Fathers to Saul)*
DR. CHAIM TADMOR *(The House of David)*
DR. JACOB LIVER *(Exile and Return)*
DR. MENACHEM STERN *(Hellenistic and Roman Periods)*
DR. SHMUEL SAFRAI *(Bar Kochba and Crisis in the Old East)*
DR. CHAIM H. BEN SASSON *(The Middle Ages)*
DR. SHMUEL ETINGER *(The Renaissance and Modern Times)*
RABBI JACK COHEN *(The Jews in America)*
RABBI ISRAEL GOLDSTEIN *(Two World Wars)*
COL. NETHANEL LORCH *(The War of Independence)*
DR. SHAUL ESH *(The Holocaust)*
COL. MOSHE PERLMAN *(The Rise of Israel)*
PROF. ROBERTO BACKI *(Jewish World Population)*

Editorial Advisors	PROF. ABRAHAM SCHALITT
	RABBI BENJAMIN Z. KREITMAN
Executive Editor	ORY N. MAZAR
Managing Editor	SHLOMO S. GAFNI
Art Advisor	SHMUEL JOSEPH SCHWEIG

Editorial Assistants: JACOB CHISDAI; MOSHE EILAT; DR. OSKAR SCHMALTZ; ISHAI SCHACHAR. *Research Assistants:* SHLOMO ARONSON; HANAN BAR-ADON; LOTTE DAVIS; ZEVI HELLER; HANOCH RAVIV; YONA SERI; ZEVULUN SERI; EITAN SHANI; SHLOMO SHOSHANI; EFRAIM STERN; EFRAT YEIVIN. *English Version:* MICHAEL M. BERNET; ARIE HAUSLICH; JANE KRONHOLTZ; YEHUDA LEV; NEHEMIA MAYERS; BATIA RABIN; DR. ANSON F. RAINEY; HEDDY RAPOPORT; DR. RUTH REIGBI; EMANUEL SHIMEONI. *Production Manager:* IRVING KLIGFIELD. *Graphic and Production Assistants:* RUTH BAUM; HANNA GAFNI; ARIE HAAS; ROBERT HELLER; ZEHAVA KEREM; ROLF KNEUBUHL; ZEVI STEINER; HELEN ZAROVITZ. *Maps:* CARTA, JERUSALEM. *Staff Photographers:* HANAN BAR-ADON; SHLOMO BERON; WERNER BRAUN; ZEEV DEKEL; ITZHAK EFRONI; MICHAEL MEIR; YEHEZKIEL MAY; CHAIM MINZBERG.

PEKI'IN IN UPPER GALILEE, ONE OF THE VILLAGES IN ISRAEL IN WHICH JEWS HAVE LIVED CONTINUOUSLY THROUGHOUT THE GENERATONS.

TRADITIONS OF HEROISM:
THE STATUE OF MORDECHAI ANILIEWITZ, LEADER OF THE WARSAW REVOLT, RECALLS THE HEROISM OF THE FIGHTERS OF THE WARSAW GHETTO. BEHIND THE STATUE THE RUINED WATER TOWER OF KIBBUTZ YAD MORDECHAI STANDS AS A MEMORIAL TO THE VALOR OF THE DEFENDERS OF THE KIBBUTZ THAT WAS NAMED IN HONOR OF ANILIEWITZ.

TABLE OF CONTENTS

THE ILLUSTRATED HISTORY OF THE JEWS

THE ILLUSTRATED HISTORY OF THE JEWS

FROM FATHERS TO SAUL

A PORTION OF THE GILGAMESH EPIC ON A CLAY
TABLET DATING FROM THE 15TH-13TH CENTURY B.C.,
FOUND NEAR MEGIDDO.

Forty years ago, hardly a historian considered any of the biblical traditions concerning the period preceding King Saul as real historical material. Some thought these traditions were myth, others saw in them the work of post-exilic scribes writing about the nebulous beginnings of tribal Israel. If this attitude has completely changed, it is due to two main factors. First, our improved understanding of the language of the Bible has resulted in the elimination of many rash emendations of the text, made to support untenable fancy theories. Secondly, the unprecedented advance of archeological research has revealed and interpreted entirely new material on the political history, sociology, religion, literature and daily life of the Ancient East. Today the historian treats the early Bible stories, from the Patriarchs to Saul, as serious history. Various types of evidence can be used. First, there are the personal names in the patriarchal story. Of the 36 Hebrew names figuring there, 27 do not recur in later biblical narratives, and most of the others reappear only in post-exilic times, when biblical names became fashionable. Of the former class of names, those that can be recognized as conforming to definite west-Semitic patterns are typical of the period between the 19th and the 17th Centuries B.C.

Secondly, there are various geographic indications. Foremost among these is the main artery of traffic between Canaan and Mesopotamia. This figures prominently both in the campaign of the four Mesopotamian kings in the days of Abraham (Gen. 14) and in Jacob's journeys, especially on his return from Padan-Aram (Gen. 31:22-33:18). Archeological surveys have proved definitely that a main "King's highway", conforming to biblical data, passed through Transjordan during the 3rd and early 2nd millennia, and that the sites along it were destroyed and mostly abandoned sometime in the early 18th Century, probably as a result of an invasion by nomadic tribes from the eastern steppe. Thereafter the highway gradually ceased to be used as a main line of communication.

Thirdly, the manners and customs reflected by the Patriarchal stories are entirely different from, and in many instances actually opposed, to later biblical legislation. They can only be understood in the light of contemporary Mesopotamian and kindred legislation as reflected in collections of laws and legal documents dating back to the 19th-15th Centuries B.C. and (at least in the case of the later ones) embodying much earlier traditions. The archives of Nuzi and the royal archives of Mari on the Middle Euphrates are a particularly valuable source.

And last, there is the story of the campaign undertaken by four Mesopotamian kings under the leadership of an Elamite suzerain into southern Canaan (Gen. 14). Only recently, with the discovery and publication of the royal archives of Mari on the middle Euphrates, could this seemingly enigmatic campaign be placed in proper historical perspective, thus forging an additional and decisive link in the chain on which hangs the chronology of the Age of the Patriarchs. From this archive we learn that sometime during the reign of Yarim-Lim, the last king of Mari (approximately 1711-1696 B.C.) the political situation in Mesopotamia and Northern Syria was summarized by an envoy of that king as

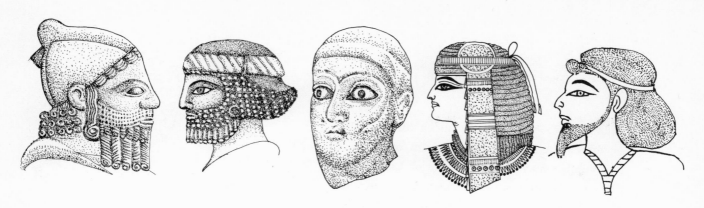

FACIAL FEATURES TYPIFYING SOME OF THE PEOPLES
REPRESENTED IN THE "TABLE OF NATIONS" IN GEN-
ESIS X.

(left to right)
ARAMEAN
ASSYRIAN
ELAMITE
EGYPTIAN
CANAANITE

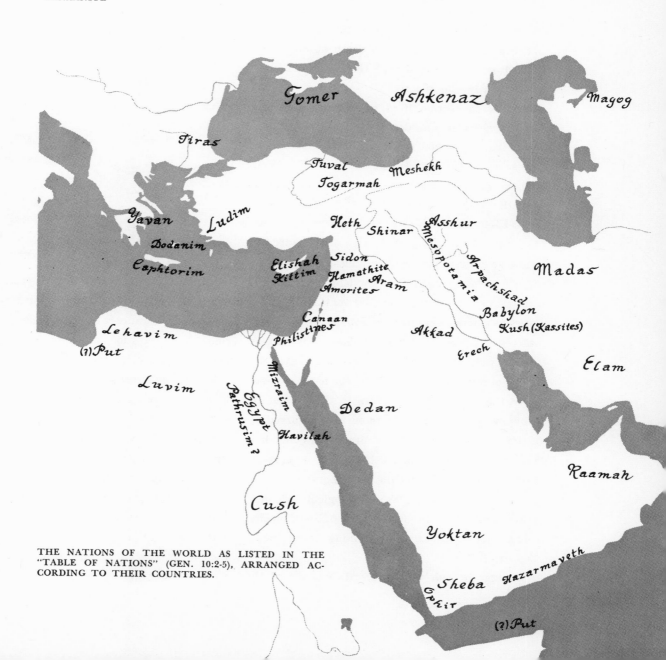

THE NATIONS OF THE WORLD AS LISTED IN THE
"TABLE OF NATIONS" (GEN. 10:2-5), ARRANGED AC-
CORDING TO THEIR COUNTRIES.

follows: "No king is powerful on his own. Ten or fifteen kings follow Hammurabi of Babel, a like number may follow Rim-Sin of Larsa, Ibal-pi-El of Eshnunna, or Amut-pi-El of Katna; twenty kings follow Yarim-Lim of Yamhad (Aleppo)". In such a political constellation it was quite likely that a confederation of Mesopotamian kings would conduct a military raid into Canaan to restore order along the important trade route of Transjordan-Egypt. Though we have no knowledge from extra-biblical sources of such a campaign, it seems highly possible that it occurred between the years 1717 (the death of Shamshi-Adad I of Assyria) and 1695 (Hammurabi's final defeat of Rim-Sin of Larsa).

In this connection it is noteworthy that the biblical narrative in describing this campaign, says: "and (the confederation of Mesopotamian kings) smote the Rephaim in Ashteroth Karnaim, and the Zuzim in Ham, and the Emim in Shaveh Kiriathaim and the Horites in their Mount Seir, unto El-paran which is by the wilderness" (Gen. 14: 5-6; RV slightly different). This wording, while keeping to geographic names, mostly those of cities, clearly states that the defeated foes were ethnic groups designated by national appellations, whose respective locations are fixed by reference to the geographic names. This implies that the cities were less important, and that the above ethnic groups roaming in the neighborhood were the main human factors in the region. In other words, the Mesopotamian raid occurred at a time when the cities were already in ruins, but their memory was still fresh enough to serve as a precise indication within the general region, a fact agreeing with the archeological evidence that attributes the destruction of settlements along this route to the beginning of the 18th Century B.C.

During the rule of the Third Dynasty of Ur

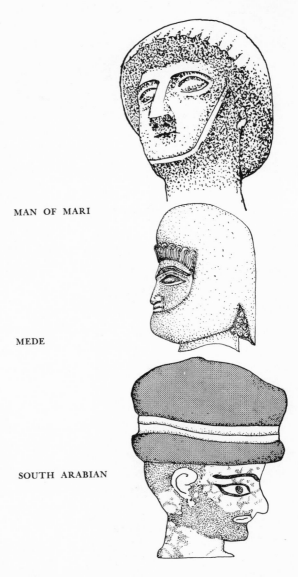

MAN OF MARI

MEDE

SOUTH ARABIAN

we first hear in cuneiform documents of a category of people called Habiru (or Hapiru), who seem to be "strangers and sojourners" in the settlements in question, are apparently outside the pale of the law applying to citizens, and belong as far as one can see to various ethnic groups. Most scholars agree that the same category of people was referred to in Egyptian texts some 600 years later as Apiru, and correspond to the biblical Ibrim (Hebrews), a far larger group than the later Israelites.

While the cuneiform documents show the Habiru from the viewpoint of the civilized and settled population of the Middle East with whom they dealt, the Patriarchal traditions present us with the story of one such group of Habiru as they themselves related it and transmitted to their descendants.

The biblical picture of the Patriarchs of Israel is deeply rooted in history. The three generations of the Patriarchs seem to reflect three stages in the vicissitudes of this clan: the final caravan-eering period of the Terahites (connected with Abraham, about 1950-1700 B.C.), the attempted settlement in the Northern Negev (connected with Isaac, about 1700-1620 B.C.), and the reversion to a mainly pastoral semi-nomadic way of life with the beginnings of intermingling with the native population (connected with Jacob and his direct descendants: Dinah, Judah, Simeon, about 1620-1580 B.C.).

The establishment of the Hyksos-dominated semi-feudal city-states in Syria and Canaan drove the semi-nomadic Israelites into the fringe-lands of the Negev and the south-western border hills of Judah, whence prolonged drought forced them to seek permission to enter Egypt towards the end of the Hyksos period there. At the time, they were allowed to continue their way of life on the borders of the eastern Delta under the patronage of the Hyksos pharaohs of the 16th Dynasty. But with the reassertion of Egyptian nationalism by the 18th dynasty these Israelite "sojourners" were gradually turned into corvée workers, Apiru of almost slave status.

It is not quite clear whether all clans of all tribes descended into Egypt. Certain indications seem to point to the probability that at least some clans, mainly Levites, remained in the region of the oasis of Kadesh-Barnea (the Qudey-

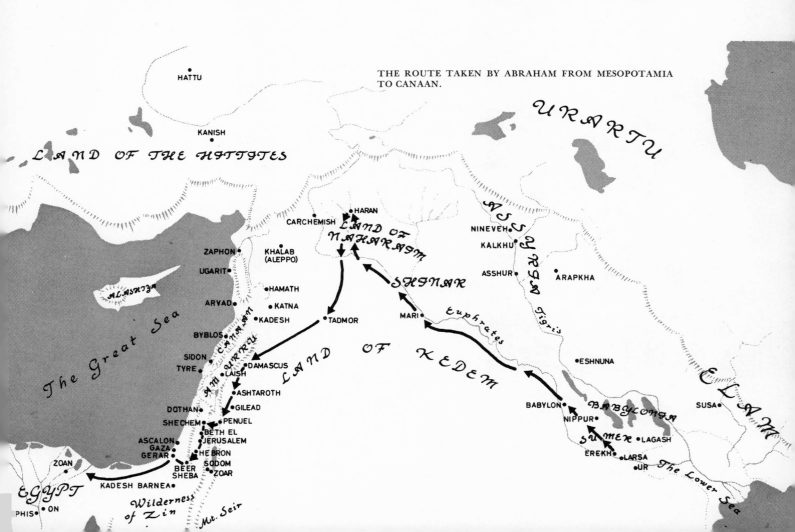

THE ROUTE TAKEN BY ABRAHAM FROM MESOPOTAMIA TO CANAAN.

rat-Quseyme region), keeping up the ancestral worship of El Shaddai, the One God.

It was there, apparently, that the new leader, Moses, arose. Possibly brought to the court of Pharaoh as a hostage in early boyhood, he grew up absorbing the spirit of the high material civilization of Egypt, at its zenith in the New Kingdom under Amenophis III "the magnificent". This pharaoh, one of the great "builders" among the kings of Egypt, is known to have employed large groups of Apiru, forced laborers, in his constructions; he would well suit the role of the "Pharaoh of oppression" of the Bible. Moses, born into the society of semi-independent Egyptian nobility and Canaanite hostages at the pharaonic court, soon clashed with the Egyptian supervisors over the forced labor of his kin, and had to flee from the court. Obviously, he could not return to his tribe, and took refuge with the Midianites wandering in and around the few less accessible oases in the mountainous southern part of Sinai. It was here among the lofty wild peaks of this massif, raising their rugged heads as if to heaven, that Moses received his great inspiration to become the redeemer of his people from Egyptian bondage. As soon as the news of the old Pharaoh's death spread, Moses hastened to Egypt to negotiate with the young Akhenaton, co-regent and successor of Amenophis III, for the release of the Hebrews, on the pretext of religious celebrations that could not take place in Egypt proper (Ex. 5:13, 8:22).

Israelite tradition, viewing the story of the Exodus from the perspective of faith, saw in it the miraculous intervention of Israel's God and made it the cardinal event in the history of Israel. For the Egyptians though, in the tempestuous times of the early reign of Akhenaton after his

STATUE OF GODDESS WITH FLOWING VASE FROM MARI.

PART OF THE ROYAL STANDARD DISCOVERED IN A
TOMB IN UR OF THE CHALDEES, REPUTED BIRTH-
PLACE OF ABRAHAM; DATING FROM THE THIRD MIL-
LENIUM B.C. IT SHOWS A BATTLE SCENE WITH CHARI-
OTS AND SOLDIERS.

SHECHEM, (19TH CENTURY LITHOGRAPHY).

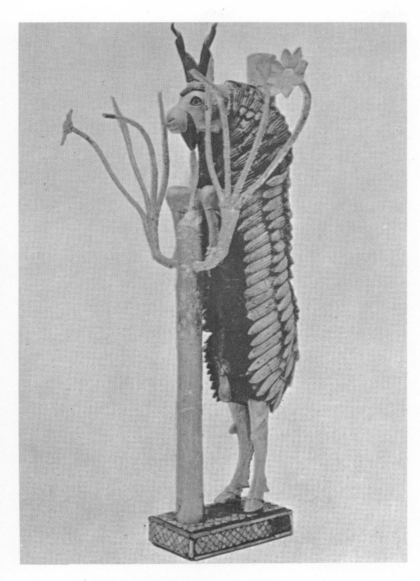

STYLIZED SCULPTURE, BELIEVED TO HAVE SERVED AS A STAND FOR LIBATION VESSELS, FOUND IN A SUMERIAN TOMB AT UR. THE DESIGN RECALLS THE BIBLICAL STORY OF ABRAHAM'S SACRIFICE WHEN "A RAM, CAUGHT IN THE THICKET BY HIS HORNS" WAS OFFERED UP IN THE PLACE OF ISAAC.

SPHINX IN THE LIKENESS OF PHARAOH KHAF-RE.

THE ENTRANCE TO THE CAVE OF MACHPELAH IN
HEBRON, TRADITIONAL BURIAL PLACE OF THE PA-
TRIARCHS.

MOUNT SINAI. THIS PEAK, WHICH IS KNOWN BY THE
ARABS AS JEBEL MUSSA ("MOUNTAIN OF MOSES") IS
GENERALLY ACCEPTED TO BE THE SITE OF THE GIV-
ING OF THE LAW.

THE OASIS OF KADESH BARNEA IN NORTHERN SINAI, WHERE SOME OF THE ISRAELITES MADE THEIR HOME BEFORE ENTERING THE HOLY LAND.

A VESSEL FOUND AT LACHISH, THAT BEARS AN INSCRIPTION IN THE EARLIEST KNOWN FORM OF ALPHABETIC WRITING.

(Top) A VIEW OF THE RIVER JORDAN
(Bottom) MOUNT TABOR, FROM WHICH BARAK LAUNCHED
HIS ATTACK ON THE CANAANITES.

father's death, it may have been of little importance, and it has left no trace in contemporary Egyptian records.

This early dating of the Exodus to about 1360 B.C. seems to hit an insurmountable snag in the biblical record of the forcible employment of the Hebrews in the construction of Pithom and Ramses. For the city of Ramses (Ex. 1:11) at least, certainly could not have been built before the days of Ramses II (1290-1224 B.C.), after whom it was named (Per-Ramses). But these two names must be viewed in conjunction with other Egyptian names occurring in the stories of the Patriarchs and their descendants in Egypt. Of the four Egyptian names figuring in the story of Joseph, Potiphar, Potiphera, Asenath, Zaphnath Paaneah, the former two never occur before the 14th-13th Centuries B.C., and became common only in the 9th Century B.C. and later, while the latter two only appear from the latter date onwards. But in the course of the oral transmission of these traditions the names of the leading personalities were brought up to date from time to time; and the same applies to the "geography" of the bondage. The famous Pithom and Ramses built by forced foreign labor took root in later popular tradition as the site of the Hebrew bondage in Egypt.

THE ZIGGURAT OF UR. IT WAS BUILT BY UR-NAMMU OF THE THIRD UR DYNASTY (2074-1960 B.C.) AND IMPROVED AND REBUILT BY NABU-NAID, THE LAST OF THE CHALDEAN KINGS (550 B.C.).

It was in Sinai that Moses proved himself the master builder of a nation. Inspired by ethical monotheism, the heritage of Abraham, he well understood that the slaves he had led out of Egypt (cf. Ex. 12.38) would have to be thoroughly transformed if they were to become equal to the task he planned for them. He led the Israelites to the southern wilderness of Sinai, partly because he wished to avoid the main caravan routes to Canaan, where Egyptian domination and reprisals may have been feared, for the latter seem to have still maintained some sort of a hold on Canaan in the early days of Akhenaton; and in part, it was probably because he wished the newly liberated clans to experience the exaltation that he had drunk from this awe-inspiring region. He also seems to have realized that his great hope lay in those still young and in future generations, who would be close enough to their forbears' stories of the amenities of civilized life in settled agricultural areas, and yet removed from the spirit-breaking subservience of slave labor in Egypt. Exposure to Egypt and its God-King meant spiritual as much as social oppression. The Exodus was accordingly much more than just a physical undertaking. It was more truly and profoundly an act of liberation from intolerable spiritual bondage. The Ten Commandments given in thunder and lightning on Mount Sinai are mankind's first declaration of spiritual independence, the resolute proclamation of a new and different faith. The rejection of Egypt, like Abraham's migration from Mesopotamia, was basic to all that was to follow. The Bible tells us again and again that it was God who freed the Israelites from the bondage of Egypt for the express purpose of making them His own people. Hence the remembrance of the Egyptian experience becomes a dominant note, echoed through all the portions of the Scriptures, together with the covenant between God and Abraham. Only an indelible spiritual experience could sink so deeply into the national consciousness.

Some decades of wandering among the mountainous massif of southern Sinai, guided by the allied clan of Jethro the Midianite, brought the tribes to the oases of Kadesh-Barnea, where the new generation, now matured, was ready to send out groups of clans into Canaan to conquer and settle.

PHARAOH THUT-MOSE (THOTMES) IV IN BATTLE AGAINST HIS ASIAN FOES. THE ILLUSTRATION IS FROM THE SIDE OF A CHARIOT FOUND IN THE ROYAL TOMB.

Meanwhile, in the Asiatic provinces of Egypt the situation had drastically changed. In the north the Hittites, under the energetic leadership of Shuppiluliuma, emerged from Anatolia and extended their sway over Northern Mesopotamia and Northern and Central Syria. In Canaan proper, too, Egyptian control lapsed almost entirely, and in the resulting anarchy the local princes of many city-states vied with each other to enlarge their diminutive domains at the expense of their immediate neighbors. They relied frequently on the help of roving bands of Habiru, who found opportunity during this period of disorder to infiltrate into the fertile parts of Cisjordania. Among such infiltrating Habiru bands were most probably some mixed Hebrew clans, not of pure Israelite descent, who may have penetrated into the Jezreel valley through the natural gap in the mountainous massif forming the backbone of Cisjordania, at Beth-Shean. These were to become later the tribe of Asher (a son of one of the "maids" and not of a matron-wife of Jacob), for Pharaoh Seti I (1311-1290 B.C. approximately), who already in the first year of his reign reimposed effective Egyptian control in Canaan, mentions Asher in the list of nations and territories conquered by him.

About the same time, part at least of the main body of Israelites concentrated at Kadesh-Barnea in the south made an attempt to penetrate into Western Canaan from the south, but were repelled by the King of Arad (Num. 14: 40-46; 21:1).

This defeat turned the attention of Moses and the Israelites to the possibility of penetrating into Canaan by the devious route through Transjordan. Biblical traditions become seemingly contradictory at this point. The main body of tradition is very clear: it explicitly states that the Israelites turned eastward, asked for permission to pass through Edom and Moab, were refused it, travelled round these countries, forced a way through the Amorite Kingdom of Sihon, conquering both it and the neighboring kingdoms of Jazer and Bashan and descended into "the plains of Moab on this side of the Jordan" (Num. 21:4-22:1), where Moses divided Transjordan between two and a half tribes, at their request (Num. 32). When Moses died there (Deut. 34), Joshua led the tribes across the Jordan, near Jericho, conquered western Canaan in several campaigns, and divided it between the remaining nine and a half tribes (Josh. 1-19).

At the same time, other traditions interspersed in the Bible seem to contradict this uniform picture. To begin with, we have in the Book of Numbers (33:41-49) a different version of the route that the Israelites took from Kadesh Barnea through Transjordan. According to this, the Israelites crossed the Arabah and passed unmolested through the heart of Edomite, Moabite and Sihonite territories into the plains of Moab. Moreover, this version says nothing of either a request for permission to travel through the above-mentioned territories, or of a military clash with Sihon, let alone the existence of an Amorite kingdom in the region.

Then again, the first, introductory chapter of the Book of Judges describes the conquest of

Canaan in a different light. According to this source, groups of tribes fought for their territories. Thus, Judah and Simeon crossed the Jordan opposite Bezek (northeast of Shechem), took Bezek and Jerusalem, and spread southwards into Mount Judah. The Josephites settled in Mount Ephraim after the conquest of Beth-El. Archeological evidence shows that Canaanite Beth-El was destroyed by conquest about the beginning of the second quarter of the 13th Century B.C. in the early years of Pharaoh Ramses II (1290-1274 B.C.).

This source says nothing of the allotment of tribal territories, but merely lists such Canaanite strongholds as had not been reduced by the invading Israelites (Judg. 1:31-36), but which

JERICHO, AN IMPORTANT OASIS FROM PRE-BIBLICAL TIMES, AS IT LOOKS TODAY.

probably succumbed only to the hosts of King David.

Other archeological evidence shows that Transjordan south of the Yarmuk River was not resettled till the early 13th Century, while the founding of the Amorite kingdom of Sihon, carved out from erstwhile Moabite territory in the days of the first king of Moab, must be connected with the Amorite incursion into Damascene territory following the Egypto-Hittite clash at Kadesh on the Orontes in 1285 B.C.

Bearing all these facts in mind we now can attempt to piece together the various bits of seemingly contradictory evidence into a hypothetical whole. Some fragmentary clans of mixed Israelite-Hebrew parentage succeeded in infiltrating into the northern part of the country some time before the accession of Seti I (1311 B.C.). These comprised later Asherite families and possibly also Naphtalites. This may be considered the first wave of Israelites to enter Canaan. The second wave, probably consisting of Leah tribes (Reuben, Simeon, Levi, Judah, Issachar and Zebulun), passed unopposed through Transjordan, crossed the Jordan opposite Bezek and split; the first-mentioned four turned southwards, the last two passed northwards into Lower Galilee.

A third wave of Israelite invaders, comprising the Rachel tribes (Ephraim, Manasseh and Benjamin), had to by-pass the Edomite and Moabite kingdoms, which had risen meanwhile, and fought its way through the Amorite kingdom of Sihon (founded after 1285 B.C.) to the plains of Moab. They crossed the Jordan opposite Jericho, which they took and destroyed, occupied Beth-El, made a pact with the Gibeonites and settled in Mount Ephraim. Their entry can be dated by archeological evidence from the excavations of Beth-El (see above), further supported by the fact that Ramses II erected in 1272 B.C. a

triumphal stele at Beth-Shean, which may possibly be connected with an Egyptian attempt to quell disturbances in the area caused by the then recent penetration of Rachel tribes into mountainous Samaria. This invasion was probably led by Joshua, and being the latest, impressed upon later tradition the belief that it was he who was responsible for the conquest of Canaan as a whole.

Some fifty years later the northern tribes, probably with the active assistance of the House of Joseph, and perhaps even led by the aged Joshua, made bold by the deterioration of effective Egyptian hold over their Asiatic possessions, attacked Hazor, the great Canaanite center of a local vassal ruler, probably around 1225 B.C. These may have been the local disorders that prompted the newly enthroned Mernephtah (1224-1214 B.C.) to undertake in his third year a military campaign into Canaan commemorated in the so-called "Israel Stele", which he erected in his fifth year at Thebes:—

"The princes are prostrate, crying 'Shalom'
(Peace)!

"Plundered is Canaan with every evil;

"Carried off is Ashkelon; seized upon is Gezer;

"Yenoam is made as that which does not exist;

"Israel is laid waste, his seed is not;

"Kharu (Canaan) is become a widow for
Egypt" . . .

By about 1220 B.C. the conquest of Canaan by the Israelites, such as it was, was completed although several Canaanite enclaves still withstood them.

Now began their adjustment to their new surroundings, and their gradual transition to the state of settled agriculturists. The Book of Judges (Chapter 8) describes a first clash with the powerful clan of Cushan-rishataim on the borders of the Shephelah, the geographical trough in the western foothills of Mount Judah, which was resolved by the courageous leadership of the local chieftain, Othniel son of Kenaz, allied with the Calebites of Hebron. This encounter may still be considered as an aftermath of the Conquest.

Of a more serious nature was the attempt made by the Transjordanian Moabites to follow in the steps of the Israelites and establish their suzerainty over them. This challenge was answered from Mount Ephraim, a region very sparsely settled in pre-Israelite days, and now with an overwhelmingly Israelite population. Thus it was presented with the opportunity to keep up the traditional spirit of independence characteristic of the nomads and semi-nomads. The Benjaminite Ehud of the Gera clan (I Chron. 8:3; Judg. 3:14-30) led the successful revolt against the Moabite yoke.

Meanwhile the victory of Pharaoh Ramses III over the Sea Peoples (about 1190 B.C.) brought the Phillistines and their ally Thekel to the southern and Sharon coasts of Canaan respectively. They were allowed by the Egyptians to settle there as nominal vassals of Pharaoh. The Philistines, spreading from the seaside inland, and the Israelites, probing their way from their mountain fastnesses into the maritime plain were bound to clash. The Israelites, under Shamgar the son of Anath, probably supported by the local pre-Israelite population, inflicted a defeat on the Philistines in one of their encounters, perhaps in the eighties of the 12th Century B.C.

After the destruction of Hazor, the commander of its chariotry, Sisera, tried to maintain the Hazorite hegemony in Galilee (Harosheth of the Gentiles). At the instigation of the prophetess Deborah, a Josephite, a combined effort of several tribes led by the Naphtalite Barak defeated Sisera's chariotry in the plain of Megiddo. They were helped by bad weather, which turned the plain into a quagmire which deprived the chariots of their superior maneuverability. This final defeat of an organized Canaanite force in Galilee, which probably occurred about 1180 B.C. opened the way to fresh incursions from the desert border-lands. The Midianites were not slow to exploit this opportunity, and started periodic intrusions into Cisjordania, spoiling the threshing floors and grazing their flocks on the still unharvested crops. Again, the challenge was taken up by a Josephite clan. Gideon of the Manassite clan of Abiezer routed the Midianites in a night attack on their encampment, probably some time during the second half of the 12th Century B.C.

So far the leaders that helped to ward off the various attacks were ordinary people, or, at most, honored elders, driven into action by exceptional dangers which inspired them and their tribes to extraordinary efforts. By this time it had dawned on some Israelites that self-preservation and survival demanded some sort of a centralized organization capable of providing permanent security. And so a son of Gideon by a Canaanite woman from Shechem, Abimelech, tried his hand, after the death of his father, at the establishment of a monarchy in the Josephite territory, leaning mainly on the support of the descendants of pre-Israelite notables of Shechem (Judg. 9:2). The attempt, during the late 12th or the early 11th Century B.C. failed owing to the undisciplined spirit of the would-be subjects of such a monarch.

Gideon's repulse of the Midianites brought peace to the Valley of Jezreel, so that a succession of local elders ruled peacefully in the valley and surrounding mountainous districts (Judg. 10.12: 8 ff).

Serious menaces loomed, however, both in the east and west. In Transjordan the Ammonites, possibly pressed by border nomads, made an attempt to invade the Gileadite territory of the

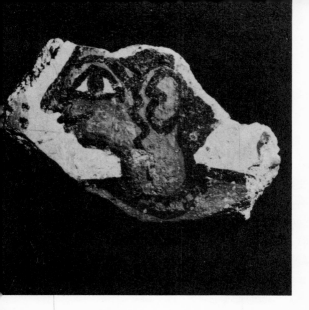

(Top) A PAINTED POTTERY FRAGMENT FROM THE 13TH CENTURY B.C., SHOWING A WOMAN'S HEAD. IT WAS FOUND AT BETH SHEAN.
(Right) A CLAY COFFIN FOUND IN THE BETH SHEAN EXCAVATIONS: SUCH COFFINS WERE USED FOR THE BURIAL OF PHILISTINE SOLDIERS, THIS ONE POSSIBLY FOR A MEMBER OF THE GARRISON MAINTAINED AT BETH SHEAN BY PHARAOH RAMSES III.

Israelites, but were repulsed, at least temporarily, by the Gileadite warrior Jephtah.

The threat to Israelite independence from the west proved of a more permanent nature. The Philistines stubbornly and gradually extended their rule over the hinterland. The small mixed tribe of Dan (also traditionally a son of a "handmaid" of Jacob) could not raise organized opposition to the invaders under a local "judge". The story of their partisan resistance to the Philistine conquest crystallized around the legendary figure of Samson. In the final count the Danites were compelled to abandon their territory and, migrating northwards, settled round the town of Laish (Leshem), which they conquered and renamed Dan, probably about 1100 B.C.

This flight created a territorial vacuum, into which began to pour clans of the neighboring tribes of Ephraim, Benjamin and Judah, for the Philistines were not interested in colonizing the territory, but only in extracting tribute from the local farmers.

It seems that the Benjaminites gained the upper hand in this contest, thus incurring the envy

CANAAN DIVIDED AMONG THE TRIBES OF ISRAEL.

and hatred of the other Josephites and Judahites. The incident of the concubine at Gibeah (Judg. 19) was sufficient, therefore, to provoke civil strife on a large scale, in which the Benjaminites were decimated by the combined hosts of Israelite tribes. But this victory weakened one of the main forces of resistance to Philistine penetration into the main stronghold of Israelite independence, Mount Ephraim.

It seems that the main sanctuary of the Israelites since the days of the conquest was situated at Shechem. The disgrace brought on the city by the downfall of Abimelech probably cast a shadow also on its importance as a religious center, and about the end of the 12th Century a new shrine rose at Shiloh, to which the Tabernacle and the Ark of the Lord were brought, and where the family of Eli officiated. It also served as a center of annual pilgrimages for, at least, the inhabitants of Mount Ephraim. Some of the pilgrims, like Hannah the wife of Elkanah, dedicated there their sons to the services of the Lord, and so the feet of Samuel were set on the path of national service.

The weakness of the Israelite tribes finally enabled the Philistines to score a decisive victory at the battle of Eben-Haezer (I Sam. 4). They penetrated into the heart of Mount Ephraim, destroyed Shiloh, and set up control over at least the southern part of this territory (cf. e.g., I Sam. 10:5). This event is probably to be dated to about 1050 B.C.

Samuel recognized, as part of his spiritual vocation, the need to drive out the Philistines and reestablish Israelite independence. How he set about his task and what he achieved is part and parcel of the history of Israel under the monarchy.

THE ILLUSTRATED HISTORY OF THE JEWS

THE HOUSE OF DAVID

ISRAEL UNITED AND DIVIDED

AN IVORY CARVING OF A WINGED CHERUB FOUND IN
THE CITADEL OF THE ISRAELITE KINGS IN SAMARIA.

THE HOUSE OF DAVID

The destruction of Shiloh (1050 B.C.) marked the end of one period and the beginning of another in the history of Israel, since it was followed by Philistine domination of the land of

JERUSALEM DURING THE REIGN OF SOLOMON.

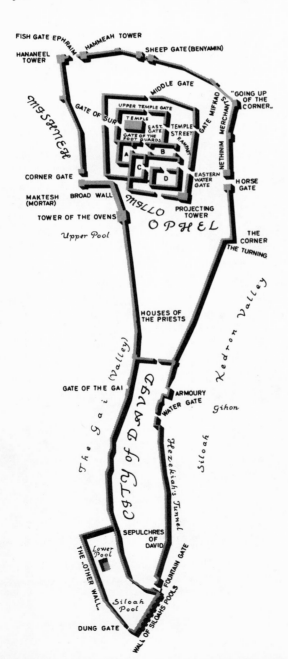

Benjamin and of the southern part of Mount Ephraim. This, in turn, placed Israel for the first time in danger not only of subjugation but of annihilation. Yet these developments, which would normally have sown disunity and led to the disintegration of the tribes dwelling in the center of the country, had the opposite effect: they fostered new unity and led to the establishment of the united Kingdom of Israel within one generation. The kingdom was founded in the days of Samuel, at a time when the prevailing tendency was towards the institution of a centralized monarchy. On the other hand the rule of the elders and patriarchs was still recognized—in fact Samuel was to a large extent their representative. This duality is apparent in the acts of Samuel, who, though opposed to the monarchy, nevertheless annointed and crowned the first King, Saul, son of Kish.

The beginning and end of Saul's reign (1026-1004 B.C.) were marked by relentless wars against the Philistines. His reign opened with a victory over the Philistine garrison in the land of Benjamin, followed by the liberation of the whole area of Mount Ephraim. After Judah, Gilead and Galilee had been annexed too, the first kingdom was formed, having as its capital Saul's native town, in the hill country of Benjamin. Saul drew his support mainly from the military class, the army formed of the "elite" of the people, who were in part volunteers and in part recruits organized into units of "hundreds" and "thousands". Although typical monarchic patterns were already apparent in Saul's kingdom —such as the distribution of land-estates to the King's ministers and the formation of a military organization—it retained some of the charismatic features that had characterized Israel's leadership at the time of the Judges. As leader "by the grace of God", Saul stands out as the last of the Judges and the first of the Kings of Israel; his tragic death in the war against the Philistines on Mount Gilboa and the Philistine domination of most of his kingdom created a second serious crisis which, like the destruction of Shiloh before it, was the challenge that led to the reunification of Israel's tribes. This unification was the work of David, a native of Bethlehem in Judah, Saul's son-in-law, who ruled in Hebron as King of Judah under Philistine auspices.

A new and revolutionary stage in Israel's history opened when the elders of Israel invited David to rule over Israel as well (1000 B.C.). David's first objective was to cast off the Philistine yoke and then to reunite all Israel under a stable monarchy. His efforts to consolidate the territory of the eastern tribes led to wars with Israel's neighbors beyond the Jordan: the Ammonites, the Moabites and later the Edomites. His success against these nations brought him into direct conflict with the powerful Aramean states. The military struggle between them determined the fate of Syria and Palestine for a long time. During the 10th and most of the 9th Centuries the great powers, which had dominated the area for many years, grew steadily weaker. Egypt declined from the 12th Century on, while Assyria was forced to defend itself against the heavy pressure of the Aramean tribes. The latter spread out along Assyria's borders and established their states nearby, the most important being Aram-Zoba. In three separate battles David met the army of Zoba—and emerged the victor. Aram-Zoba and Aram-Damascus became vassals of Israel, and David's sphere of influence ex-

tended to the borders of the neo-Hittite kingdom of Hamath and reached out to the Mediterranean coast, north of Tyre and Sidon. Hamath became Israel's close ally, linked by economic and political interests. Most important was David's alliance with Hiram, King of Tyre, which led to close trade relations and to the penetration of Phoenician technical skill, art and architecture into Israel.

Together with the territorial expansion of David's kingdom major changes were introduced in the organization of the government and of the army. A complex body of royal officials ("The King's Servants") was set up to assist the king in the administration of civil affairs including various branches of economic life. Some of David's ministers bore foreign names, and it may well be assumed that in setting up the corps of officials David copied governmental patterns from the Canaanite city-kingdoms. The royal government was located in Jerusalem which, until its conquest by David, had been a Jebusite city outside the territory of Israel's tribes. Jerusalem henceforth was to become the domain of the king who conquered it ("the City of David"), drawing overwhelming advantages from its favorable geographic position—situated as it was between the land of Joseph and that of Judah. It very soon became the king's residence, the administrative capital and the ritual center of the united kingdom. The dynamic changes introduced by David, which were fully implemented within a generation or two, bypassed to a very large extent the ancient well-rooted institutions of Israel. They undermined the authority of the traditional patriarchal leadership (that is, the elders of Israel and the chiefs of the community) and aroused dissatisfaction which found expression in Absalom's revolt and even more in the revolt of Sheba, the son of Bichri of the tribe of Benjamin, who aimed at the secession of Israel from Judah under Mephiboshet, Saul's grandson. Once the revolts had been put down by the might of David's trained professional army, the kingdom shifted to a new policy, which gave precedence and privilege to Judah over the other parts of Israel. On David's death in 965 B.C., he bequeathed the kingdom to Solomon, his young son, thus establishing a royal dynasty, whose authority was confirmed by divine commitment and which was to reign in Jerusalem and Judah for 400 years, until the destruction of the First Temple. David rose in popular tradition to the role of King-Messiah, "the Singer of Israel", whose descendants would occupy his throne and remain forever in the gracious covenant of God.

The state that Solomon inherited from his father included, in addition to the Israelite commonwealth, the Aramean Kingdoms, Edom, Moab and Ammon in Transjordan, as well as the Philistine cities. It became a political and economic factor of decisive importance in the region lying between Egypt in the South and the neo-Hittite kingdoms of northern and central Syria. The privileged status of Israel's king received formal recognition in his marriage to Pharaoh's daughter, an act contrary to Egyptian custom.

David's victories had made vassals of Israel's neighbors. Continuing control during the reign of Solomon of these extensive regions necessitated the creation of a large army consisting chiefly of chariots and horsemen. These were stationed in special "chariot towns" such as Hazor, Megiddo and Gezer, located at strategic points along the country's main highways. Another innovation in the organization of the kingdom was the division of the original areas of the northern tribes into twelve districts, each of which was obliged to provide food for the king's household and court for one month every year (I Kings, 5). It appears that Judah was not included in the district scheme and that it enjoyed special privileges which bound it closely to the royal family and to Jerusalem. It can also be assumed that Judah was exempted from the corvée, that is, the obligation to supply a labor force for the king's building schemes. These included fortified towns and numerous buildings put up by Solomon throughout his realm — chiefly in Jerusalem, which grew and expanded greatly. These forced laborers numbered 70,000 "burden-bearers" and 80,000 "hewers of stone" or mountain quarrymen, who were reinforced by 30,000 men sent out in rotation to the Lebanon for the purpose of cutting down cedar trees. Their efforts resulted in the erection in Jerusalem, at the beginning of Solomon's reign, of royal and public buildings and foremost among them the Temple, designed by Tyrian craftsmen on the Phoenician pattern. The building of the Temple, which made Jerusalem a holy city and the religious-national center of the kingdom, served as the starting point of Solomon's great construction drive, which covered the entire country. This impressive construction program was an indication of the extensive changes undergone by Israel's society and of the degree to which the dynasty had been consolidated. Another innovation in Solomon's kingdom was the development of trade on a large international scale. This was made possible by Solomon's sole control of the "King's highway" the route passing over the crests of the hills of Transjordan and of the "Via Maris", the maritime road along the coast of Palestine, two main overland routes of trade between Mesopotamia, Anatolia and Syria on the one hand, and Egypt on the other. Solomon's control over the main caravan towns

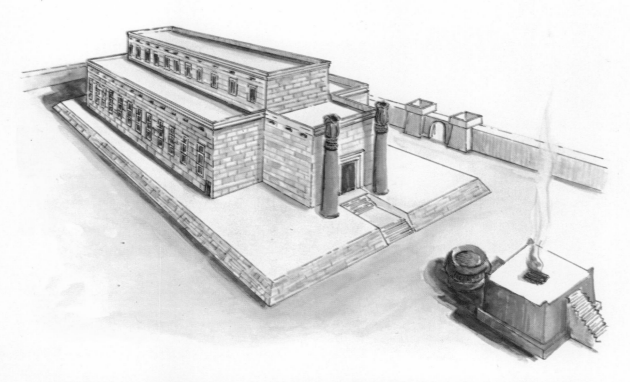

THE TEMPLE OF KING SOLOMON AS IT IS BELIEVED
TO HAVE APPEARED.

A HORNED ALTAR FROM THE ISRAELITE PERIOD,
FOUND AT MEGIDDO.

RUINS OF THE CITY GATE OF MEGIDDO.

ANCIENT ROCK-HEWN CONDUIT THAT SERVED AS PART OF THE WATER SYSTEM OF MEGIDDO.

PILLARS OF A BUILDING FROM THE TIME OF KING
AHAB, EXCAVATED AT HAZOR.

COLLONADE FROM THE ROYAL PALACE IN SAMARIA.

IVORY CARVINGS FROM THE CITADEL OF THE ISRAEL-
ITE KINGS IN SAMARIA.

ENVOY OF JEHU, KING OF ISRAEL, PAYING HOMAGE
TO SHALMANESER, KING OF ASSYRIA (841 B.C.).

CAVALRYMAN WITH SHIELD AND ARMOR — A RELIEF
FROM TELL HALAF (GOZAN) IN NORTHERN SYRIA.

THE ASSYRIAN KING SARGON II WITH HIS ATTENDANTS
—RECONSTRUCTION OF A WALL PAINTING AT KHORSA-
BAD.

REMAINS OF THE STABLES IN MEGIDDO.

between Edom and Palmyra, which gave him almost a monopoly of the Arabian trade—myrrh, frankincense and ivory—is illustrated in the colorful tale of the South Arabian queen of the Sabaeans (Sheba) who came with a richly laden caravan to Solomon's court to establish trade relations. The desire to have direct access to the products of Arabian trade induced Solomon and Hiram of Tyre to send out a joint sea expedition from Ezion Geber (Elath) on the Red Sea to Ophir in East Africa. This intensive mercantile activity, conducted by the new class of "King's merchants", which grew and flourished during Solomon's reign, did not impede a similar growth in agriculture. On the contrary, territorial expansion and the utilization of the new metal, iron, in agricultural tools gave new impetus to the development of the agricultural economy and to the creation of surpluses which served as a basis for barter trade between Israel and its neighbors, chiefly Tyre (I Kings 5:25). This prosperity came to an end in the last years of Solomon, when the region underwent many political changes. In Egypt, a dynasty hostile to Solomon came to power. Aram-Damascus and apparently also Edom rebelled against Israel and became independent. Royal expenditures grew, while revenues declined, thus leading to the sharpening of conflicts within the kingdom, that is chiefly between Judah and all the rest of Israel, which continued to bear the heavy tax burden. Against this background a revolt broke out, headed by Jeroboam, a gibbor hayil, a respected landowner and patrician from Mount Ephraim. Though the trouble began while Solomon still ruled, the actual division of the United Kingdom of Israel occurred only after Solomon's death and the accession of his son in 928 B.C. Rehoboam refused to yield to the gathered delegates of "the Congregation of Israel" in Shechem, who de-

manded that he "make lighter the grievous service of his father and the heavy yoke which he put upon them". The old slogan "What portion have we in David? Neither have we inheritance in the son of Jesse", which had been heard at the time of Sheba's rebellion against David, sounded again. But unlike David, who had speedily routed the secessionists, Rehoboam was unable to prevent the ten tribes from establishing their own independent kingdom. Its first king, Jeroboam, was crowned by the "Congregation of Israel" with the support of the Prophets headed by Ahijah the Shilonite. From that time onward, two kingdoms co-existed in Palestine. The Northern Kingdom of Israel included the greater part of Solomon's territory, whereas the southern one comprised the lands of Judah and Benjamin.

The first act of Jeroboam (928-907 B.C.) was to reinstate in Israel the ancient holy towns of Dan and Beth-El, which had been eclipsed by Jerusalem during the period of David and Solomon, and to erect in Beth-El a royal shrine similar to that of Solomon. These Israelite royal shrines differed from the Jerusalem Temple in their symbolism: the invisible deity of Beth-El and Dan was imagined as standing on a calf in the old Syro-Phoenician style, while in Jerusalem it was "enthroned above the Cherubim". Jeroboam also altered the dates of the religious festivals restoring the northern tradition in which they occurred a month later than in Jerusalem. In Beth-El a new priestly class had to be created, since the Levites remained loyal to Rehoboam.

Jeroboam's reign was marked by two serious crises. In his fifth year, Pharaoh Shishak of Egypt invaded Palestine, looting and destroying a considerable part of the Kingdom of Israel. Towards the end of Jeroboam's reign Abijam, son of Rehoboam, King of Judah, captured the southern part of Mount Ephraim as well as the sacred city of Beth-El. These events hastened the end of Jeroboam's dynasty, which lasted only one generation, and brought about the rise of a new line—that of Baasha. Baasha's reign (906-883 B.C.) was marked by wars between Judah and Israel. These wars started towards the end of the

THE MOABITE STONE ON WHICH MESHA, KING OF MOAB, BOASTS OF HIS VICTORY OVER KING AHAB.

reign of Rehoboam, who refused to accept the splitting of the kingdom but refrained at first from waging war on Israel; they increased in intensity during the time of Abijam (911-908 B.C.) and ended during the reign of Asa (908-867 B.C.).

During the reigns of Jeroboam and Baasha the principal institutions of government in the northern kingdom were developed although serious social and economic difficulties existed. During this and the subsequent periods a decisive role was played by the army, which represented the gibborei ha-hayil—"the men of substance", the landed aristocracy, who were the social center of gravity of the State. Actually, the change of dynasties in Israel came in the wake of severe military defeats: the dynasty of Jeroboam disappeared a short time after the defeat by Abijam, while the Baasha dynasty fell after the invasion of Galilee by Ben Hadad I, King of Damascus (I Kings, 14:20). Stability returned to Israel only during the short reign of Omri, an army chief who founded a new dynasty. Symbolizing this stability was the erection of Samaria, the new capital, situated in Omri's home-territory in the enclave of Issachar in Ephraim. Upon his death in 871 B.C., Omri bequeathed to his son Ahab a realm which soon became one of the most important kingdoms in Syria.

During the reigns of Jehoshaphat and Ahab the first chapter in the history of the relations between Judah and Israel, that is the period of warfare, came to an end. It was replaced by a new era of alliance between the two related countries. The advantage of political and economic cooperation appeared to have been greater than the ephemeral benefits of fratricidal war. This alliance between Israel and Judah received formal expression by royal marriages between the two dynasties: Jehoshaphat's son Joram married

Athaliah, daughter of Omri, and the way was thus opened for close cooperation between Israel and Judah. At the same time, Ahab concluded an alliance with Ethbaal, King of Tyre, who gave him his daughter Jezebel in marriage. Israel emerged at this time as a center of economic and political activity, linking Judah, which had recently renewed its hold over the copper mines of Edom, with the trade routes of Transjordan and Tyre. A period of economic prosperity opened for the whole region, from Phoenicia to the Red Sea.

The Israelite expansion in Gilead, which began in Omri's reign, led finally to fierce wars between Israel and the kings of Aram Damascus, but towards the end of Ahab's rule a peace pact was concluded between them. This union of former enemies originated in the campaigns of the Assyrian kings Ashurnasirpal II and Shalmaneser III, who terrorised Northern Syria by ravaging the big cities, decimating the population and carrying off huge amounts of plunder and loot.

A military alliance, headed by the kings of Damascus, Hamath and Israel, was formed to counter the Assyrian threat. This alliance, which included twelve states and was actively supported by Egypt, fought bravely against the Assyrian armies on numerous occasions (in the years 853, 849, 848, 845) and succeeded in repelling them and preventing Shalmaneser III from laying his hands on Southern Syria, Phoenicia and Palestine.

Ahab's political achievements—territorial expansion and the economic prosperity of Israel—could not conceal serious internal problems. The position of the King, of his ministers and officials grew in importance and the tyranny of the royal court over the Israelite elders and respected land-owners increased, thus arousing opposition to Ahab and to his dynasty among wide sections of the population. The main opposition was directed against Jezebel, Ahab's queen, who introduced her native cult of Tyrian Baal into Samaria.

The center of the resistance to Ahab's dynasty is to be found in the prophetic movement headed by Elijah the Gileadite, and his spiritual successor, Elisha. The struggle of the prophets against the ruling dynasty grew in intensity during the reign of Jehoram, Ahab's son (851-842 B.C.) and finally was instrumental in overthrowing Ahab's dynasty. The actual liquidation of this dynasty was the work of Jehu, the army commander described in biblical historiography as the executor of the prophecies of Elijah and Elisha and as their agent; assisted by the army officers he rebelled against Jehoram and was proclaimed by them as king.

Jehu's accession to the throne inaugurated a

TWO HEBREW OSTRACA FROM TEL-QASILE NEAR TEL AVIV.
(Upper) "OF THE KING, 1100 (MEASURES) OF OIL, (FROM) HIYAHU."
(Lower) "GOLD OF OPHIR TO BETH-HORON, 30 SHEKELS."

new period of political decline in Israel and subservience to Aram. For Jehu's revolt, which put an end to the worship—and the worshippers—of the Tyrian Baal, also severed the links uniting Israel to Tyre and Israel to Judah. King Ahaziah of Judah was put to death by Jehu together with Jehoram, Ahab's son, and the result was Israel's political isolation and internal weakening. On his accession to the throne, Jehu paid tribute to Shalmaneser III, King of Assyria (841 B.C.) hoping that the latter would become an ally and protector in his war against Aram. But before long Jehu found it impossible to withstand the increasing pressure of Hazael, king of Aram, who conquered Gilead, imposed his dominion upon Ammon, Moab and Edom and towards the end of Jehu's reign penetrated deep into the territory of Israel, reached Philistia and received Judah's capitulation. The reigns of Hazael and of Ben-Hadad III, his son, were a period of total decline for the Kingdom of Israel. Jehu's son, Jehoahaz, had to become an Aramean vassal. At this time of acute danger to the very existence of the kingdom of Israel, unexpected assistance came from the King of Assyria, Adadnirari III, who on numerous occasions defeated Aram-Damascus and thus in fact saved Israel. A few years later, Jehoash, son of Jehoahaz (800-784 B.C.), managed to restore to Israel the territories it had lost in Transjordan, while Jeroboam, his son, (784-748 B.C.) gave Aram a crushing blow, occupied Damascus and established his hegemony over southern Syria as in Solomon's days: "He restored the border of Israel from the entrance of Hamath as far as the Sea of Arabah". (II Kings 14: 25-27).

While upheavals and changes of dynasty were a constant phenomenon in 9th Century Israel, the Davidic dynasty in Judah remained stable and indeed deeply rooted. The Kingdom of Judah was given its first organizational structure by Jehoshaphat, who seems to have divided the country into twelve administrative regions, along Solomon's lines, for the purpose of levying troops and collecting taxes. A second administrative achievement of Jehoshaphat was the establishment of a judiciary system in Israel by the appointment of judges from among the Levites, with a view to strengthening the king's prerogatives and the central authority of Jerusalem.

Jehu's rebellion against Jehoram (842 B.C.) in which Ahaziah, king of Judah, Jehoshaphat's grandson, was killed, marked a turning-point not only in Samaria but also in Jerusalem, as it brought about a dynastic crisis by raising Athaliah the Israelite to the throne as queen of Judah. Six years later this in turn led to a counter-revolution when Jehoiada the chief priest of the Temple raised to the throne Joash, a seven year old son of Ahaziah. Most of Joash's long reign was marked by political decline, in which various forces—the priests of the Temple on the one hand and the king and his ministers on the other—were in constant conflict. The internal struggle in Jerusalem continued also during the reign of his son Amaziah, the only king of Judah who tried to resume the military struggle against Israel. Yet Amaziah's war against Israel ended with the fall of Jerusalem at the hands of the Israelite king and with the destruction of its walls. Amaziah was removed from the throne and the ministers appointed as regent in his stead his young son Azariah (Uzziah), who was still a boy of sixteen. With the accession of Azariah to the throne (785) there began a new era in Judah's history which lasted over 50 years and which was characterized by territorial expansion and intensified economic activity: these developments were basically similar in time and content to those which took place in the kingdom

of Israel during the reign of Azariah's contemporary, Jeroboam II (784-748 B.C.). While Jeroboam was occupying Damascus and imposing his hegemony upon Southern Syria, Azariah was expanding his realm in Edom and on the Negeb, conquering Elath and reaching Kadesh-Barnea, the home of the semi-nomadic Meunite tribes. But his greatest military feat was the conquest of Ashdod in Philistia. In Judah itself a strong army was raised, organized and equipped with modern weapons, while Jerusalem's walls were fortified. At the same time Azariah directed his attention to the development of agriculture and livestock: "And he built towers in the wilderness, and hewed out many cisterns, for he had large herds; both in the Shephela and in the plain; and he had farmers and vine-dressers in the hills and in the fertile lands; for he loved the soil" (II Chronicles 26:10). During the reign of Azariah's son, Jotham, who acted as regent because of his father's illness (II Kings 15:5) Judah began to expand even in Transjordan, and took possession of southern Gilead, subjugating the Ammonites as well. This expansion, coinciding with the Israelite enterprise in Bashan (recently captured by Jeroboam from the Arameans), paved the way for renewed Judean and Israelite settlement in the northern part of Transjordan and in time permitted the rise of a new social force, the great landowners of Gilead, whose influence increased in Samaria towards the end of Jeroboam's reign and chiefly after his death.

It may be doubted whether it was mere chance that the sudden decline of Israel and the frequent crises it underwent after the death of Jeroboam II (in 748 B.C.) should have coincided with a period so fateful to western Asia—the rise of Assyria under Tiglath-Pileser III (745-727 B.C.). This ruler, who restored Assyria's might and laid down the patterns of an Empire, invaded

Syria in 743, only a few years after the death of Jeroboam, and started annexing the Syrian states, exiling their peoples and turning the states into provinces of Assyria. A decisive task devolved at that time upon Judah which, being the biggest and most important state in Palestine and Southern Syria, inherited after Jeroboam's death Israel's role of political hegemony in the region. Thus Judah formed and headed a new alliance directed against Assyria which included North Syrian and Phoenician states. Unfortunately, only a few fragmentary records of these events have survived, but it is nevertheless clear that the allies were defeated by Tiglath-Pileser and that North Syria and most of Central Syria were conquered by the Assyrians (738). At the same time Israel and Aram paid tribute to Tiglath-Pileser, thus recognizing Assyrian sovereignty.

The year 738 also marks the beginning of the swift decline of Judah. The main tributaries, Edom and Northern Philistia, became independent and together with Aram and Israel started to harass Judah's borders. The campaign of Tiglath-Pileser III in Philistia in 734, subjugating for the first time all the coast as far as the

Egyptian border, laid the basis for events to come. The tension between Judah, whose king Ahaz — Azariah's grandson — had paid tribute to Assyria, and the allies Israel and Aram, increased and resulted in an open war between them. Pekah the new King of Israel (735-733) and his ally Rezin, King of Aram, defeated Judah's army and marched on Jerusalem in order to dethrone Ahaz and to place in his stead a certain Ben-Tabeel, apparently a Gileadite prince (Isaiah 7). At this stage of political upheaval Tiglath-Pileser intervened. He besieged Damascus, conquered it and turned it into an Assyrian province (733-732 B.C.). He invaded Israel, conquered Galilee and Gilead, banished their populations and annexed them as provinces to Assyria, leaving to Hoshea, the new king of Samaria, only the land of Ephraim. But the destruction which befell almost two-thirds of Israel did not lead to political stability. The extremists again had the upper hand and during the reign of Shalmaneser V (726-722 B.C.), the revolt against Assyria was resumed. Hoshea relied on the assistance of the Egyptian Pharaoh who feared the expansion of Assyria close to his borders. But the Assyrians were determined, on this occasion, to liquidate the Kingdom of Samaria. Hoshea was imprisoned (724 B.C.). Shalmaneser invaded the country and besieged Samaria which fell in the year 722 (that is the 6th year of the reign of Hezekiah, king of Judah). Two years later, Sargon II, who founded a new dynasty in Assyria, marched again on Samaria and exiled 27,290 persons, leaving only the poorest elements. Samaria, too, became an Assyrian province (called Samerina) and in place of its inhabitants, who were exiled to Northern Mesopotamia, Chaldeans and Arabs were settled.

The destruction of the Kingdom of Israel and the banishing of considerable numbers of its

ARAMAIC INSCRIPTION ON LIMESTONE FROM THE FIRST CENTURY B.C. WHICH READS: "HITHER WERE BROUGHT THE BONES OF UZZIAH, KING OF JUDAH—NOT TO BE OPENED!"

THE "OPHEL OSTRACON" FOUND IN JERUSALEM BEARS
A LIST OF NAMES IN ANCIENT HEBREW SCRIPT FROM
THE PERIOD OF THE KINGS OF JUDAH.

population found echoes in the prophecies of Isaiah, who witnessed these momentous events. Accordingly, the Judean prophet, who was close to the royal court in Jerusalem, explained that the destruction by the king of Assyria, the "rod of God's anger", was a fitting retribution for a sinful kingdom. The prophecies of Isaiah, who began his vocation at the time of the sudden decline of the Kingdom of Judah, were the continuation of the prophecies of Amos and Hosea, who were active in Israel at the time of Jeroboam II and of Menahem, kings of Israel. This new prophetic movement in Israel and Judah came into being during the period of the great decline of the two kingdoms which occurred after a time of expansion and prosperity. The social background of this decline lay in the conflicts and tensions among the social classes, the pauperization of the small land-owners and the rise to power of the king's ministers and his officials — the "King's Servants". Amos and Hosea in Israel, like Isaiah and Micah in Judah, were "literary prophets" of a new type, concerned in their prophecies not with narrow political questions, as was the case of the bnei ha-nebi'im, prophetic guilds of the 9th Century, but rather with public preaching on moral issues. To this were added new themes in the prophecies of Isaiah: the expectation of the coming "day of the Lord", a universal vision of the end of days when "nation shall not lift up sword against nation, neither shall they learn war any more", when "a shoot out of the stock of Jesse" shall judge with righteousness all the nations. In the eschatalogical vision of the End of Days, a decisive role was reserved for Jerusalem, and for the "mountain of the Lord's house" to which "all nations shall flow". The people will then abandon paganism, and the "word of the Lord will go forth from Zion" to the whole world. These themes, typical of the period of universal crisis during which Isaiah lived and worked, contrast starkly with the difficult conditions reigning in Palestine: the destruction of the Kingdom of Israel and the decline of Judah to the rank of a small country, vassal to the great all-powerful Assyrian Empire.

THE KINGDOM OF DAVID AND SOLOMON.

THE ILLUSTRATED HISTORY OF THE JEWS

THE HOUSE OF DAVID

THE KINGDOM OF JUDAH

THE IMPRINT OF A ROYAL SEAL: "OF THE KING, HEBRON". AT THE RIGHT IS THE HANDLE OF A VESSEL BEARING AN IMPRINT WITH THE SAME DESIGN. THIS ONE READS: "OF THE KING, ZIPH".

THE HOUSE OF DAVID

The destruction of the Kingdom of Israel had great repercussions in Judah, which now considered itself as the "remnant of Israel" and the natural heir of the exiled kingdom. Against this background it is possible to comprehend the efforts of Hezekiah (727-698 B.C.) to establish close contact with those of Israel's tribes (especially in Galilee) who had not been exiled. According to the tradition preserved in the book of Chronicles (II Chron. 30) he intended to have them cooperate in his efforts to purify the

A DESCRIPTION OF THE CUTTING AND COMPLETION OF THE SILOAM TUNNEL IS GIVEN IN THIS HEBREW INSCRIPTION FROM THE REIGN OF HEZEKIAH WHICH WAS FOUND IN THE TUNNEL ITSELF.

Temple from Assyrian and Aramean elements which had penetrated the official ritual during the reign of his father Ahaz. This activity took place in the shadow of the Assyrian Empire, whose frontiers were not far from Jerusalem. But Assyria's close proximity to Judah did not prevent efforts by vassal kings of Palestine to liberate themselves from the imperial yoke. In the year 712, Ashdod, the main port of Northern Philistia, rebelled in conjunction with its neighbors, including Judah, but the revolt failed and Ashdod became an Assyrian province. A new and more widespread revolt broke out upon the death of Sargon II, in a battle fought in Asia Minor in the year 705. This revolt, against which the Prophet Isaiah spoke out vehemently, was the work of the remaining vassal states of Southern Syria headed by the king of Judah. The rebels relied on the assistance of the Nubian kings of the 25th dynasty who had come to power in Egypt some time before. Fearing that Jerusalem might be besieged, Hezekiah fortified the city and took steps to ensure its water supply by digging a tunnel — the "Siloam tunnel" — which brought the water of the Gihon spring to the city. In 701, Sennacherib, Sargon's son, set out to suppress the revolt in Palestine. He again defeated the Philistine cities and near Elteqeh in the coastal plain encountered the Egyptian auxiliary army which had come to assist the rebellious allies. After the Egyptians retreated, Sennacherib threw all his might against Hezekiah. The fortified towns of Judah, the most important of which was Lachish, were captured and Jerusalem was besieged, while many thousands of people were led into exile. Hezekiah had no alternative but to yield unconditionally. He was forced to pay the king of Assyria a heavy trib-

INTERIOR VIEW OF THE SILOAM TUNNEL.

THE SIEGE OF LACHISH (701 B.C.). A MURAL FROM THE
PALACE OF SENACHERIB IN NINEVEH.

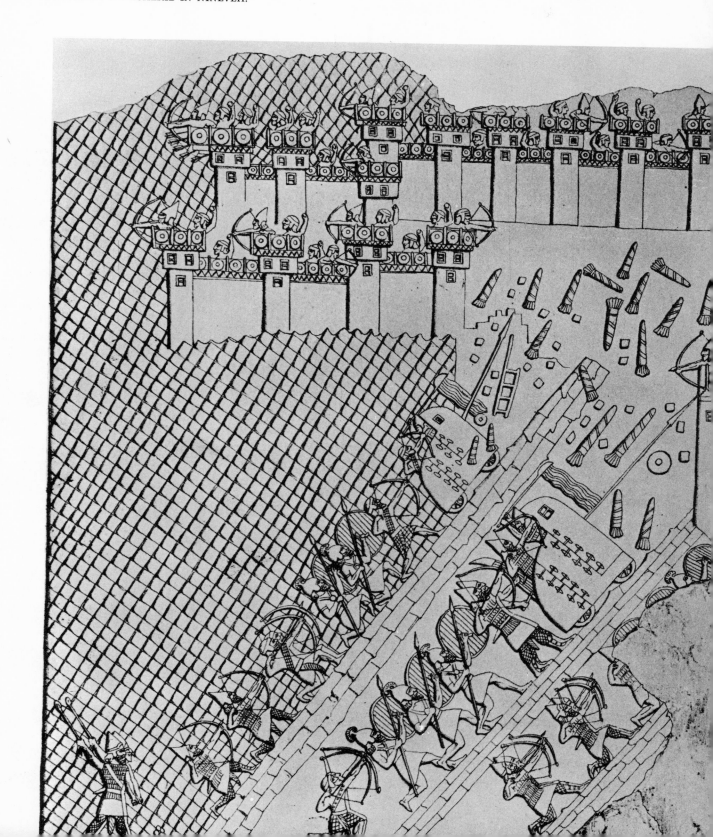

GENEOLOGICAL TABLES

THE UNITED KINGDOM OF ISRAEL

SAUL 1026-1004
DAVID 1004-965
SOLOMON 967*-928

JUDAH

REHOBOAM 928-911
ABIJAM 911-908
ASA 908-867
JEHORAM 851*-843
AHAZIAH 843-842
ATHALIAH 842-836
JEHOASH 836-798
AMAZIAH 798-769
UZZIAH (AZARIAH) 785*-733
JOTHAM 758*-743*
AHAZ (JEHOAHAZ) 743*-727
HEZEKIAH 727-698
MENASSEH 698-642
AMON 641-640
JOSIAH 639-609
JEHOAHAZ 609
JEHOIAKIM 609-598
JEHOIACHIN 597
ZEDEKIAH 596-586
FALL OF JERUSALEM 586

ISRAEL

JEROBOAM I 928-907
NADAB 907-906
BAASHA 906-883
ELAH 883-882
ZIMRI 882/1
OMRI 882/1-871
AHAB 871*-852/1
AHAZIAH 852/1-851/0
JORAM 851/0-842
JEHU 842-814
JEHOAHAZ 817*-800
JOASH 800-784
JEROBOAM II 789*-748
ZECHARIAH 748/7
SHALLUM 748/7
MENAHEM 747/6-737/6
PEKAHIAH 737/6-735/4
PEKAH 735/4-733/2
HOSHEA 733/2-724/3
FALL OF SAMARIA 722

ASSYRIA

ASHUR-DAN II 934-912
ADAD-NIRARI II 911-891
ASHURNASIRPAL II 883-859
SHALMANESER III 858-824
ADAD-NIRARI III 810-783
TIGLATH-PILESER 745-727
SHALMANESER VI 726-722
SARGON 721-705
SENNACHERIB 704-681
ESARHADDON 680-669
ASHURBANIPAL 668-627
FALL OF NINEVEH 612

EGYPT

22th DYNASTY: 935-725
SHISHAK I (SHOSHENQ) 935-914
25th DYNASTY 751-656
TIRHAKAH 689-664
ASSYRIAN CONQUEST 671
26th DYNASTY 664-525
PSAMMETICHUS I 664-610
NECHO 610-595
PSAMMETICHUS II 595-589
APRIES 589-570

BABYLON

NABOPALASSAR 626-605
FALL OF NINEVEH 612
NABUCHADREZZAR 604-562

Note: The dates for the kings of Israel and Judah are given according to the system proposed in the article of H. Tadmor in the Encyclopaedia Miqra'ith (the Hebrew Biblical Encyclopedia), vol. IV, Jerusalem 1963, pp. 245-310.

*Kings marked with an asterisk were co-regent with their predecessors during the overlapping years.

ENTRANCE TO THE SILOAM TUNNEL WHICH WAS CUT
BY KING HEZEKIAH TO CARRY THE WATERS OF THE
GIHON STREAM INTO JERUSALEM.

JUDEAN CAPTIVES FROM LACHISH BEING TAKEN INTO
EXILE BY THE ASSYRIANS (701 B.C.).

ROCK-CUT TOMBS IN JERUSALEM FROM THE PERIOD
OF THE KINGDOM OF JUDAH.

EXCAVATIONS OF THE ROYAL FORTRESS OF JUDAH,
AT RAMAT RAHEL ON THE OUTSKIRTS OF JERUSALEM.

CAPITAL OF A PILLAR FROM THE
FORTRESS AT RAMAT RAHEL.

POTSHERD WITH HEBREW INSCRIPTION FROM THE FORTRESS OF HASHAVIAHU, NORTH OF ASHDOD.

ENTHRONED FIGURE OF A KING OR NOBLE, PAINTED ON A CLAY FRAGMENT FOUND AT RAMAT RAHEL.

THE CITY OF LACHISH ON THE EVE OF ITS DESTRUC-
TION ABOUT 600 B.C.—A RECONSTRUCTION.

RUINS OF A FORT FROM THE 7TH CENTURY B.C., GUARDING THE APPROACHES TO EIN-GEDI, AN OASIS ON THE SHORES OF THE DEAD SEA.

POTTERY, DATING FROM THE KINGDOM OF JUDAH, DISCOVERED AT EIN-GEDI.

SECTION OF THE RUINS OF BABYLON, SHOWING THE
ISHTAR GATE, DATING FROM THE REIGN OF NEBUCH-
ADNEZZAR II (SIXTH CENTURY B.C.).

ute, which included according to Assyrian custom the surrender of the best part of his army to serve in Sennacherib's forces. But why did Sennacherib go back to Nineveh, sparing Jerusalem from conquest and total destruction, and the people of Judah from exile and annihilation? It is possible that Sennacherib was satisfied with what he had achieved in Judah, or perhaps his return was motivated by internal troubles in Assyria. Some claim that the reason was a plague that had broken out among his troops. In any event, the salvation of Jerusalem from "the host of Sennacherib" strengthened the prevalent Judean belief in the holiness of the city, of the Temple of God and of the Davidic dynasty. Yet the fact was that partially devastated Judah remained an Assyrian vassal, and became even further subjected during the reign of Manasseh, son of Hezekiah (698-642 B.C.) — that is at the time of the great kings of Assyria, Esarhaddon and Assurbanipal. These were the last decades of greatness for Assyria, whose armies, fighting against Egypt and North Arabia, were crossing Palestine at will. Judah's total subjection to Assyria was also evident in religious practices and general culture: Manasseh, who accepted the integration of Judah as a full-fledged vassal state within the Assyrian Empire, abolished the religious reforms of Hezekiah and introduced, in Jerusalem and Judah, Assyrian and Syro-Phoenician cults, chiefly the worship of the "Heavenly Host". At the same time the practice of magic and divination grew in importance, in line with the prevalent customs in Assyria. The extreme acts of Manasseh aroused a strong opposition movement centered around the prophets' disciples, the Jerusalem priesthood and the elders. This opposition came into the open at the beginning of the reign of Josiah, Manasseh's grandson (639-609 B.C.) who reached maturity at the time of As-

syria's sudden decline during the last years of Assurbanipal. The momentous events that shook the Assyrian Empire at the time — civil war in Assyria, the revolt of Babylonia resulting in the foundation of the Chaldean dynasty in Babylon by Nabopalassar (626) — had far-reaching repercussions in Judah. By 628, the 12th year of Josiah's reign, the king of Judah was already independent enough to undertake a major religious reform involving the purging of the Assyrian and Aramean rituals dating back to the days of Manasseh, the destruction of altars throughout the land, and the reinstatement of Jerusalem as the only legal site for the worship of God and the offering of sacrifices. The reform affected not only

THIS BABYLONIAN RATION LIST FROM THE YEAR 592 B.C. MENTIONS THE NAMES OF JEHOIACHIN, THE EXILED KING OF JUDAH, AND HIS FIVE SONS.

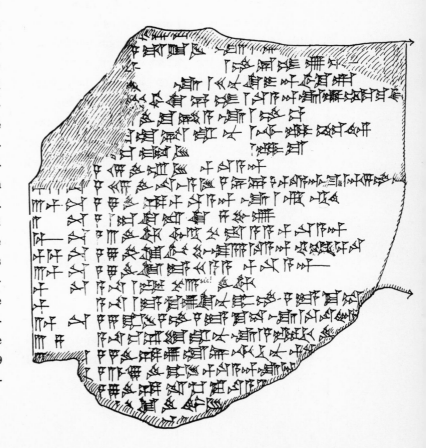

Judah but also considerable parts of Samaria which Josiah annexed to his realm; chief among these being Beth-El and its ancient Israelite altar, which Jeroboam I had built some three hundred years previously. This reform movement, which aimed at purifying the country of "the sins of Manasseh", was merely the expression of Judah's renaissance, in which purification of religious practices went hand in hand with the expansionist aspirations of Judah in the direction of Samaria, Galilee and Philistia. The centralization of worship in Jerusalem served in addition to reinforce the central royal authority in the capital. The crowning achievement of Josiah was the covenant made by the king and his people before God to abide by the "Book of the Law" (presumably an early version of Deuteronomy), which was discovered in the Temple during the repairs undertaken in 622 B.C. (the 18th year of Josiah). This covenant was in fact the first attempt in the history of Israel to give a legal basis to the Torah's commandments and precepts. The covenant's main feature was an undertaking to serve God in the correct manner, in "the city which the Lord had chosen out of all the tribes of Israel", that is Jerusalem, and "to keep his commandments and his testimonies and his statutes" (II Kings 23:3). But apparently the covenant could not put an end to syncretistic practices such as the veneration of "The Queen of Heaven" which was deeply rooted in Judah from the reigns of Ahaz and Manasseh.

Towards the end of Josiah's reign, Judah was faced by a new and serious crisis which affected most of western Asia: the Assyrian Empire collapsed under the combined attack of the Babylonians and the Medes; its chief cities fell one after another. In 612 B.C. Nineveh was captured and two years later Harran in Syria, the stronghold of the last Assyrian king. Nothing availed Assyria,

not even the assistance of Egypt which, at this time of international crisis suddenly changed her traditional policy of rivalry into one of alliance.

When Pharaoh Necho came, in 609, to the assistance of the Assyrian army, which was engaged in battle near Harran, Josiah attempted to prevent the Egyptian forces from crossing his territory. It is difficult to know what led him to such a decision. It may be that he feared Egyptian domination or that he dreaded a renaissance of Assyrian might. In a battle waged near Megiddo, which lies on the main route leading north, Josiah was killed, and when Necho returned to Judah a few months later, he exiled Jehoahaz, the son of Josiah, crowned his brother Jehoiakim (609 B.C.), and placed Judah under Egyptian domination. However, it did not last long, for in 605 Nebuchadnezzar, son of Nabopalassar, defeated and annihilated the Egyptian garrison near Carchemish on the Euphrates and occupied all of Syria including Judah. Here begins the Babylonian period, the last chapter in the history of Judah.

The struggle between Babylonia and Egypt did not end with the conquest of Syria and Palestine by Nebuchadnezzar. In 601 a new campaign was fought; the Babylonians reached the Egyptian frontier but were repelled and retreated. This battle between the armies of Necho and Nebuchadnezzar was apparently the final event leading to the revolt of Jehoiakim against Babylon; the Judean king and his ministers were pro-Egyptian and thought they could rely on Egyptian military might. But four years later, as the Babylonian armies marched on Judah and besieged Jerusalem, Jehoiakim died and his son Jehoiachin (Konyahu) became king. On the 2nd of Adar (16th of March) 597 the Babylonian forces entered Jerusalem and the young Jehoiachin was exiled to Babylon together with some 10,000 of his people, including "craftsmen and smiths", priests and soldiers, the elite of Jerusalem and Judah. Mattaniah, Jehoiachin's uncle, was made king and changed his name to Zedekiah. During the reign of this ruler, who was the last of the Davidic dynasty (596-586 B.C.), tensions and conflicts in the royal court grew in intensity. The moderates, headed by King Zedekiah, were ready to bear the Babylonian yoke, while the extremists, the partisans of rebellion, turned to the Pharaoh for succor. This conflict was sharpened by the fact that Nebuchadnezzar considered the exiled King Jehoiachin as the legitimate king of Judah even in captivity, and this undermined the status of Zedekiah. Even the fiery sermons of Jeremiah, the Prophet from Anatoth, who wielded his greatest influence during Judah's last days and who warned that the Babylonian threat would result in catastrophe and the destruction of the Temple, could not prevent the revolt: the partisans of rebellion had the upper hand and swept Zedekiah in their wake. In 591, when Pharaoh Psammetichus of Egypt marched on Phoenicia, Judah allied herself closely with him and a short time later rebelled against Nebuchadnezzar, relying on the assistance of Pharaoh's army. The Babylonian reaction was immediate. In 588, the Chaldean army marched on Judah, conquered its fortified cities and fortresses and besieged Jerusalem, which fell in Tammuz (July) 586 after a prolonged siege. Zedekiah tried to escape but he was captured by the Babylonians and suffered a bitter fate for having violated his oath as a vassal. His sons were slaughtered before his eyes, and he himself was blinded and led chained into exile.

The end had come for the Kingdom of Judah. "Now in the fifth month, on the seventh day of the month, which was the nineteenth year of Nebuchadnezzar King of Babylon, came Nebu-

zaradan the captain of the guard, a servant of the King of Babylon, into Jerusalem. And he burnt the house of the Lord, and the king's house; and all the houses of Jerusalem, even every great man's house, burnt he with fire. And all the army of the Chaldeans, that were with the captain of the guard, broke down the walls of Jerusalem round about. And the residue of the people that were left in the city, and those that fell away, that fell to the King of Babylon, and the residue of the multitude, did Nebuzaradan the captain of the guard carry away captive." (II Kings 25: 8-11). The period of the First Temple had come to an end; of the Kingdom of Judah there were left only "the poorest of the land", which the Babylonians had spared to be "vinedressers and husbandmen". Fortunately for the future of the Jewish people, the Babylonians did not adopt the Assyrian policy of systematic banishment and did not send into Judah exiles from other parts of their Empire. The land of Judah remained desolate, to be rebuilt only on the return of her exiles from Babylon.

THE CITIES OF LACHISH AND AZEKAH IN JUDAH ARE MENTIONED ON THIS HEBREW OSTRACON FROM LACHISH.

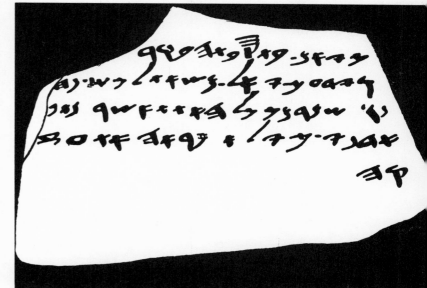

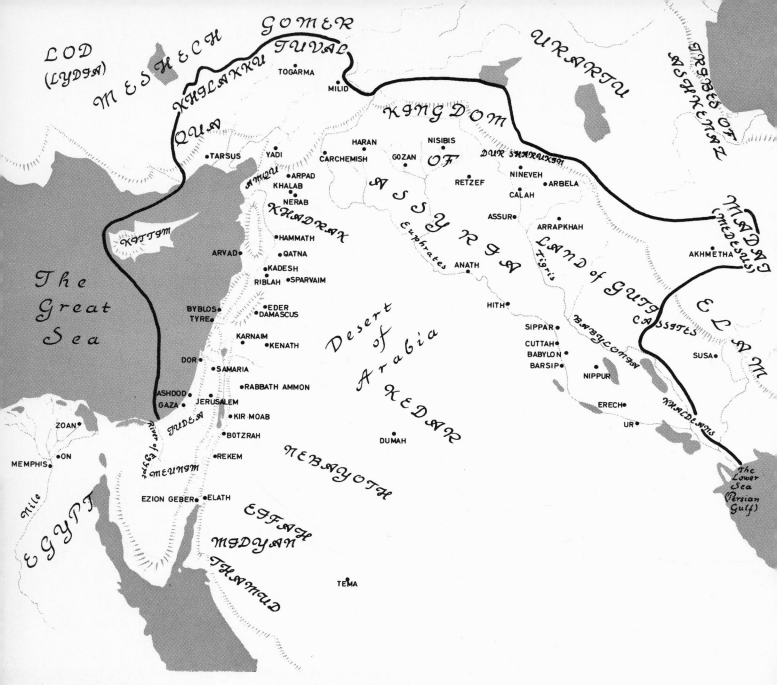

LOD
(LYDIA)

MESHECH

GOMER

TUVAL

KHILAKKU

QUA

TOGARMA

MILID

KINGDOM

URARTU

TRIBES OF
ASHKENAZ

HARAN

NISIBIS

GOZAN

DUR SHARUKIN

OF

TARSUS

YADI

CARCHEMISH

RETZEF

NINEVEH

ARBELA

ARPAD

ASSYRIA

CALAH

MADAI
(MEDES)

KHALAB

NERAB

ASSUR

ARRAPKHAH

AKHMETHA

KHADRAX

Euphrates

LAND OF GUTI

HAMMATH

ANATH

Tigris

CASSITES

ELAM

ARVAD

QATNA

KADESH

RIBLAH

SPARVAIM

HITH

SUSA

The
Great
Sea

KATTIM

BYBLOS
TYRE

EDER
DAMASCUS

SIPPAR

CUTTAH
BABYLON
BARSIP

NIPPUR

KARNAIM

KENATH

Babylonia

DOR

SAMARIA

ERECH

ASHDOD
GAZA

JERUSALEM

RABBATH AMMON

Desert
of
Arabia

UR

The
Lower
Sea
(Persian
Gulf)

Chaldeans

River of Egypt

JUDEA

KIR MOAB

KEDAR

ZOAN

BOTZRAH

MEMPHIS

ON

REKEM

DUMAH

NEBAYOTH

EGYPT

Nile

MEUNIM

EZION GEBER

ELATH

EFAH

MIDYAN

THAMUD

TEMA

THE ASSYRIAN EMPIRE.

EXILE AND RETURN

A JUDEAN COIN FROM THE LATE PERSIAN PERIOD.
THE BEARDED FIGURE, POSSIBLY REPRESENTING A
GOD, SITS ON A WINGED CHARIOT. HE HOLDS A FAL-
CON IN ONE HAND AND A GOBLET IN THE OTHER.

EXILE AND RETURN

The destruction of Jerusalem and the Temple, the fall of Judah and the loss of the kingdom marked the end of an era in the history of Israel. The days of the Babylonian exile that followed and, no less, the days of the return to Zion, put the people of Israel to one of the sorest trials in its history, of which the worst aspects were spiritual and religious crises. The Temple and the

SEAL OF GEDALIAHU, SON OF AHIKAM.

dynasty of David had made the people feel by their presence that the Lord was with them and that they would endure. Their destruction filled the Jews with a sense of desolation and loss. The ability of the people of Israel in these circumstances to endure and even to nurture a hope of redemption was the work of those selfsame prophets who had foretold the dispersion, the so-called "prophets of doom" — Jeremiah and Ezekiel. For these prophets, who had warned again and again of calamities to come, also foresaw the resurgence of Israel, the renewal of the Kingdom of the House of David, and the achievement of national independence.

The authority with which their prophecies as a whole were invested after the Destruction (which the prophets had foretold with cruel clarity) gave sense and significance to the Exile, which no longer was considered meaningless. The prophecies of deliverance uttered by these selfsame prophets were now believed to be God's own word. This vision of redemption strengthened them in their exile and led to a stronger bond with the House of David as a symbol of hope and revival.

The wars that had been fought by the Babylonians in Judah in 587 B.C. had brought heavy destruction to the land, which had suffered before from Babylonian oppression. The last kings of Judah had never willingly bore the Babylonian yoke, and their attempts to regain the independence of their kingdom had brought retribution upon them. The Babylonian army had destroyed the land and dispersed its people into exile, and many had fled to neighboring countries.

From archeological evidence, as far as it goes, the period of exile was one of total destruction

SEAL OF "YAZNIAHU, SERVANT OF THE KING." IT WAS FOUND IN ONE OF THE GRAVES AT MIZPEH AND ITS OWNER WAS PROBABLY A SOLDIER WHO JOINED GEDALIAH THERE AFTER THE DESTRUCTION OF JERUSALEM.

of extensive regions of the land of Judah. Many towns lay waste throughout the days of exile, and Jerusalem, the capital, was not rebuilt and re-settled until the return to Zion. Devastation was less in Benjamin, where many Jews remained throughout the period of the dispersion. At Miz-peh, in the land of Benjamin, survivors from other parts of Judah were concentrated; most of them were the "poorest of the land" left behind on pur-pose by the Babylonians to be vinedressers and husbandmen. There were also among them army officers, who had escaped from the Chaldeans and had returned when calm had been restored.

Nebuchadnezzar, King of Babylon, appointed Gedaliah ben Ahikam as governor of those who remained. He had been, in the days of Zedekiah, the chief minister "over the household". But his rule did not last long. Gedaliah was killed by Ishmael ben Nathania of the royal family, who disagreed with his policy. After the assassination the officers and many of those who remained, in-cluding Jeremiah the prophet, sought refuge in Egypt.

At the very same time, neighboring peoples

RECONSTRUCTION OF THE ISHTAR GATE IN BABYLON.

invaded the country and spread over wide regions — the Edomites in southern Judah, and the Philistines in the west. Central Judah, including Jerusalem, remained waste; it was not made a governorate of the Babylonian Empire, and the Babylonians did not resettle it. It seems that the official status of the country remained as it had been before the destruction. However, part of the land of Benjamin was made imperial domain, and the poor of the land who remained in Judah tilled the soil as serfs.

Besides this remnant in Judah, there lived in Palestine and neighboring countries groups of Jews who had escaped from Judah. These had in part assimilated with the Israelites in northern Samaria, in Galilee, and in Transjordan. After the assassination of the governor Gedaliah, those Jews who had escaped to Egypt under the leadership of the army officers found Jewish communities already in existence there. The refugees settled mainly in the region of the Nile Delta, but the prophet Jeremiah, who was among them, refers to Jewish communities in upper (southern) Egypt. Some of these had escaped to Egypt during the wars with the Chaldeans, but others were mercenaries who had been brought there by the kings of Egypt shortly before the Babylonian conquest, when Egypt had ruled over Judah, and were settled as mercenaries in the city of Elephantine on the southern border of Egypt. These maintained their own community life and religious worship, and even built a temple to the God of Israel. Details of all this have come down to us in the many papyri of the Persian period. Their contacts with Jews elsewhere were slight.

The most important Jewish center after the dispersion was in Babylon itself. Jews had been brought there from the very beginning of Babylonian rule in Judah.

It would appear that the Exile to Babylon began on a limited scale in the days of King Jehoiakim. In the spring of the year 598 B.C. after the surrender of Jehoiachin, his son, to the Chaldeans, there were brought to Babylon the "princes and the mighty men of valor" and the royal family. Together with these, the Chaldeans exiled craftsmen and smiths. Many of these exiles were settled by the Babylonians in special settlements in southern Mesopotamia, on the banks of the river Chebar, one of the largest artificial canals of the Euphrates in the vicinity of Nippur. There they kept their traditional patriarchal social structure, and were led by the elders, and in this way they were able to maintain their national and religious identity. At the outset the Jews engaged mainly in agriculture; only later did they begin to engage in trade. The craftsmen among them were occupied in some of the vast building schemes of Nebuchadnezzar and some of them were brought to the city of Babylon.

King Jehoiachin and his family enjoyed a special status on the fringes of Nebuchadnezzar's court. This we learn from Babylonian documents found in the ruins of the king's palace in the city of Babylon. In these documents — lists of rations distributed to those attached to the court — Jehoiachin and his sons are mentioned with their full titles, "King of Judah" and "Sons of the King of Judah".

The comparative ease enjoyed by the exiles at the time of Jehoiachin enabled them to develop a communal life of their own. They were joined by those exiles brought to Babylon after the destruction of Jerusalem, and by still others, following the revolt in Judah and the neighboring states five years after the Destruction. Within the boundaries of the Babylonian Empire, and apparently even in the land of Babylon itself, dwelt the descendants of the exiled Ten Tribes of Israel,

A VIEW OF JUDEA, LOOKING SOUTHEAST FROM ZORA.

CLAY CYLINDER BEARING CUNEIFORM INSCRIPTION IN
WHICH CYRUS ASSERTS HIS CLAIM TO THE THRONE
OF BABYLON.

TOMB AT PASARGADAE, TRADITIONALLY ASCRIBED TO
CYRUS.

TRIBUTE BEARERS FROM VARIOUS COUNTRIES: SECTION
OF A TABLET FROM THE AUDIENCE HALL OF THE PER-
SIAN ROYAL PALACE AT PERSEPOLIS.

brought there by the Assyrians more than a century before. Of these, the ones who still kept up the religion of their fathers joined the exiles of Judah, and probably later participated in the return to Zion.

Outstanding among the Jews in Babylon was the prophet Ezekiel, who had been exiled with Jehoiachin; from afar he reacted sharply to events in Judah. His prophecies also reflected the spiritual and religious crises that faced the Jewish exiles, and he dwelt on the personal relationship between the individual and his God. He saw the Exile as a purifying furnace for Israel. Return and future redemption were to him not dependent on the will of the people but were destined by God to occur at His will, irrespective of the desires of the exiled Jews.

During the long reign of Nebuchadnezzar, the Babylonian Empire flourished. There was no change in the position of the exiles or of the land of Judah, but hopes of a redemption and a return

BEARDED PERSIAN SOLDIERS WITH SPEAR, BOW AND ARROWS. FROM A MURAL ON A GLAZED TILE WALL IN BABYLON.

to Zion were kept alive by the very fact that Jehoiachin was allowed to retain his royal titles.

The last twenty years of the Babylonian Empire, from the death of Nebuchadnezzar to the conquest of Babylon by Cyrus, King of Persia, in 539 B.C., were times of unrest and imperial decline. The position of the Jews there and in Judah remained static. Evil-Merodach, who ruled after the death of Nebuchadnezzar, showed favor to the exiled king Jehoiachin. However, if any hopes were thereby kindled in the hearts of the Jews, they were ill-founded. The last king of Babylon, Nabonides, shook the foundations of the Empire by his quarrel with the priests of Marduk, who were exceedingly powerful in the city of Babylon. This period marked the beginning of

Jewish settlement in Northern Arabia. Nabonides tells in his inscriptions of the many years he spent in the deserts of Arabia, and of the establishment there of garrisons, among whom were men of Palestine and Syria. Some of these were undoubtedly exiles from Judah, and the towns mentioned in the inscriptions (Theima, Yathrib [Medina], Chaibar and others) are known as Jewish centers in Northern Arabia in the pre-Mohammedan period.

A radical change in the situation of the Jews came only after the conquest of Babylon by Cyrus, King of Persia; even before this, after the victories of Cyrus in Asia Minor and the disintegration of the Babylonian Empire, they pinned their hopes on his success. The Prophet of the

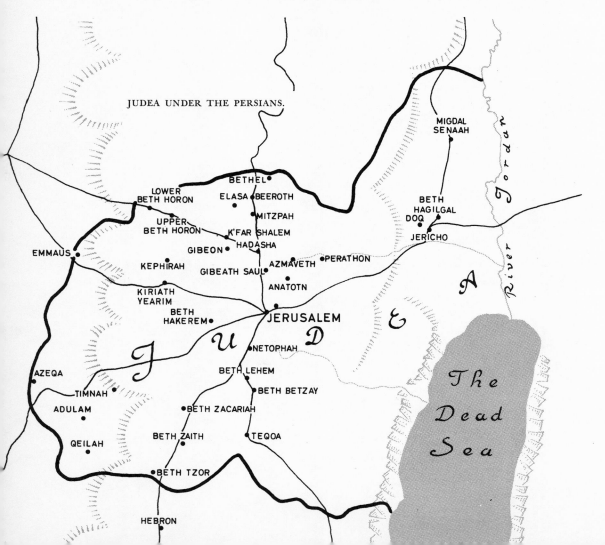

JUDEA UNDER THE PERSIANS.

INSCRIPTION OVER THE ENTRANCE TO THE CATA-
COMB OF THE TOBIAD FAMILY, GOVERNORS OF AMMON.
IT DATES FROM THE PERSIAN PERIOD. THE TOBIADS
WERE FIERCE OPPONENTS OF NEHEMIAH.

Deliverance, whose pronouncements have come down to us in the book of Isaiah (from chapter 40 onwards) gave expression to these hopes.

The conquest of Babylon by Cyrus was a turning-point in the history of Israel. The Persian King's policy of tolerance was manifested in the restoration of temples in Babylon itself, and in the return of the various peoples exiled by the Babylonians to the countries of their origin. This was the setting for the policy of Cyrus towards the Jews, which permitted the return from Babylon, the beginning of the rebuilding of the Temple, and the resettlement of Jerusalem. A special decree of Cyrus to this effect opened the period of the Return to Zion. In addition to the decree, he issued an administrative order — never carried out in practice — to cover the expenses of the rebuilding from the imperial treasury. The practical effect of the royal decree was limited. It permitted the Exiles of Judah to return to Jerusalem and there to build a House to the God of Israel, and allowed those Jews who remained in Babylon to give silver, gold and other possessions to the House of the Lord in Jerusa-

lem. The real importance of Cyrus' decree, however, was that it gave official status to the Temple that was to be built in the future. At the head of the returning Jews were Sheshbazzar Prince of Judah, son of King Jehoiachin; Jehoiachin's grandson Zerubbabel; Joshua son of Jozadak, the High Priest; and the leaders of the priests. The appointment of members of the House of David as governors of Judah under the King of Persia, aroused renewed hopes of independence, but it is doubtful whether the Persians really meant this to happen. Judah was no more than a province, distant and poor, and those who returned there never received the support of the local Persian administrators. When the rebuilding of the Temple began, they were faced with many difficulties. Peoples from the neighboring provinces had penetrated into and settled Judah. In particular the Samaritans, descendants of the northern tribes who had remained in Samaria and mixed with non-Israelite exiles brought there by the Assyrians, opposed the independent efforts of the returned exiles. They tried to obtain for themselves some influence in Jerusalem and in the building of the Temple. When this was refused them, they succeeded by intrigues in halting the work. In spite of these delays, the returned exiles were reinforced by successive waves of returning Jews, who continued to arrive in Judah in the reigns of Cyrus, Cambyses and Darius. Ultimately, they were joined by most of the descendants of those Jews who had never gone into exile.

The contrast, between the hopes of redemption aroused by the decree of Cyrus and hard reality, produced a crisis among the Jews. This was particularly severe since, from the start, all their hopes had been based upon the favor of the king of Persia and it now became apparent that there was little hope of real assistance from that quarter. As a result, the rebuilding of the Temple and the reestablishment of the state were slowed down.

About twenty years after the conquest of Babylon by Cyrus, the Persian Empire underwent a period of severe trial. When Darius ascended the throne he found himself in the midst of rift, disruption and continued revolt in the various countries of his Empire — among them Babylon and even Persia itself. In Palestine, however, there was comparative peace and quiet. The echoes of this turmoil, which shook his empire, undoubtedly aroused national and religious ferment, and renewed hopes of independence in Judah. These hopes were given voice by the prophets Haggai and Zacharia, although their prophecies were uttered after the establishment of Darius' rule on a firm basis. They envisioned tremendous changes to come in the world, and called upon the people of Judah to rise and build the Temple with their own hands. The prophets blamed the obstacles and the impediments to revival on the people's own neglect of this work, and promised repeatedly that after the Temple was rebuilt, redemption would come, and the House of David would rise again. And so, in the second

year of Darius, the Jews began to build the Temple. They completed the work four years later, in 516 B.C. At the head of the builders were Zerubbabel, son of Shealtiel of the dynasty of David, and the High Priest Joshua.

From Zachariah's pronouncements it may be inferred that during the building dissension arose between Zerubbabel and the High Priest regarding the hegemony over the people of Judah. The Persian authorities were involved in these quarrels and, by order of the Persian satrap, work on the building of the Temple temporarily ceased. It was resumed by direct command of Darius, now at last with the aid of a substantial grant from the Imperial treasury. Darius originated the custom that among the offerings in the Temple sacrifices should be offered for the life of the king and his sons. This custom persisted almost throughout the period of the second Temple, and came to symbolize the dependence of Judah on the king of Persia and, subsequently, on the Hellenistic and Roman kings.

In order to frustrate any attempt at revolt, the Persians no longer appointed the governors of Judah from the House of David. Thus ended the strife between the High Priest and the descendants of David. Henceforward the High Priest held undisputed sway and the House of David was removed from positions of influence in Judah.

The Temple, completed at last, became the center of the social and religious life of Judah, but the political status of Judah remained unchanged. With the consolidation of the Persian Empire the likelihood of national independence appeared to be further away than ever. From now on, these hopes found expression in messianic visions of a magnificent new era, which could come at the End of Days. This new conception of salvation was a result of the fact that the Jews were now reconciled to political reality. Henceforward

PART OF THE AUDIENCE HALL (THE APADANA) OF THE PERSIAN ROYAL PALACE AT PERSEPOLIS.

they envisaged salvation as wholly God-given and beyond the influence of the power of men.

Politically, during these years of marking time, Judah fitted into the mosaic of small states in the Persian satrapy of Syria-Palestine. The rise of the Temple hierarchy, the fact that all Judah in some way centered round the Temple, and the tendency of the Persians not to interfere in the religious customs of their subject peoples — all these helped to establish the autonomy of the community, so much so that the High Priest, despite the presence of an official Persian governor in Jerusalem, became in fact the undisputed leader of the people of Judah.

During this period of comparative peace, the population increased and spread beyond the borders of Judah. Consecutive Jewish settlement was extended, particularly towards the north, in southern Samaria and the low hill-country. Jews also resettled in the Negev, the Sharon Valley and Transjordan. At that time began the process of intermarriage with those same people of the country who had been rejected by the returned exiles who saw in such merging a serious danger to national and religious existence. Intermarriage was now particularly prevalent among the ruling class of Judah, the wealthy, the priests, and even the family of the High Priest himself. Marriage links with the ruling families of their neighbors strengthened the political position of the leaders of Judah, but conversely also provided a foothold within Judah for these neighbors. At the same time, social conflicts were sharpened. The people groaned under the heavy taxes levied by the Persians; the upper classes accumulated great landed possessions, and formerly independent farmers were forced to become tenants and serfs.

After a period of sixty years, Judah was once again awakened to new life, religious and political, by an influx of Jews from Babylon. The Jewish community of Babylon had shared the general economic prosperity of that country under Persian rule, and had cherished the spiritual heritage of the people: the Mosaic Law and the preachings of the Prophets. As in the days of the first return, this new influx into Judah was led by men invested with authority by the King of Persia. Foremost among them was Ezra, a "scribe of the Law of Moses", who in the seventh year of the reign of Artaxerxes I (457 B.C.) led a caravan of Jews into Judah. The charter he carried from Artaxerxes gave permission for the Jews of Babylon to come to Jerusalem, and gave full authority to Ezra to appoint judges and magistrates, not only in Judah, but over the Jews in the region of the Empire "beyond the river" (Euphrates). This seems to have been a political act on the part of the Persians, designed to conciliate the Jewish population of the Empire during a period of serious revolts against Persian rule in Egypt. However, Ezra did not receive executive powers, and therefore, despite all his efforts, he was unable to change the situation in Judah radically. Nevertheless his efforts did inaugurate a new period of religious and national activity among the Jews, which led to fundamental changes later.

THE EXCAVATIONS OF YEB, A JEWISH MILITARY SETTLEMENT AT ELEPHANTINE IN SOUTHERN EGYPT.

The resurgence of national fervor in Judah was expressed shortly after that, in an attempt to complete the fortification of the walls of Jerusalem without royal permission, at a time when Megabysos, the Satrap of the Persian territories "beyond the river", was in revolt against Artaxerxes. This move was used by the Samaritans and others of the neighboring states as a pretext to obtain the King's sanction to march in force against Jerusalem and to destroy these works. At this moment of crisis, Nehemiah, a high court official of Artaxerxes, stepped forward. He succeeded in persuading the King to appoint him governor of Judah, with permission to refortify Jerusalem (445 B.C.). Nehemia was given full authority, and a military force was put at his disposal. He managed to arouse the people to the effort of closing the breaches in the walls, and completing the fortification system of Jerusalem. This work was strongly resisted by Judah's neighbors, who, surprisingly, found an ally in the High Priest Eliashib. The High Priest, as head of the Temple hierarchy, preferred to extend the temporal influence and power of the Temple above the consideration of religious principles, and, moreover, he feared the increasing influence of

the Jewish governor in the community. He therefore hoped to bring the Samaritans and other peoples of the country closer to the Temple, against the policies of Ezra and Nehemiah.

Nehemiah strove to regulate the life of the Jewish community, to ensure its continuance according to the Law of Moses, and to carry out the proper maintenance of the Temple service. In order to realize these aims, a "sure covenant" was made to which the heads of the people, including Nehemiah, subscribed. This covenant called on all Jews to acknowledge the supreme authority of the Law of Moses and to annul all marriages contracted with their Gentile neighbors. It forbade further intermarriage, and included regulations designed to provide means for the maintenance of the Temple, and others designed to keep Jews separate from their neighbors.

Ezra and Nehemiah molded the Jewish way of life for many generations to come — Ezra by the force of his spiritual authority, and Nehemiah by his more physical achievements, foremost among them the transformation of Jerusalem into the walled and densely populated capital of Judah.

The controversy between those who demanded the segregation of the people and those who favored extending Judaism, particularly among the Samaritans, had already started at the beginning of the return, and was not settled until about the

AERIAL VIEW OF THE PERSIAN CITY OF SUSA (SHUSHAN), SCENE OF THE BIBLICAL BOOK OF ESTHER.

THE SEALS OF TWO JUDEAN LOCAL GOVERNORS WHO RULED AFTER THE TIME OF NEHEMIAH, FOUND AT RAMAT RAHEL ON THE OUTSKIRTS OF JERUSALEM

hemiah (end of the 5th Century B.C.), found in the Jewish colony of Elephantine in Egypt, indicate the widespread influence of Jerusalem on far-off Jewish settlements. One of these documents, a royal order apparently originating from Jerusalem, instructs the Jewish soldiers in Elephantine in the ritual of celebrating Passover. Another document, a letter to Bagohi, Governor of Judah, requesting his support in obtaining permission to rebuild the local Temple destroyed by the Egyptians, mentions that they have already applied once before in this matter to Johanan the High Priest, and to the priests and Jewish nobles in Jerusalem.

After Nehemiah, Judah was ruled by a succession of governors, some of them probably Jews, as we may infer from seals found at Ramat Rachel just outside Jerusalem. One of these seals bears an inscription probably reading "Yahud (Judah), Yohiyezer the Governor" and another refers to one Ahiyo. However, in communal affairs, the priests and nobles of Judah held sway.

In the 4th Century B.C., silver coins were minted in Judah, carrying the inscription "Yahud". This right to mint coins is an indication of the great degree of autonomy granted to Judah towards the end of Persian rule. It is likely that during this period there was no resident governor in Judah, and that the High Priest also fulfilled the function of head of the province, a position certainly held by him in the Hellenistic period, after the conquest of the East by Alexander the Great.

From the point of view of Jewish history, the end of Persian rule and the inclusion of Judah in the Hellenistic world did not mark the end of an era. Contact with Hellenism, which was to influence Israel so deeply in the future, did not at the outset entail any essential change in the political status or the spiritual life of Judah.

end of the Persian period. It persisted even after Nehemiah had forcibly expelled from Jerusalem the son of the High Priest, who was the son-in-law of Sanballat, governor of Samaria and leader of the Samaritans. In the course of time the Samaritans were gradually ousted and finally completely excluded from the Temple in Jerusalem. Samaritan worship became centered in Shechem, a site hallowed by patriarchal tradition, and they founded a temple nearby on Mount Gerizim. This separation between the Jews and the Samaritans occurred in a period of which little is known, between Nehemiah's reforms and the conquest of the East, by Alexander the Great.

Interesting documents of the period after Ne-

THE PERSIAN EMPIRE.

DARIUS I OF PERSIA SITTING ON HIS THRONE: SECTION
OF A TABLET FOUND IN DARIUS' PALACE AT PERSEPOLIS.

PART OF A LETTER WRITTEN BY THE JEWS OF YEB TO
BAGOHI THE GOVERNOR OF JUDEA IN WHICH THEY ASK
HIS HELP IN OBTAINING PERMISSION TO REBUILD THEIR
DESTROYED TEMPLE.

(*Top*) SILVER SAUCER FROM THE PERSIAN PERIOD, FOUND
IN A TOMB IN SOUTHERN ISRAEL.
(*Bottom*) DECORATIVE URN FROM THE SIXTH CENTURY
B.C., FOUND AT BAT YAM NEAR TEL AVIV.

AHASUERUS, KING OF PERSIA, AND ESTHER, HIS JEWISH
QUEEN, ON THEIR THRONES. THIS MURAL, FROM A
3RD CENTURY SYNAGOGUE IN DURA EUROPOS, MESO-
POTAMIA, SHOWS THE THRONE DECORATED WITH
LIONS AND EAGLES IN THE STYLE OF THE BIBLICAL
DESCRIPTION OF THE THRONE OF KING SOLOMON.

THE HELLENISTIC CHALLENGE
AND THE MACCABEES

THE SO-CALLED "ABSALOM MONUMENT" IN THE KIDRON
VALLEY NEAR JERUSALEM. A TYPICAL MONUMENT FROM
THE FIRST CENTURY.

THE HELLENISTIC CHALLENGE AND THE MACCABEES

Until the 4th Century B.C. Palestine was within the sphere of influence of the Eastern Empires and the country's history was determined by changes in the balances of power among them. After the 4th Century and up to the Islamic conquest, Palestine came under the influence of a civilization whose inspiration and primary foundations were rooted in Greece. The beginning of this period was marked politically by the establishment and ascent of the Greco-Macedonian powers which emerged from the kingdom of Alexander the Great. It soon became apparent that a united Macedonian empire had no chance of survival and after a period of agitation three powerful states emerged in the Eastern Basin of the Mediterranean: the Ptolemaic Kingdom, whose center was in Egypt, but whose influence and dominion considerably overlapped the frontiers of the Nile country; the Seleucid Kingdom, exceeding in area and population each of the other king-

doms, and including a great part of the ancient provinces of the Persian state; and the Macedonian Kingdom in Europe.

The 3rd Century B.C. saw the zenith of the Hellenistic states; they led the world in military arts, in politics, organization and culture. Busy with wars though they were, the Macedonian conquerors succeeded in organizing, in Egypt and in the countries of Asia under their dominion, a huge settlement enterprise, unparalleled in the history of the Ancient World. Towards the end of his life, Alexander had envisaged a fusion of the oriental and Macedonian elements. His successors abandoned this policy, which they considered unworkable. They openly gave precedence to the Greco-Macedonian elements, and consequently endeavored to reinforce them to the greatest possible extent. Moreover, in view of their military activities, the Hellenistic kings required a large and well-trained army, that was made up

THE HELLENISTIC EMPIRE.

chiefly of Greeks. They were therefore compelled to create permanent sources of loyal Greek power within their kingdoms. This object was attained by the allocation of large areas of land to Greek settlers, in return for military services rendered; in this manner, they created a stable military reserve which was economically dependent on them. The Macedonian kings also depended on the Greeks for services in administration, technology and economy. At the beginning of the Hellenistic period, the Greek element had already spread considerably throughout the East. Greeks had become the effective rulers in the Eastern countries: they were the courtiers, the commanders, the executives and the engineers.

The conquest of Palestine by Alexander in the year 332 B.C. was swift. The cities of Palestine with the exception of Gaza, did not rise against the invading armies. After the death of Alexander in 323, a series of wars swept the countries of the East, including Palestine. The country changed hands several times, and its cities and population suffered considerably. In the year 301 Palestine was finally conquered by Ptolemy I, King of Egypt; it remained under Ptolemaic rule until 200 and its history was determined by

RECONSTRUCTION OF THE TOBIAD PALACE AT ARAK EL AMIR, WHICH WAS BUILT IN THE SECOND CENTURY B.C.

events in Egypt. The Ptolemaic rule in Palestine in the 3rd Century was not secure. The Seleucids had claims over the country, since the government of an area so close to the center of their own kingdom was of great concern to them. The Ptolemies, too, attached great strategic importance to the country as an advanced base for the defence of Egypt, and it was hardly less important to them economically. During most of the 3rd Century, the Ptolemies had the upper hand. Only with the succession of Antiochus III (223-187 B.C.) was the situation reversed, and the initiative taken by the Seleucids. In the year 200, their armies won a decisive victory near Panion, which is close to the sources of the Jordan. With this victory, the country passed from Ptolemaic to Seleucid rule.

The Ptolemies, during their rule, generally succeeded in maintaining order and in consolidating their regime, owing chiefly to their efforts to conciliate the local population. It is not too much to say that of all the foreign rules that existed in Palestine between the Persian and Roman pe-

riods, the Ptolemaic regime left the greatest imprint on the administration of the country and on
its way of life.

The Greek domination was accompanied by the
settlement of Greeks in the land. Prior to the
Macedonian conquest, the country's population
had been mainly Semitic, comprising Jews, Phoe-
nicians, Edomites and Nabateans. After the Macedonian conquest, this was no longer the case.
Greek merchants and soldiers were already prominent in Palestine during the Persian period,
but the number of Greeks who came to settle in
the country was relatively small. Now, overnight,
they became the lords and masters of the land,
settling on it at an ever-increasing rate. Greek
towns and garrisons were created, and even the
established cities underwent a change. In point
of fact, all the important Greek cities in Palestine
were old cities that had accepted the Greek way of

ARAMAIC INSCRIPTION FOUND ON A JEWISH GRAVE-
STONE IN ALEXANDRIA, EGYPT.

life and adopted the organizational pattern of
the Greek city.

The most important social centers of the new
culture were Gaza and Ascalon in the south and
Acre in the north. In addition to the Greek
coastal towns, urban Greek centers sprang up
east of the Jordan and around the Sea of Galilee.
Urban civilization was much less developed in
Transjordan than in the coastal area, but in the
course of time the Hellenized inhabitants of
Transjordan developed an urban culture no less
sophisticated than that of their neighbors. Prominent among the cities of Transjordan was Gadara,
which had produced writers of world renown already during the Hellenistic period.

In the hinterland, the process of Hellenization
was slower and less pervasive. The only exception
was Samaria, which was highly Hellenized owing
to the fact that, as early as the beginning of the
Hellenistic period, it had been settled by Mace-
donians. Hellenistic elements were also found in
Marissa. This city, situated on the road to Jerusalem from the south-west, was at an important
crossroads and served as a Ptolemaic administrative center in the south of the country. The
propagators of Hellenism in this part of the land
were Hellenized Sidonians.

Judea was, at the beginning, one of numerous
units which formed part of the Ptolemaic area
of dominion, and later a part of the Seleucid area
of dominion in Southern Syria. Thus, the Judean
state existed continuously as a political unit from
the time of the Persian period. The Hellenistic
kings considered Judea as a national entity,
"ethnos", with Jerusalem as its capital. The Jewish ethnos enjoyed a large measure of autonomy,
but its rights were confined to the State of
Judea: the Jewish ethnos was considered by the
authorities as a territorial-geographical concept.
Until the decrees promulgated by Antiochus Epi-

WELL-PRESERVED ROUND TOWER FROM THE HELLEN-ISTIC PERIOD FOUND IN SAMARIA.

phanes, Jerusalem was not a city-state, but its status in relation to the Jewish territory somewhat resembled the relation of those cities enjoying polis status to their territories.

The government of autonomous Judea was in the hands of the High Priest and of the "gerusia", the council of elders. The office of High Priest was hereditary. Jews and Gentiles alike considered the High Priest as the leader of the nation. He was responsible for the proper functioning of the Temple, the safety of Jerusalem and the regular supply of water to the city. He headed the "council of elders", which was responsible for the collection of the royal taxes. The "gerusia" comprised the priesthood and most prominent elders, who represented the interests of the provincial towns of Judea. Historical sources also mention popular assemblies in Jerusalem. These assemblies did not meet at fixed periods, but were summoned by the leaders only on special occasions, particularly when far-reaching changes in the political regime were expected.

The Torah served as the law of the land and this Law was also sanctioned by its foreign rulers. As a result, the Jewish autonomous authorities were empowered to enforce the Mosaic laws on all of Judea's inhabitants and to ban all trace of paganism from the land. In the center of the religious and social life of Judea stood the

Temple. According to the historian Polybius, the Jews were "a nation centered around the famous Temple of Jerusalem". The priests constituted the privileged class in Judea and it was they who administered the Temple.

From the social point of view as well, the priests formed the most exalted class. Side by side with the High Priest's family, a number of priests and their families were prominent, fulfilling important functions in Jewish society. The members of the aristocratic priesthood married mainly within their own ranks during the period of the Second Temple; but whenever their interests dictated a different course of action, they did not hesitate to marry into influential families which did not form part of the priesthood.

The prolonged Hellenistic administration of Palestine, the practices of the Ptolemaic and Seleucid administrations, the material achievements

REMAINS OF HASMONEAN FORTIFICATIONS IN JERU-SALEM.

of Hellenistic culture in the spheres of agriculture, urbanism and finance, were all instrumental in bringing far-reaching changes to Judea. We must bear in mind that the Jewish population centers in Palestine, in Judea and elsewhere, were surrounded by foreign populations, ethnically heterogeneous. The question arose: would Judea manage to survive as a living cultural force, or would it lose its specific national, religious and cultural identity, just as it had lost its political independence and become another one of the numerous units making up the Hellenistic culture of Palestine? Around 200 B.C. the victory of Hellenism appeared certain; its external glitter, its aggressive militarism and the fact of its dominance, seemed likely to defeat the Jewish culture. It was evident that Judea was being Hellenized. The upper classes, priests and laymen alike, were adopting more and more the mentality and way of life of their peers in the non-Jewish parts of Palestine.

GRECO-HEBRAIC INSCRIPTION ON STONE MARKING THE BOUNDARY OF THE CITY OF GEZER.

Not all the Jews of Palestine lived within the administrative boundaries of autonomous Judea. Since the end of the Persian period, the number of Jews in Palestine had been continuously on the rise, and the country's boundaries, from Beth-Zur in the south to Beth-El in the north, had become too narrow to contain them all. The Jewish community thus overflowed the confines of Judea, and the neighboring districts, such as Lydda, were also inhabited by Jews. These Jews,

of course, aspired to political unification with Jerusalem, and during the period the anti-Jewish laws of Antiochus, many of the Jews dwelling in the mountains north and north-east of Jerusalem, as well as the inhabitants of the plain of Lydda, were among the most fervent warriors. Jewish settlements were also to be found in Transjordan, in Galilee and in the coastal towns. Jewish centers existed in the Diaspora too, in Egypt and Babylonia. The inhabitants of Judea had special links with Babylonia, from which many of them had returned, but during the reign of the Ptolemies the Jews of Palestine were cut off from the densely-populated Jewish communities of Babylonia and the other countries under Seleucid dominion. In contrast, their ties with Egyptian Jewry became closer. At the beginning of the Hellenistic period, the migration from Palestine to Egypt increased. This migration was partly voluntary, partly compulsory, since many Jews were taken prisoners by the Ptolemaic troops passing through the country. The Ptolemaic rule fostered these ties, as is evidenced by the fact that Hebrew literary works written in Palestine were soon translated into Greek to answer the needs of Greek-speaking Egyptian Jews.

Antiochus IV (175-164 B.C.) began to take an interest in the affairs of Palestine soon after his accession to the throne, and showed a greater concern for Jerusalem than did his predecessors. Jason, the High Priest whom he appointed, introduced far-reaching changes in the government of the city and in its social order. Apparently, the purpose of these measures was to convert Jerusalem into a polis, to be called Antiochia. The development of the new polis involved the introduction of Greek political and cultural institutions, such as the gymnasium, into the traditional Jewish society of Jerusalem. Jason's term of office was rather short. The war against Ptolemaic

(Top left) COIN THOUGHT TO HAVE BEEN MINTED BY ANTIOCHUS VII.
(Top right) COIN MINTED BY MATTATHIAS ANTIGONUS (44-37 B.C.). IT SHOWS A SEVEN-BRANCHED CANDELABRUM AND PART OF THE NAME "ANTIGONUS".
(Center) COIN FROM THE TIME OF ALEXANDER JANNAEUS (103-76 B.C.) WITH EIGHT-RAYED STAR. THE HEBREW INSCRIPTION READS: "YEHONATHAN THE KING".
(Bottom) COIN MINTED BY JOHN HYRCANUS II (67-40 B.C.) SHOWING DOUBLE HORN OF PLENTY, WITH A POPPYHEAD BETWEEN THE HORNS.

Egypt was imminent and Antiochus apparently had misgivings as to Jason's loyalty at this critical period. He was replaced by Menelaus, who did not hail from the ranks of the high priesthood, and whose position depended entirely on his devotion to the throne. A new leaf was thus turned in the relationship between the Hellenistic kings and Judaism. The High Priest, who had hitherto presented the interests of the nation, now acted as a representative of Antiochus, and as his instrument in carrying out his policy towards the Jews.

Meanwhile, some momentous events had taken place in that part of the world. The Ptolemaic kingdom, desirous of reconquering Palestine and Southern Syria, declared war on Antiochus; the latter, however, very soon took the lead into his own hands. In the year 170 or 169 B.C. he invaded Egypt and defeated Ptolemy's armies, but did not succeed in conquering Alexandria. In 168 his armies again invaded Egypt, this time endangering the very existence of Ptolemaic rule in Egypt. It was only due to the intervention of

THE MONUMENT TRADITIONALLY KNOWN AS "ZECH ARIA'S TOMB" IN THE KIDRON VALLEY, EAST OF JERUSALEM.

Rome that the Ptolemaic kingdom was saved.

The wars of Antiochus Epiphanes were closely linked with other momentous events in Judea. On his way back from his Egyptian campaign, Antiochus — assisted by Menelaus — plundered the Temple of Jerusalem, outraging the feelings of the Jews by this violation of their nation's most sacred objects. In 168 Jason returned to Jerusalem, probably backed by the Ptolemies, and

once more seized power.

Antiochus conquered Jerusalem, and in order to ensure his rule brought in foreign settlers and established them in the citadel of Jerusalem. These new settlers brought their idols with them, to which the extremists among the Hellenized, with Menelaus at their head, made no objection. Many Jews could not bear the new tyranny, and their souls rebelled against the idolatrous practices that swept the city. They left their birthplace and went to live in the deserts to the east and southeast of the city, or in the villages and provincial towns in the northwest. In 167 B.C. the observance of the Jewish laws was proscribed and the death penalty imposed on any Jew found circumcising a child or keeping the Sabbath. Moreover, the authorities forced idol worship and other forbidden customs on the population, in particular the eating of pork. The Temple was desecrated, and was henceforth dedicated to Zeus.

(Left) WESTERN WALL OF INTERIOR OF ABSALOM'S MONUMENT.
(Right) SOUTHERN WALL OF SAME INTERIOR.

ALEXANDER THE GREAT FIGHTING THE PERSIANS. SEC-
TION OF A ROMAN MOSAIC FOUND AT POMPEII.

A LETTER FROM TOBIAS TO APOLLONIUS, AN EGYPTIAN
FINANCE MINISTER. IT CONCERNS A SHIPMENT OF ANI-
MALS SENT FROM TRANS-JORDAN TO THE KING IN EGYPT
(257 B.C.).

DOORWAY IN THE CENTRAL HALL OF A CATACOMB BE-
LONGING TO THE SIDONIAN FAMILY OF APOLLONIUS, AT
MARESHAH, THIRD CENTURY B.C.

ANTIOCHUS IV EPIPHANES.

JAFFA FROM THE NORTH; THE CITY'S ANCIENT RUINS
LIE BENEATH THIS MOUND. JAFFA WAS JUDEA'S PRINCI-
PAL SEAPORT IN THE HELLENISTIC ERA.

GENERAL VIEW OF THE TOMBS IN KIDRON VALLEY NEAR
JERUSALEM.

SITE OF THE FORTRESS OF SIMON THE HASMONEAN (SIMON MACCABEE) AT GEZER.

ENTRANCE TO ONE OF THE SEVENTY TOMBS OF THE SAN-
HEDRIN IN JERUSALEM, CONTEMPORARY WITH THE
SECOND TEMPLE.

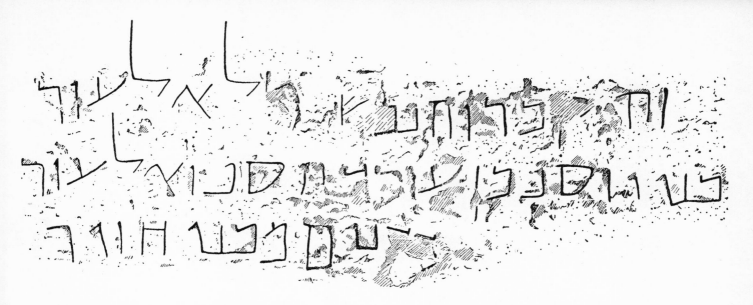

INSCRIPTION FROM THE FACADE OF THE TOMBS OF
THE PRIESTLY FAMILY OF KHEIZIR, IN THE KIDRON
VALLEY.

Polytheism was generally tolerant. Antiochus himself did not impose any religious coercion on the other nations within his kingdom. Only the Jewish religion was persecuted relentlessly. It would appear that the continuous tension in Judea made it clear to Antiochus that the opposition of the Jews to his methods was rooted in their peculiar religion. This religion he considered hostile to his entire philosophy of life. It may be assumed that political and military considerations, and in particular his anxiety over the maintenance of peace in the periphery of his kingdom, prompted Antiochus to proclaim his anti-Jewish laws.

The religious persecutions that followed, unparalleled in the history of the Jews, awakened mighty forces in the nation. Among these was the Hasmonean house, the family of the Maccabees, which led the rebellion that was ultimately to restore political and religious freedom. Judah Maccabeus and his brothers succeeded gradually in converting the undisciplined mass of Jewish warriors into an army — an army that successfully fought against the Seleucid armies sent by Antiochus. Seleucid attempts to quell the rebellion were defeated by the victories of Judah Maccabeus in the battle of Beth-Horon, Emmaus and Beth-Zur. The rebels captured Jerusalem and purified the Temple (164 B.C.). These achievements symbolized the victory of the Jewish rebellion. In the year 163 the religious autonomy of the Jews and the administration of the Temple by devout Jews were recognized by the central government as well.

Various factors determined the outcome of the battle from the military and political standpoints. Of these, some were external and some internal. The major factor was undoubtedly the boundless devotion of the Jews to their religion, as it had evolved during the many centuries preceding the decrees of Antiochus. The ideals formulated during these hundreds of years had permeated

THE TOMBS OF THE PRIESTLY FAMILY OF KHEIZIR IN
THE KIDRON VALLEY.

through to wide sections of the population; rarely indeed in ancient times did such a wide body of people accept to such a degree the aspirations of its spiritual leaders. Thus, not inconsiderable human resources were at the disposal of the Hasmoneans in their fight against the House of Seleucus. Judea and the neighboring regions were densely populated by villagers faithful to the religion of their forefathers; they could be turned into soldiers. The extremists among the Hellenized population, who sided with the Seleucids, were in the minority. Even after Judea's non-Jewish neighbors had joined the camp of the opposition, the balance of power remained with the Jews. The greatest danger threatening Judea was the large, well-trained Seleucid army. However, under prevailing conditions, the Seleucids could not throw into this war their entire military force, for while one part of the army was fighting in Judea, another section was fighting in the eastern governorates of the kingdom. The successors

of Antiochus had to face similar problems, augmented by recurrent dissensions over the succession. These discords were instrumental in helping the cause of Jonathan and Simon, the Hasmoneans who led the Jewish struggle for liberation after Judah's death.

Meanwhile, the Jewish fighters had progressed in the military sphere, and Jewish commanders ventured to match forces with the king's troops even on the plains outside the limits of Judea. In summing up the factors that led to the victory of the Jews, account must be taken of the fact that the Jewish resistance to the Seleucids was supported by foreign powers. The Roman Republic was interested in weakening the Seleucid kingdom, and even before the death of Judah Maccabeus (161 B.C.) the Roman Senate had concluded an alliance with the Jewish rebels.

The Hasmonean kingdom, which came into being as a result of the revolt, was in a constant state of territorial expansion. Jonathan the Hasmonean annexed to Judea the areas inhabited by Jews in Southern Samaria, as well as the Ekron area. Simon, by conquering Jaffa, won for Judea

PLAN OF QUMRAN, NORTHWEST OF THE DEAD SEA. IT SHOWS THE LIVING QUARTERS AND WATER RESERVOIRS OF THE SECT THAT WROTE THE DEAD SEA SCROLLS.

DECORATION OVER THE ENTRANCE TO ONE OF THE SANHEDRIN TOMBS.

an outlet to the sea. His successor, Hyrcanus (134-104 B.C.) and his two sons, Aristobulus the First (104-103) and Alexander Jannaeus, extended Judea's territory to cover all of Palestine. Edom in the south, Galilee in the north, and the area surrounding the east bank of the Jordan became completely Jewish. Jewish rule was also imposed on central Samaria and in the various Greek towns along the coast, south of the Carmel (with the exception of Ascalon). Alexander Jannaeus conquered some of the towns of the Decapolis. The Jewish Kingdom became one of the important political factors in the area at a time when the Seleucid and Ptolemaic kingdoms were on the wane and the Roman Republic was slackening its intervention in the affairs of the Near East.

The great conquests were also accompanied by changes in Judea's political regime. The Great Synod, which met at the time of Simon the Hasmonean (140) confirmed Simon and his sons after him as rulers, high priests and military commanders of the Jewish State. Simon's successors changed the traditional Jewish regime headed by high priests into a monarchy. Jonathan Hyrcanus had already maintained a mercenary corps on the model of the Hellenistic powers and his son Aristobulus crowned himself king of Judea. The process reached its climax at the time

of Alexander Jannaeus, who strengthened the royal power at the expense of the institutions representing the nation. This development slowed down during the reign of his wife Salome (76-67) who endeavoured to govern with the consent of elements influential among the Jewish masses.

The period of the Hasmonean monarchy was characterized by social and ideological effervescence. At the beginning, the Hasmonean dynasty rode on a wave of religious and national enthusiasm, but the situation was fraught with seeds of dissension. The supporters of the first Hasmoneans did not present a united front. It was difficult to find a permanent meeting ground between the extremists and the moderate Hellenized elements from among the upper classes who had taken part in the war of liberation. The struggle between the Pharisees and the Sadducees on the character of the Hasmonean state was the expression of a tension which thrived on the evolution of the regime, on the political situation of Judea, and on the tendency of most of the Hasmonean rulers towards Sadducee ideas.

The period of approximately eighty years during which an independent Hasmonean state existed (142-63) was one of consolidation and expansion of Palestinian Jewry. Even Roman rule from the time of Pompey and his successors did not completely reverse this trend, and the influence of Judaism on large parts of Palestine became an established fact for many years.

The Great Sea

TYRE

PANIAS

KEDESH

SELEUCIA

GUSH HALAV

GOLAN

PTOLEMAIS
(ACRE)

GALILEE

SHIKMONA

MIGDAL
ARBELA

Lake of Galilee

HIPPOS
(SUSITA)

GAMALA

SIHIN
SEPPHORIS

HAMATH

ABEL

DION

Mt. Carmel

GABBA

PHILOTERIA
(BETH YERAH)

HAMATH
GADARA

DOR

GADARA

YIZRAEL

ARBELA

STRATON'S
TOWER

EIN
GANNIM

SCYTOPOLIS
(BETH SHAN)

PELLA

NARBATA

SAMARIA

BETH SHAN

SAMARIA

ZAPHON

REGEV

GERASA

APOLLONIA

SHECHEM

SAMARITANS

HAMTAN

ANTIPATRIS

AKRABA

JAFFA

SARTABA
(ALEXANDRIUM)

River Jordan

PHILADEPH

LOD

HADID

GOFNA

MODIIN

TZOR

BETH HORON (LOWER)
BETH HORON (UPPER)

DOK

GEZER

JERICHO

YAMNIA

EMMAUS

ABEL

BETH
HARAM

HESHBON

ASHDOD

EKRON

JUDAEA

JERUSALEM

KH. KUMRAN

HYRCANIA

MADABA

ASCALON

BETH LEHEM

MARISSA

BETH ZUR

ANTHEDON

GAZA

HEBRON

ADORAIM

ARISTOBOLIAS

MACHAERUS

GERAR

YUTA

EIN
GEDI

Dead Sea

IDUMAEA

MASSADA

RAPHIAH

KERAK

BEER SHEBA

ZOAR

NABATEANS

ABDA

THE STRUGGLE AGAINST ROME

THE TOWER OF PHASAEL, POPULARLY KNOWN AS "DAVID'S TOWER", PART OF THE CITADEL OF JERUSALEM.

THE STRUGGLE AGAINST ROME

The direct intervention by the Romans in Syria and the annexation of Syria to the Roman Republic, proceeded directly from the victories of Pompey over the kings of Pontus and Armenia, and the eradication of piracy from the maritime lanes. It would have been possible for Rome to conquer Syria and Palestine sooner, but reasons connected with the internal development of the republic and the limitations of the administrative apparatus, prevented the complete domination of the eastern countries by Rome at an earlier stage. These difficulties, however, did not deter Pompey, and once the decision to annex the whole of Syria had been reached, the conquest of Judea became imminent. It was only a matter of time to see the manner in which Judea would be incorporated within the political boundaries of the Republic. The civil war that broke out between Aristobulus the Second and Hyrcanus the Second, the sons of Alexander Jannaeus, only hastened this intervention and determined the character of the association between Rome and Judea; it could not change the basic trend of events. Pompey's intervention tipped the scale in favor of Hyrcanus. Aristobulus' supporters and the partisans of political freedom were determined to fight the Roman invaders to the bitter end. The Temple Mount, where the Jewish warriors had dug themselves in, fell to the enemy after a siege, and the first military clash between Rome and the Jewish nation ended in the loss of the independence of the Hasmonean state in the year 63 B.C.

The Hasmonean kingdom ceased to exist. The office of High Priest reverted to Hyrcanus the Second, who was also appointed "Ethnarch" (President) of the Jewish nation. Pompey also reduced Judea's territory by taking away some of the conquests of John Hyrcanus and Alexander Jannaeus, such as Samaria and the Greek towns along the coast and in Transjordan. Pompey had time only to lay the foundation of a renewal of the Greek urban way of life in the areas that had previously formed part of the Hasmonean Kingdom. This project was carried out mainly under the first pro-consuls of Syria, chiefly Gabinius. In contrast, most of the territories of Edom retained their Jewish character, as did the strip of land east of the Jordan, between the Sea of Galilee and the Dead Sea.

The first years of Roman rule were marked by recurring revolts throughout the land instigated by Aristobulus and his sons in their efforts to restore themselves to power. These attempts all ended in defeat, but they demonstrated the weakness of Roman rule. Gabinius aimed at the complete destruction of Jewish unity, which he tried to achieve by dividing the country into five regional Sanhedrins; this, however, only served to undermine the prestige of Hyrcanus, who was dependent upon the Romans. The victories of Julius Caesar over his Roman rivals were a turning point in the Palestine situation (48-44 B.C.). Caesar acted in conjunction with the pro-Roman Jewish leaders of Palestine. He abolished the administrative divisions of Gabinius, and the leadership of the Jews was again entrusted to Hyrcanus. Jaffa was returned to the Jews and the question

THE INSCRIPTION COMMEMORATES THE BUILDING OF A SYNAGOGUE IN JERUSALEM BY THEODOTUS, A JEW FROM THE DIASPORA. FROM THE FIRST CENTURY.

THE HERODIAN KINGDOM.

of the tribute which Judea was compelled to pay to Rome was settled. During this period the son of an Edomite family that had embraced Judaism during the time of John Hyrcanus and had reached the highest grades of the Hasmonean administration, became more and more prominent at the side of Hyrcanus. His name was Antipater.

The events following Caesar's death brought about the gradual and almost total extinction of the Hasmonean dynasty and the rise of Antipater's family. During the Parthian invasion of Palestine, Hyrcanus was taken prisoner, while the attempts of Antigonus, the son of Aristobulus, to retain the monarchy failed. In the year 40 B.C. Herod, the son of Antipater, was recognized by the Romans as King of Judea. In 37, Jerusalem fell into the hands of the Roman legions after a prolonged siege, and Herod, faithful ally of the Romans, was enthroned as King of Judea.

Herod's kingdom prospered chiefly after the victory of Octavian over Antonius. His country was no smaller than the Hasmonean state at the time of its greatest extension. The fact that the constitution of Herod's kingdom was not overly Judeo-theocratic made it easier for the Roman authorities to annex to it the large Greek towns of Palestine. In the eyes of the Romans, Herod was a friend, king, and ally; and as a result, he was entitled to the ceremonial protocol pertaining to royalty. In the sphere of foreign policy he was kept within the limits drawn by the central Roman government, but in the field of internal policy he had unlimited control over his subjects. He held the supreme judicial authority and could impose the death penalty; he had the right to levy taxes as he saw fit, to found new towns, to transfer residents and to confiscate landed property. His power was absolute and neither the autonomy of the Greek towns nor the Jewish Sanhedrin could prevail against it. The Sanhedrin

JERUSALEM AT THE TIME OF THE SECOND TEMPLE, SHORTLY BEFORE ITS DESTRUCTION. THE THIRD WALL SHOWN ON THE MAP WAS NEVER COMPLETED.

lost its former prestige completely and ceased being an element of the administrative machine. The center of power shifted to the Royal Sanhedrin, that is, to the King's Privy Council.

In order to increase his royal prestige, the King devoted himself to the erection of splendid edifices and new towns. The largest towns he built were Caesarea, which became Jerusalem's rival, and whose port was the most important along the Palestine coast, and Sebaste, that is, Samaria. He also built lavishly in Jerusalem and Jericho. In Jerusalem he built a royal palace and a new temple (Herod's Temple) to replace the temple of Zerubbabel. His activity extended beyond the country's borders. He supported many Greek towns and institutions and helped to introduce the Olympic games; an Athenian inscription attests to the fact that the Athenians respected him for his efforts on their behalf. He also promoted the interests of the isle of Rhodes. These

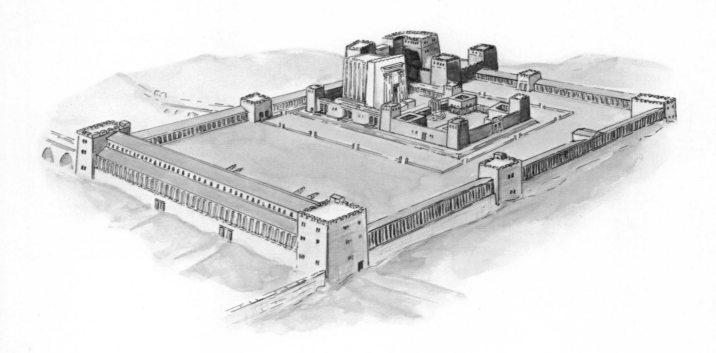

THE TEMPLE OF HEROD AS IT IS BELIEVED TO HAVE APPEARED.

THE WAILING WALL IN JERUSALEM. PART OF THE
WESTERN WALL, IT IS THE ONLY SURVIVING REMNANT
OF THE TEMPLE BUILT BY HEROD.

A SECTION OF THE WALL OF THE OLD CITY OF JERUSA-
LEM. THE LOWER COURSES DATE FROM THE PERIOD
OF THE SECOND TEMPLE.

THE GOLDEN GATE IN THE WALL OF THE OLD CITY OF JERUSALEM.

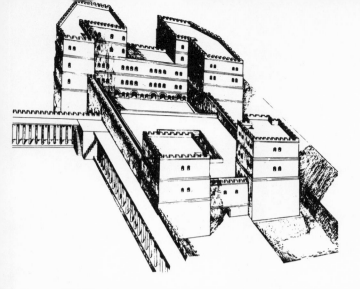

RECONSTRUCTION OF THE CITADEL ANTONIA BUILT BY HEROD IN JERUSALEM.

activities turned Herod into an international figure.

The splendor of Herod's kingdom found its main expression in his royal court, which resembled other royal courts of the Roman East in every way, with the same ceremonials and the same endless intrigues. Persons of Greek culture filled the court and the dominant language was Greek. Many at court, whether permanent residents or visitors, were foreigners. Among the courtiers there were world famous literary figures, who took great pains to propagate the king's fame. But the other side of the coin included murder and assassination. Among the king's victims were his wife, Miriam the Hasmonean, and her two sons, Alexander and Aristobulus, as well as Antipater, the king's son by his former wife.

Although Herod was also active in the Jewish interest, especially in the countries of the Diaspora, and had hoped to win the sympathy of his Jewish subjects in Palestine itself by the construction of the Temple, he was hated by most of the nation. His absolutist rule and his respect for physical strength were contrary to the traditional Jewish way of life. He had taken the throne by brute force in expelling the Hasmoneans with the assistance of Roman legions. In Jewish opinion, his Edomite ancestry made him unfit for the throne, while his sympathetic attitude to Hellenism and the non-Jewish character of

his regime increased the general suspicion. His arbitrariness in the appointment of high priests and the relative liberties he took with regard to the religious interpretation of the Torah added fuel to the fire. Public discontent grew towards the end of his reign, plots were hatched against the King and the Jewish masses waited for the chance to rebel. When the King died, in the fourth year B.C., it seemed that the time was ripe; rebellion seethed throughout Palestine and it was only with difficulty that public order was restored by the military might of Rome.

Throughout the period leading up to the destruction of the Temple, the Jewish population was ruled by Roman procurators. There was but one short interval during which the rule over all parts of Palestine was concentrated in the hands of a Jewish king, Agrippa the First (41-44). After the removal of the Ethnarch Archelaus, son of Herod, Judea, Samaria and Edom became one province, while Galilee, the Jewish part of Transjordan, the Gaulan and Trachonitis continued to form part of the states of Herod's sons, Herod Antipas and Philippus.

After the dismissal of Archelaus, in the year 6, Augustus had a number of alternatives. He could choose another ruler from Herod's dynasty, but a suitable one was not available, since the dynasty was opposed by most of the nation. Alternatively, Augustus could annex Archelaus' state directly to Syria. But there were serious arguments against such a course of action, because of the special character of the Jewish population, its religion and its political heritage. It was therefore decided to transform Judea into an autonomous unit headed by a procurator from the Roman equestrian order.

Upon Judea's transformation into a Roman province, Jerusalem ceased to be the political and administrative capital of the country. The center

(Top) COIN OF THE REIGN OF AGRIPPA THE FIRST (41-44)
(Bottom) A SILVER SHEKEL FROM THE THIRD YEAR OF
THE REVOLT AGAINST THE ROMANS (66-70) WITH THE
INSCRIPTION "SHEKEL OF ISRAEL, YEAR THREE"

of government shifted to Caesarea.

The Roman rule in the country gave a large measure of autonomy to existing Jewish institutions and even made use of them whenever necessary. These institutions were entrusted with responsibility for the maintenance of law and order. The most exalted institution of the Jews was the Jerusalem Sanhedrin, which was the Supreme Tribunal. In the administrative field, the Sanhedrin's prerogatives at that time were limited to Judea proper, whereas in the sphere of religion and religious laws, the Sanhedrin's authority extended over the whole Jewish population of Palestine.

When examining the Sanhedrin's competence, a distinction must be made between theory and the actual facts of the situation as it existed towards the end of the Second Commonwealth, after the Roman authorities had reduced the Sanhedrin's prerogatives — already curtailed by both Herod and Archelaus. The Supreme Tribunal, nevertheless, retained the power of decision in religious affairs and in everything connected with the Temple. The right to impose the death penalty was, in principle, taken away from the Jewish institutions and transferred to the Roman administration. However, in matters directly affecting the Temple sanctity, the Jews were entitled to decide in questions involving life or death, although this right was to a certain extent subject to the supervision of the Roman Government. The strictness of this supervision varied with the personality and policy of the procurators.

The members of the Sanhedrin hailed from the priestly class, the Levites and the common people. The high-ranking priests formed a cohesive group within the Sanhedrin. With them sat the elders, and the scribes who were the representatives of the Pharisees. In the Sanhedrin there were also representatives of the provincial towns as well as persons hailing from beyond the borders of Judea proper.

Towards the end of the Second Commonwealth Jews made up the majority of Palestine's population, most of which was concentrated in Judea, Galilee and Perea, that is Jewish Transjordan. But many Jews also lived outside these areas and even in Greek towns. Most Jews lived in rural areas, but a considerable number were concentrated in settlements that were urban in size and sometimes in organizational structure. Some of the latter were purely Jewish areas, like Jerusalem, or predominantly Jewish, like Tiberias, Jericho or Yavneh. From existing historical sources it can be gathered that the country was densely populated. Considering the size of Jerusalem's population, it can be stated that Judea, which stretched from the Jordan to Jaffa was numerically the largest of the Jewish centers of Palestine. Jerusalem overshadowed all the other Jewish cities in the country. It was the administrative capital only of Judea proper, but its institutions had power of decision in the religious and social life of all the Jews in the whole country. The Temple, on the one hand, and the Pharisean centers of Torah study, on the other, made it "the most famous city in the Orient and not only in Judea" (Pliny). Jerusalem was the bond that united the Jewish population, and it drew Jewish pilgrims from the Diaspora, as well as proselytes. Its powerful fortifications were a source of pride and confidence to the Jewish community as a whole. It was the center of spiritual creativeness and the residence of the representatives of the School of Hillel. Scholars from other places went to live in the capital. Jerusalem's seminaries became teeming centers of study, to which came those in search of knowledge, from all parts of the country and from the Diaspora.

The Galilean center was second in importance to Judea. Its remoteness from Judea contributed to the emergence of a recognized Galilean type of Jew. Towards the end of the Second Commonwealth Galilee was prosperous, and noted for its many towns and large villages. Some of the most important religious and political movements originated in Galilee. It was there that Christianity was born and that the extremist movement headed by the son of Yehuda Hizkiah came into being. From Gischala (Gush Halav) in Galilee hailed Yohanan, son of Levi, one of the two principal leaders of Jerusalem during the siege, and Eleazar, who brought about the conversion of the Adiabene royal dynasty.

The priestly class continued, to a large extent, to form the elite of Jewish society in the last years of the Second Commonwealth. The priests were in real control of the Temple and they were the mainstay of Jewish ritual. They enjoyed considerable material advantages, in accordance with the privileges extended to them by the Torah. In Jerusalem they were prominent because of their large number and there were priests in all parts of Palestine. The priests, who owed their social prestige to their ancestry, endeavored to prevent the accession into their ranks of elements of doubtful extraction. From Herod's time onward, a closely-knit oligarchy of high priests, took shape. These oligarchic families considered the position of high priests as their monopolistic right, and married only within their own ranks.

The Roman-Hellenistic period is characterized by an increase in the number of Jews throughout the civilized world. Hundreds of thousands of Jews lived in Babylon, Syria, Cyprus, Asia Minor, Egypt, Cyrenaica, the Dodecanese Islands, Greece and Italy. Their number grew from generation to generation by the combined effect of natural increase, migration from Palestine and conversions to Judaism, which reached record proportions during the generation preceding the destruction of the Temple. Babylonia was the greatest center of Jewish settlement outside the boundaries of the Roman Empire. Its Jews lived in densely populated areas where they constituted the majority of the population and there were towns entirely inhabited by Jews. The Jews of Babylonia had their own centrally organized institutions and they were considered one of the most important ethnic elements of the Parthian kingdom.

The most important Jewish diaspora within the Roman Empire was the Egyptian one, whose origins go back to the First Commonwealth. In the years preceding the destruction of the Temple, the number of Jews living in Egypt approached one million. These Jews lived in numerous settlements in the Nile Valley stretching from Alexandria in the north to the borders of Nubia in the south. Their occupations were highly varied; many worked the land as farmers, vine-dressers or agricultural laborers; others were craftsmen. During the Ptolemaic period, Jews were prominent in the service of the Government and of the Army. In Alexandria, rich Jews, bankers and merchants, lived side by side with the craftsmen and the poor. In Cyrenaica, close to Egypt, the Jews constituted one of the main elements of the population. There were also large Jewish populations in all the big cities of the Empire's Oriental provinces. It was so in Antioch, Syria's capital, and in the various towns of Asia Minor. Special importance devolved on the Jewish inhabitants of Rome, capital of the Empire, on account of their closeness to the imperial court.

The Jews of the Diaspora developed their own organizational patterns. The centers of the Jew-

THE ARCH OF TITUS IN ROME, BUILT TO MARK THE ROMAN VICTORY OVER THE JEWS IN THE YEAR 70.

ish communities were the synagogues where the Jews gathered for prayer and also for various public and social purposes. The Jewish communities were generally headed by elected leaders. The Alexandrian community was headed until Augustus' reign by an Ethnarch and later by a Council of Elders (Gerusia). The Jews also had their own tribunals and some of the big towns had Jewish Archives. The Roman Emperors recognized Jewish particularism and granted the Jews legal privileges which permitted them to live according to their laws and customs. These privileges often gave rise to conflicts between the Jews and their Greek neighbors in the big towns.

Greek was the spoken and written language of most Jews living in Egypt, as in other parts of the Roman Empire. By the third Century B.C. the Torah had been translated into Greek in Egypt, and this translation, known as the Septuagint, was circulated throughout the Diaspora and was utilized by the hellenized Jews in their religious rituals. The Jews also developed an extensive literature in the Greek language, comprising poetic, historical and philosophical works. This Jewish-Hellenistic literature was not merely Greek literature written by persons of Jewish extraction, but rather Jewish literature written in Greek. It was mainly a body of literature revolving around Judaism, its problems and history, rather than a literary trend based on subjects typical of Greek thought. Whatever the object of this literature, whether it was written as a response to internal Jewish needs, or whether it was directed towards the outside and had an apologetic role, it was always, even in its moderate aspects, aggressive. Its greatest figure was Philo of Alexandria, who combined all that was best in Greek literary and philosophical culture with his unrestricted loyalty to the Jewish religion and nation.

The Jews of the Diaspora maintained close ties with the homeland. Jews who were faithful to the Jewish religion considered Jerusalem as the capital city of all Jews everywhere and viewed the Jewish settlements outside Palestine as "colonies", originating in Jerusalem, the metropolis.

The close relationship existing between the Jews of the Diaspora and Palestine was naturally of great political importance. The Imperial Roman Government, in the pursuance of its Palestinian policy, had to take into account the probable reaction of the masses of Jews living throughout the Empire and outside it. This relationship between the Jews of the Diaspora and the Homeland had also social, economic and cultural repercussions. Immigrants from the Diaspora occasionally determined the character of Jewish society in Palestine; the donations of the Jews of the Diaspora (the half-shekel) helped to increase the splendor of the Temple of Jerusalem and to enrich its treasures; moreover, the pilgrimage to Jerusalem resulted in the formation of close ties among Jews belonging to distant communities and served as a vehicle for the propagation of new ideas throughout the Jewish world.

The years preceding the destruction of the Temple were marked by eschatological effervescense. Large sections of the nation believed in the imminence of the "Kingdom of God" on earth. This vision of the end of days went hand in hand with a belief in the nation's redemption and in the destruction of the wicked rule of Rome. Important sections of the nation gave the eschatological expectations an active political interpretation. This was the theory preached by the Zealot party, whose origins went back to the beginning of the direct Roman rule of the country. The Zealots believed in the exclusiveness of God's kingdom and in the logical conclusion this implied, namely that to accept the domination of the Roman em-

peror was tantamount to a serious offence against religious law. In the opinion of the Zealots, it was not enough to bide their time; it was necessary to act on their religious convictions, to rebel against Roman rule and to force other Jews to this line of action, despite their reluctance. Whereas the Jewish nation had rebelled against the Seleucid dynasty, under the leadership of the Hasmonean dynasty, only when there was a direct threat to the values of the Jewish religion, the Zealots preached rebellion in the name of the principle of freedom, which to them had the force of a religious precept.

Beside the eschatological activists, there were also other prophets who preached the imminence of the Kingdom of God, to be attained by miraculous intervention and not by violent human acts.

Christianity was born against this background. Its founder, Jesus of Nazareth, fell victim to the opposition of the oligarchy of high priests to all those who change and to the suspicion of the Roman rulers of Jewish· messianic movements. The disciples of Jesus, particularly Paul, a hellenized Jew from Tarsus in Asia Minor, turned the original Jewish eschatology of Jesus into a religion with universal power of attraction.

The last years of the Second Commonwealth were characterized by fanatical loyalty to their religion on the part of the Jewish masses. At this period there are no reports of any serious attempt on the part of the Jews of Palestine to resume the process of Hellenization and to make far-reaching concessions to the dominant Greco-Roman civilization at the expense of Jewish tradition. The religious interpretation of Mosaic law, which had been developed by the great Pharisee scholars, covered large areas of the nation's life. Extremist purist trends took root among Pharisee groups and among esoteric organizations, like the Essenes. The masses were ready to

COIN BEARING HEAD OF TITUS.

BRONZE COIN MINTED BY VESPASIAN (69-79) TO COMMEMORATE THE VICTORY OVER THE JEWS. THE PALM TREE SIGNIFIES JUDEA; THE MALE IS THE TRIUMPHANT EMPEROR IN UNIFORM; AND THE FEMALE IS REPRESENTED BY A MOURNING JEWISH WOMAN. THE INSCRIPTION READS "IUDAEA CAPTA."

sacrifice their lives in an effort to prevent any attempt directed against the nation's sacred values. This was the situation during the rule of Pontius Pilate and on the occasion of the attempt of Caligula to place his statue in the Temple. This scheme was frustrated, but many realized at the time that the very existence of the Jewish religion could not be guaranteed as long as the Jews were dependent on the goodwill of a foreign government.

The Roman Emperors recognized the principle of the uniqueness of the Jewish nation. But in fact many conflicts arose between the Roman administration and the Palestine Jews. Many of the Procurators, especially the later ones, were unfit for their posts. Some of them were of Greek-Oriental extraction and were therefore prejudiced in favor of the hellenized towns in their struggle against the Jews. The fact that the Roman garrison in Palestine was made up chiefly of natives of the hellenized towns, hostile to the Jews, also contributed towards the disruption of the relations between the Jews and the authorities.

To all these factors must be added the social tension existing within the Jewish population; the exploitation of the masses by the upper classes, the struggle among the priestly oligarchic families, the taking over of the rural areas by the extremist Zealots whose activities eventually spread to Jerusalem and resulted in anarchy. Large sections of the population lent a willing ear to the extremists' propaganda and were ready to participate in actions directed against the Romans.

The crisis became particularly acute at the time of the procurator Florus. The support given by the Roman administration to the Greco-Syrian inhabitants of Caesarea and the fiscal excesses of Florus in Jerusalem itself, in the year 66, were the direct causes of the conflagration. The leadership in Jerusalem passed into the hands of the extremists who broke all contact with the Imperial authorities. The rebels were successful at first, soundly defeating the Roman governor of Syria who had rushed to crush the rebellion while it was still in the bud. As a result of this victory, moderate elements also joined in the revolt. To eschatological expectations were added realistic considerations: verified reports as to the weakness of the eastern Roman legions, the expectation that Jews in various countries would join in the revolt and that the Parthian kingdom would intervene. None of these hopes materialized. The Parthians did not lift a finger; the rebellion did not have a unified command and a relentless internal war characterized all the operations. In the year 67 Vespasianus, the Roman commander, con-

CAESAREA, THE ROMAN CAPITAL OF JUDEA AND THE PRINCIPAL PORT OF THE PROVINCE, BUILT BY KING HEROD.

quered Galilee. After he became Emperor, the command was transferred to his son, Titus. Titus conquered Jerusalem, in the year 70, after a prolonged siege during which the Jews had fought valiantly against superior forces. The burning of the Temple by the Romans ended a great period in Jewish history.

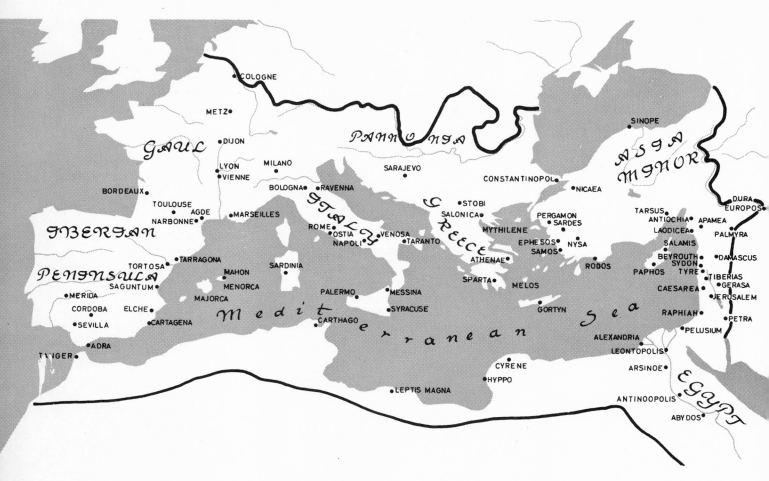

THE ROMAN EMPIRE.

ENTRANCE TO THE "TOMBS OF KINGS" IN JERUSALEM,
BUILT AT THE CLOSE OF THE SECOND TEMPLE ERA FOR
THE KINGS OF ADIABENE, THE MESOPOTAMIAN ROYAL
DYNASTY WHICH CONVERTED TO JUDAISM.

DETAIL FROM ARCH OF TITUS, SHOWING ROMAN SOL-
DIERS TRIUMPHANTLY CARRYING THE SEVEN-BRANCHED
CANDELABRUM TAKEN FROM THE TEMPLE.

THE FORTRESS OF MASADA WAS THE SITE OF THE LAST BATTLE BETWEEN THE JEWISH ZEALOTS AND THE ROMAN LEGIONS DURING THE REVOLT IN 66-70. NOTE THE MOUND BUILT BY THE ROMANS TO FACILITATE BRINGING UP BATTERING RAMS.

SIMON BAR-KOCHBA—
SOVEREIGN OF ISRAEL

COINS FROM THE BAR KOCHBA REBELLION.
(Top center) BRONZE COIN FROM THE SECOND YEAR OF
THE WAR SHOWING A LAUREL WREATH AROUND THE
WORD "JERUSALEM."
(Bottom left) REVERSE SIDE OF THE COIN.
THE INSCRIPTION AROUND THE PITCHER READS "SEC-
OND YEAR OF THE FREEDOM OF ISRAEL".
(Bottom right) BRONZE COIN SHOWING A HARP AND BEAR-
ING THE WORDS, "FIRST YEAR OF THE REDEMPTION
OF ISRAEL".

SIMON BAR-KOCHBA—SOVEREIGN OF ISRAEL

The more than 500 years between the destruction of the Temple and the conquest of Palestine by the Arabs marked a transition period, between the independence of Israel as a people living in its own political and social framework, and the period of exile when the nation was dispersed as a minority, large or small, without any center of independent national leadership and without any active political initiative.

During this period the nation had no political independence. From a religious viewpoint the times were regarded as abnormal, as the Temple, in which only it was possible to carry out complete religious observances, lay in ruins, and the communal leadership, the Sanhedrin, deemed itself lacking in full authority as long as the Temple was not functioning. Nevertheless, many of the fundamental elements of a people's life, whose absence generally characterizes a life in exile, were still in existence during the first half of this period.

Long after the destruction of the Temple, the Jews together with the Samaritans still constituted the majority of the population of Palestine. Up to the beginning of the 4th Century most of the land in Palestine was held by Jews, independent farmers, each with his small holding. Economically the position of the people in this period was satisfactory. Besides agriculture and the processing of agricultural produce, many crafts flourished, such as the manufacture of clothing and utensils, for which Palestine became famous from the middle of the 2nd Century onwards. Later on, however, the masses of Jewish farmers were stripped of their lands and as the economic foundation of the country was undermined, emigration increased and petty commerce became more widespread.

During almost the whole of this early period there existed an independent national leadership. This leadership found its chief expression in the Patriarchate and the Sanhedrin, which were founded soon after the destruction of the Temple. These two institutions embraced all the principal aspects of the life of the people. They constituted the representation and the national leadership of the nation both in Palestine and in the Diaspora, as well as forming the supreme religious authority. The Supreme Court, and the

(Top) ROMAN INSCRIPTION TO THE GOD SARAPIS, OFFERED BY SOLDIERS OF THE THIRD LEGION WHILE PASSING THROUGH JERUSALEM DURING THE REIGN OF EMPEROR TRAJAN.
(Bottom) "THE SEAT OF MOSES" FROM THE SYNAGOGUE AT CHORAZIN, DATING FROM THE THIRD CENTURY.

Great School in which the judges and the teachers of the Law were ordained, revised and determined points of the Law and taught the Law to individuals and communities; to them the people came, from the country itself and from the Diaspora, to study the Law.

As the years passed, the position of the national leadership was strengthened. Commissaries, who were sent by the Patriarch and by the Sanhedrin to supervise the communities and their institutions, were also authorized to appoint and to transfer leaders of the communities. The leadership first attained decisive sovereignty within the nation, and was ultimately recognized by the Roman government, which helped it by recognizing its authority to collect taxes, in Palestine and in the Diaspora, for the maintenance of the Patriarchate and the Sanhedrin. The Patriarchate remained in existence for over 300 years and except for one brief interruption, was directed by descendants of Hillel, who in turn claimed to be members of the House of David. This lent to the national leadership a halo of almost regal brilliance. Even when the Romans abolished the Patriarchate in 429 the Sanhedrin remained in existence.

The Diaspora generally accepted Palestinian hegemony, although there were occasional struggles for independence on the part of the Babylonian community, which had enjoyed a long tradition of self-rule under the Head of the Exile, and whose consciousness of independence was strengthened by its large and concentrated Jewish population and by its widespread study of the Law from the end of the Tannaic Period (the end of the 2nd Century). But Babylonian Jewry, like that of other communities, accepted the authority of Palestine in the teaching and in the study of the Law. Its dependence on Palestine lessened only in later generations, when the Jewish com-

munity in Palestine had dwindled and declined in strength.

Political activity continued throughout the period. Economically this was expressed in the struggle for the retention of the land in the hands of small Jewish farmers, in the encouragement of migration to Palestine and the preservation of the Jewish community there, and in the fostering of the spirit of Rabbinic law throughout the social order. Politically, this activity found expression in the refusal to recognize Roman rule and the economic system that Rome had sought to impose on the country, and in the long succession of attempts to revolt and to restore political freedom. Some of these attempts, made with the collaboration of the communities of the Diaspora,

A BUNDLE OF LETTERS SENT BY BAR KOCHBA TO ONE OF HIS OFFICERS IN THE EIN GEDI GARRISON, RECENTLY DISCOVERED IN THE "CAVE OF THE LETTERS".

such as the revolt in the days of Trajan (115-117) and Hadrian (132-135) were on a major scale while others were limited uprisings, especially those in the second half of this period. This activity also took the form of efforts to exploit political constellations with a view to liberating the

THE ROMAN FORTIFICATIONS AT BETAR.

people in gradual stages. The second half of the period marked the beginnings of acceptance of foreign rule, although right up to the end of the period there were occasional resurgences of rebellion.

The importance of this period in Jewish history is twofold:

a) After the destruction of the Temple the nation was no longer able to base its life on the state and on the Temple, which had been the focal point of a life devoted to the Law and its commandments. The bases of Jewish life that were laid down in the days following the destruction of the Temple constituted the foundation for the continuation of the nation's life and its hopes for the future in the long days of exile, when it had no central national leadership and rarely any hope of attaining any.

b) During this period the Oral Law became crystallized as the sum total of the Halachic and Agadic literatures. The process of the codification of the Halacha began with the destruction of the Temple and reached its climax with the creation of the classic compendium of the Oral Law, the Mishna. This was the result of a long and complex process of creation of the Oral Law, a creation that took many generations of compilers and that reached its highest development during the two or three generations preceding its completion. The Mishna became the main basis for the study of the Law and for the laying down of the Halacha, a basis for the life and thought of the nation both at home and abroad. On the foundation of the Mishna were built, during the following two to three centuries, the two great edifices of the Oral Law: the Jerusalem and the Babylonian Talmuds.

A short time after the process of compilation of the Halachic literature was begun, there began too the crystallization and compilation of the Agada. A great part of the Agadic literature was edited only after the period under discussion, but its compilation dates from this period.

The hegemony of Palestine over the Diaspora and the many ties between Palestine and the Diaspora were of great importance during this period. The Mishna was accepted by the Diaspora as well and displaced all other compendia of the Oral Law. In this way the homogeneous reli-

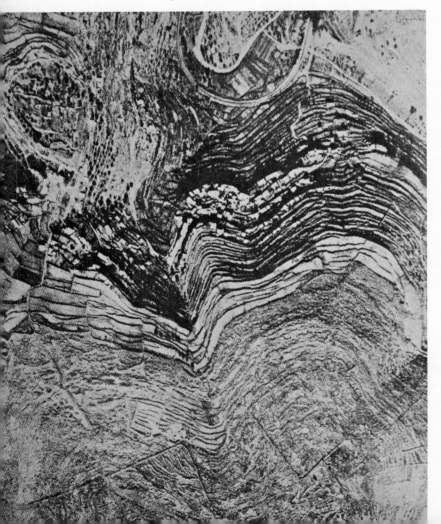

BIRD'S EYE VIEW OF THE TERRACED SLOPES OF BETAR.

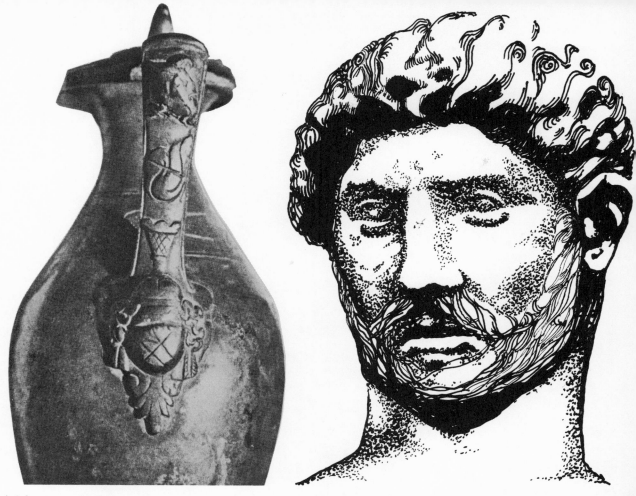

(Left) BRONZE CONTAINER FOUND IN THE CAVE OF LETTERS. PRESUMABLY IT HAD BEEN CAPTURED FROM THE ROMANS. THE RELIEF ON THE HANDLE WAS DELIBERATELY DEFACED IN PART.
(Right) BUST OF HADRIAN, THE ROMAN EMPEROR WHO SUPPRESSED THE BAR KOCHBA REVOLT.

gious and social framework of the nation was preserved. Even the two Talmuds that arose from the Mishna, those of Jerusalem and of Babylon, resembled each other far more than they differed, for the many connections between Palestine and the Diaspora ensured a common allegiance in the fields of thought and Law.

The war that culminated in the destruction of the Temple and the conquest of Jerusalem lasted for more than four years and dealt a terrible blow to the Jewish people in Palestine. Even without accepting the exaggerated casualty figures given by Josephus and Tacitus, there is no doubt that the number of Jews from Palestine and from the Diaspora who died together in the war, was very high. To them we must add the many prisoners who were sold into slavery or forced labor and those who were sent into the arena to fight wild beasts for the entertainment of foreign cities. Economically and agriculturally too, the long years of war were ruinous. Entire cities were laid waste in the fighting and after the conquest. The

valleys, and in particular the terraced areas covered with fruit trees, suffered greatly. The ground around Jerusalem had been "laid bare as if it were virgin soil" from the rooting up of trees for building siege works. But the Jewish community was not basically affected. Only a few of the destroyed Jewish settlements were not rebuilt within the space of a generation. Even in the foreign cities along the coast, where the Jewish communities were wiped out during the war years, the Jews were settled again within the first or second generation after the destruction of the Temple.

The laying waste of the country, the conquest of Jerusalem and the burning of the Temple, the subsequent abolition of the national-religious institutions, the High Priesthood and the Sanhedrin, by which the people were governed, all these

JERICHO

JERUSALEM

KH.
KUMRAN

Kidron

Judea
of
Desert
Desert

Dead Sea

David

Arugot

EIN GEDI

CAVES

Hever

CAVES

Tseelim

MASSADA

Halashon

caused great confusion and a general spiritual collapse. The city of Jerusalem and the Temple within it had served as more than just the capital city. They had formed the nucleus of the newly arising community at the beginning of the Second Commonwealth and provided the background for all the events in the life of the people as long as the Temple existed. The Temple was not only the place where the people worshipped God and atoned for their sins, it was also the connection with the other dominating aspects of their lives, such as the Sanhedrin, the synagogue and the teaching of the Law. Many sets of commandments were linked with the Temple and the worship of God that was carried on within it. Its destruction left a vacuum in the spiritual and practical lives of the Jews. A central foundation of their lives was lost and their faith in their whole way of life was undermined.

Among the people arose many ascetics, men who forswore the amenities of civilization and went off to live alone in caves, waiting in fasting and self-punishment for the Last Judgement which they prophesied was soon to come.

Politically and administratively Judea was now an independent province, where before the destruction of the Temple it had been a province annexed to Syria. After the destruction of the Temple, the Tenth Legion was stationed in Judea and command of the country was put into the hands of the Legion's commander. At Vespasian's orders extensive areas of the country were expropriated and handed over directly to Roman soldiers who had completed their service and to others, both non-Jews and Jews, who had collaborated with the Roman authorities. In many cases the Jewish proprietors stayed on their lands, no longer as owners but as tenants, and had to pay part of their produce, or its value, to the new owners. The burden of taxation grew

even heavier after the destruction of the Temple, and we find many complaints in the literature of the period regarding the pressure of taxes and mortgages. These complaints date from immediately after the Temple's destruction. A particularly irksome tax was that of two drachmas which had to be paid to the Capitol, the temple of the Roman god, Jupiter, in place of the half-shekel that every Jew in Palestine and abroad had paid to the Temple in Jerusalem. This tax was imposed on both men and women, and collected even on behalf of children. From literary sources and Egyptian papyri we learn that the tax was collected from Jewish communities throughout the Roman Empire and from converts to Judaism. More objectionable than the financial burden of the tax was the degradation that its payment implied.

The first emergence of a new national center was connected with the name of Rabbi Yohanan ben Zakkai, one of the greatest scholars and spokesman of the Sanhedrin during the days of

(Left) A COIN FROM THE FIRST YEAR OF THE REVOLT OF BAR KOCHBA. THE INSCRIPTION READS: "SIMON, NASSI (SOVEREIGN) OF ISRAEL".
(Right) A COIN MINTED BY THE EMPEROR HADRIAN SHOWING THE EMPEROR PLOWING WITH A COW AND A BULL. IN THE BACKGROUND IS THE STANDARD OF THE FIFTH MACEDONIAN LEGION. DURING HIS REIGN THE ROMANS RENAMED JERUSALEM "AELIA CAPITOLINA".

CHASED LEADEN LID OF A COFFIN FROM THE 3RD OR 4TH CENTURY, FOUND IN THE JEWISH CATACOMBS AT BETH SHEARIM.

the Second Commonwealth. Rabbi Yohanan had left Jerusalem during the siege having seen no reason or justification for the continuation of the war. The Romans permitted him to settle in Yavneh, a town in the low hill-country of Judea. There he began, either with the knowledge of the Roman authorities or without, to weld the people together again, to fill the vacuum caused by the destruction of the Temple, and to reconstitute the Sanhedrin. He announced the New Moon and the occurrences of leap years which had always been the prerogative of the Sanhedrin, as it determined the dates when the Holy Days were to be celebrated.

The activities of Rabbi Yohanan ben Zakkai were limited, either through fear of interference by the Roman authorities or because not all of the scholars who remained after the Destruction were prepared to join the new center. The Sanhedrin, however, was very active in the period of his successor, Rabbi Gamliel, known as Rabbi Gamliel of Yavneh, son of Rabbi Shimon ben Gamliel, one of the rulers in the days of the revolt preceding the destruction of the Temple. With his elevation the leadership of the Sanhedrin returned to the House of Hillel. Rabbi Gamliel came to the leadership in the year 96 with the decline of the Flavian dynasty and was recognized by the Roman authorities. In his time the center became established as the supreme spiritual and jurisdictional institution of the nation. From all parts of the land people came to Yavneh to bring their questions, while emissaries from the Patriarch and the Palestine community reached the furthest communities of the Diaspora and provided them with leadership. The order of prayers was determined and the arrangements for the Holy Days were fixed in accordance with the new reality of Jewish existence without the Temple. The Christians, who had lived partly within the framework of the Jewish community, were removed from it and a dividing line was drawn between Christianity and Judaism. The Law of the Tannaim, with its religious-moralistic and Halachic-legalistic philosophy, reached its highest expression; the various sects that tended to divide the nation were eliminated, and all forces were united in the effort to rebuild the nation. The Law of the Tannaim became supreme, not only in the study of the Law but also in practical life.

In the days of Hadrian's rule (117-138) hopes ran high for the rebuilding of the Temple and of Jerusalem. These hopes were linked to Hadrian's deeds of restoration in the East which were based on a desire to fortify the countries bordering on the Parthian Empire. Apparently he even made certain promises to the Jews when, at the beginning of his reign, he visited the East. These hopes stimulated a great revival and a migration of Jews to Palestine and Jerusalem. It appears that the Roman Emperor was taken aback by the extent of this movement and tried to limit it. Disregarding the specifically Jewish character of Jerusalem, he gave orders that the city was to be rebuilt as an ordinary pagan Greek town. The strong sense of unity and the deep Jewish feeling among the Jewish population brought about a reaction of widespread revolt to these measures. Preparations for rebellion lasted for several years, under the inspiration and with the agreement of the scholars. At their head stood one of the most renowned Tannaim of his generation,

Rabbi Akiba ben Yosef. Of poor origin, a shepherd in his youth, he had grown up to leave his mark on the whole of the Oral Law. Many flocked to the revolt even from the Diaspora. The center of the revolt was Betar, a town lying on a steep hill south-west of Jerusalem. Its military leader was Shimon Bar Kosiba, known by the Messianic name Bar Kochba. We know of the revolt from Jewish, Christian, and Roman literary sources, from the coins which Shimon Bar Kosiba struck, from ancient inscriptions, and recently from letters and documents written at the time of the revolt and now discovered in caves in the Judean desert, where the rebels took refuge when they had to flee from the cities. Many of the letters were written by or sent in the name of Shimon Bar Kosiba, Sovereign of Israel. The initial military operations of the revolt, in 132, were crowned with success but Rome's position at the time was completely secure and she was able to concentrate a considerable number of legions on the war in Judea. After extensive battles and many casualties on both sides, the legions succeeded in subduing Betar, the last stronghold of the rebels, in the summer of 135. After the revolt Hadrian carried out his plan of re-establishing Jerusalem as a pagan city, renamed Aelia Capitolina, and Jews were forbidden to live there. They were allowed to enter it only once a year, on the 9th day of the month of Ab, to bewail the ruins of the Temple on the anniversary of its destruction. A time of persecution and decrees against their religion now fell upon the Jews of Palestine; even circumcision was forbidden. Hundreds of Jews, including the pick of the nation and its scholars, were put to death, or forced into exile. Others were sold in the slave markets of the Empire. Many towns were destroyed and the central mountain region of Judea was denuded of its Jewish inhabitants.

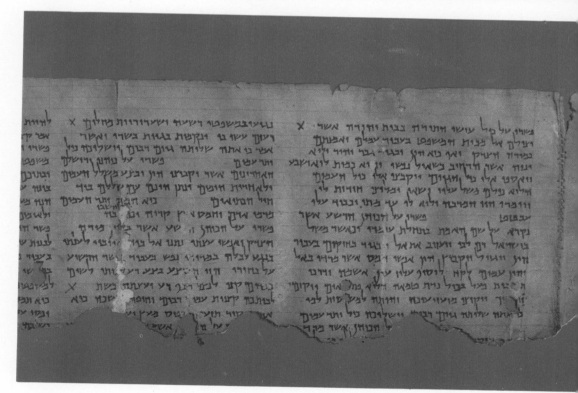

TWO FRAGMENTS OF THE DEAD SEA SCROLLS KEPT
IN THE SHRINE OF THE BOOK IN THE HEBREW UNI-
VERSITY CAMPUS IN JERUSALEM.

BETAR, NEAR JERUSALEM, WHERE BAR KOCHBA MADE
HIS LAST DESPERATE STAND.

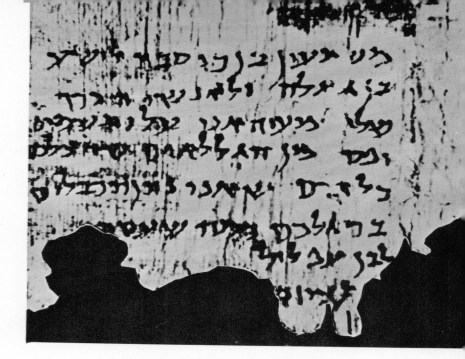

FRAGMENT OF A LETTER WRITTEN BY BAR KOCHBA
TO ONE OF HIS OFFICERS IN THE DEAD SEA AREA.
IT BEGINS: "FROM SHIMON BAR KOSIBA, TO YESHUA
BAR GALGULA."

THE "CAVE OF LETTERS" NEAR THE DEAD SEA. ITS EN-
TRANCE IS IN THE LOWER LEFT-HAND CORNER.

ISRAELI ARCHEOLOGISTS EXCAVATE THE CAVES IN THE GORGE OF TZE'ELIM, NEAR THE DEAD SEA. HERE BAR-KOCHBA'S FOLLOWERS SOUGHT SHELTER AFTER FLEEING FROM THE ROMAN LEGIONS, LEAVING THEIR LEADER'S LETTERS FOR POSTERITY.

THE CRISIS IN THE OLD EAST

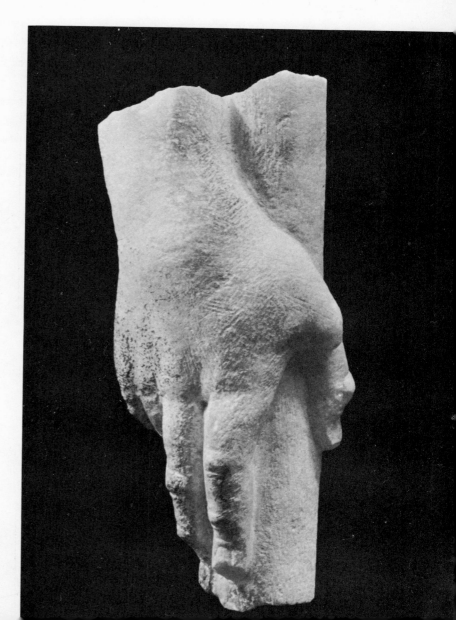

PART OF THE ADORNMENT OF A MARBLE COFFIN
FOUND IN THE BETH SHEARIM CATACOMBS IN WHICH
SOME OF THE TANNAIM OF THE MISHNA WERE BURIED.

THE CRISIS IN THE OLD EAST

The first signs of a Jewish revival and the first attempts at reorganization came from Galilee, which had suffered less than Judea. Rabban Shimon, the son of Rabban Gamliel, was permitted to assume his position as Patriarch, the seat of the Patriarch and of the Sanhedrin remaining in Galilee.

The country prospered during the Patriarchate of Rabbi Yehuda, under the civil rule of the dynasty of Severus (193-235) which treated the Jews well in gratitude for the help that the Jewish community in Palestine had given to Septimius Severus in his war against his rival, Pescennius Niger. Some members of the dynasty also showed an inclination towards Judaism or to a religious syncretism that included Judaism. Under this dynasty the legal and economic position of the Patriarchate was strengthened. Extensive tracts of land were transferred to the Patriarch Yehuda. The Jewish agricultural population grew in number as did the urban population, to the economic benefit of both. The ruins of many fine synagogues found mostly in Galilee, attest to the prosperity of the period. A long series of important laws affecting both the communal-practical and spiritual-religious life of the Jewish population was enacted during the days of Rabbi Yehuda I, his son Rabbi Gamliel, and his grandson Rabbi Yehuda II.

To these times belongs also the Mishna. Rabbi Yehuda the Patriarch was not the first to codify the Oral Law, but the Mishna was the first comprehensive code which summarized most of the subjects of the Halacha and included within it the tendencies of the various schools and their decisions on laws. Rabbi Yehuda the Patriarch, a man of humility, rich personality and elevated status helped to compile the Mishna and make it accepted as the basic book of the Oral Law, and it became, in authority, second only to the Bible. The Mishna is divided into six divisions or "Orders", each dealing with a different field of

ONE OF THE HALLS IN THE BETH SHEARIM CATACOMBS.

Jewish laws:

a) Zeraim (seeds)—laws concerning agriculture.

b) Moadim (festivals)—laws of the Sabbath and the Festivals.

c) Nashim (women)—laws of marriage, divorce and domestic relations.

d) Nezikin (damages)—civil and criminal law.

e) Kodashim (sanctity)—laws of Temple worship, ritual slaughter and permitted foods.

f) Taharot (purity)—laws for ritual purification.

Each Order is divided into tractates dealing with specific subjects. The Mishna includes all halachic laws, and even includes those no longer used after the destruction of the Temple, such as the rules for Temple worship and the laws comprising judgments that could be arrived at only by the Sanhedrin in Jerusalem; the compilers of the Mishna having regarded as only transitory the period during which the Temple lay in ruins. The Mishna is written entirely in Hebrew except for a few words in Aramaic and Greek —a Hebrew of classic precision and clarity.

The years 235-284 brought anarchy for the Roman Empire and the East, including Palestine. Under the autocratic monarchy that followed, the situation of the Jewish community in Palestine was determined mainly by economic factors. In the frequent crises that visited the East in the 3rd Century, as well as during the subsequent sta-

bilization of the regime, it was always the rural population that suffered the most. Military oppression was more severe in the villages than in the cities, and the heaviest burden of the new taxes at the end of the 3rd Century and the beginning of the 4th fell on the peasants. As agriculture was the basis of the economy of the Jews of Palestine, the Jews were the hardest hit in the country. During this period the poverty of the people and the difficulty of making a living overshadowed concern over religious or political persecution. There were also attacks by desert Arabs, especially in the frontier districts; these had the effect of further reducing the number of Jewish farmers, so that the total of Jewish farming com-

munities constantly dwindled. Emigration overseas increased because of economic difficulties and though there was some immigration into the country, it could not balance the emigration.

At the beginning of the period, in the days of the Patriarchs Rabbi Gamliel and Rabbi Yehuda II, the division between the Patriarchate and the Sanhedrin widened. Already in the days of Rabbi Yehuda I there had been disputes between those scholars who demanded a return to humility and simplicity and those who enjoyed the wealth and grandeur that was associated with the Patriarchate. Rabbi Yehuda, by the strength of his personality, was able to bridge these two worlds, but after his death they could no longer co-exist, and the schism between them grew ever more apparent. In the first and second generations after the completion of the Mishna the two authorities were finally divided, and the Patriarch no longer sat at

PLAN OF CATACOMB NO. 11.

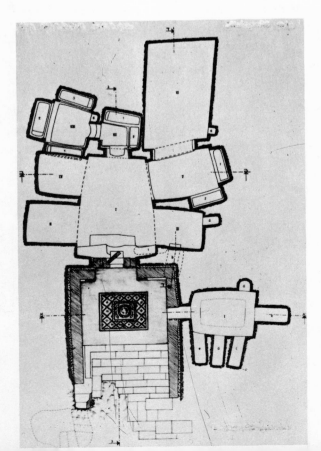

the head of the Sanhedrin. The Patriarch now served as the representative of the people and provided the political leadership, while the Sanhedrin became an independent body concerned with teaching and the determination of Halacha and civil law.

At the beginning of the 4th Century, Christianity, which had been accepted by only a small minority of the population, became the official religion of the Roman Empire, a factor which from then onwards was to have a decisive influence on the history of the Jews in Palestine and throughout the Roman Empire. The conquest of the East by Constantine in the year 324, strengthened the Christian religion and caused its influence to spread amongst the pagan population. The Empire even attempted to introduce the Christian religion into Jewish settlements by force but there were only very few converts from Judaism. The new religion of the Roman Empire affected the Jewish population also in secular matters. Roman legislation became more and more discriminatory against the Jews and imposed increasing degradation. During the second half of the 4th Century the connections between Palestine and the Diaspora became more tenuous and difficult to maintain. So as to avoid uncertainties in fixing the dates of the Festivals which were dependent on the exact determination of the hour of the New Moon by the Sanhedrin each month, a permanent calendar was calculated during the Patriarchate of Hillel the Second and sent out to all communities of the Diaspora. This lessened even more the dependence of the Diaspora on the decisions of the Sanhedrin and brought about a further reduction of the hegemony of Palestine over the Diaspora. The active political life of the people in Palestine had weakened, leading to a feeling of resignation to the prevailing political domination and to the social and economic order.

Two events, however, in the second half of the 4th Century testify to the continued vitality of the Jewish population in Palestine.

In the year 351 the Jews revolted against Gallus, the Roman governor in the East. It was an uprising, not against Christian rule, but against the corrupt and near anarchic rule of Gallus, and no violence was directed against the Christians or their churches. Apparently the rebels had depended upon other revolts breaking out simultaneously in the West and on the possibility of Persian intervention, for at that time there were several wars between Rome and Persia. The Patriarchate did not participate actively in the revolt, which was fundamentally a revolt of zealots, and the Patriarchate was not seriously affected when the revolt was finally suppressed by General Ursicinus, though considerable sections of the Jewish population in Galilee and around Lydda suffered heavily.

Again, during the short reign of the Emperor Julian, the Apostate (360-363), there was a great stir in Palestine and the Diaspora: Julian believed in the Hellenic gods and wanted to revive their worship at the expense of Christianity. He regarded the sacrifices as the most important part of the Jewish religion, and wanted to restore them too. The Emperor thought that by rebuilding the Temple and restoring Jerusalem to Jewish control he could weaken Christianity whose claim to be the "true Israel" was based to a large extent on the destruction of the Temple, which to them symbolized the decline of the people of Israel from their status of Chosen People and the transfer of this title to Christianity. Apparently also, the Emperor expected to win over the sympathies of the Jews of Persia on the eve of the war he was about to undertake in the East. Julian abolished the laws against the Jews that had been enacted during the reign of the Christian Emperors and

WALL OF THE BASILICA AT BETH SHEARIM.

also the annual tax of two drachmas that had been levied from them after the destruction of the Temple. The rebuilding of the Temple and of Jerusalem were actually started but the whole program came to nothing when Julian was murdered in Persia at the hands of a Christian soldier.

Until the last days of its existence the Patriarchate enjoyed the recognition and respect of the civil authorities, but in the last years before its abolition there were persistent attempts to circumvent the Patriarch and to limit his legal powers. When Rabbi Gamliel VI died in the year 429 the authorities refused to authorize a successor

RELIC OF TABLET BEARING GREEK INSCRIPTION, FOUND AT BETH-SHEARIM.

and forbade the collection of money on behalf of the Patriarchate.

The two centuries between the abolition of the Patriarchate and the Arab conquest, which put an end to Byzantine rule in Palestine, were difficult years for the Jews of Palestine. It was a time of suffering and degradation accompanied by a constant lowering of their legal and social status. There were only a few faint bright spots throughout the period. Though collecting of money for the maintenance of the rabbinical center in Tiberias was imperially forbidden, this institute of leadership continued to exist, and the people of Israel, wherever they lived, continued to support it. Nonetheless, its influence and its field of operations were limited compared to previous eras. At the beginning of the 5th Century more discriminatory laws against the Jews were enacted, this time with a clear Christian theological basis. Fanatic priests launched violent attacks on the Jews, all to the greater glory of Christendom, and accompanied this by the burning of their synagogues. The rebuilding of synagogues was forbidden by the Romans and this prohibition was renewed on several occasions. During this period the Christian population of Palestine increased, both through the conversion of the pagan population and by the immigration of Christians from other countries, among them men of wealth and influence who built churches and monasteries in places holy to Christianity. The numerical importance of the Jewish population decreased during this period, though it re-

(top) ENTRANCE TO THE TWENTIETH CATACOMB AT BETH SHEARIM. IT HOUSED THE REMAINS OF THE PATRIARCH AND HIS FAMILY.

(center) ONE OF THE HALLS IN THE TWENTIETH CATACOMB. THE HOLES IN THE COFFINS ARE THE WORK OF ROBBERS.

(bottom) A HEBREW INSCRIPTION ON AN ELABORATELY DECORATED COFFIN.

RELIEF SHOWING MOUNTED HORSEMAN, FOUND IN ONE
OF THE HALLS OF CATACOMB NO. 1 AT BETH SHEARIM.

mained an important factor in the life of the country right up to the end of the Byzantine period. The years from the second half of the 5th Century until the renewal of an aggressive Christian policy on the accession of Justinius (527-565) were relatively peaceful ones for the Jews. The Christians were occupied with the schism that divided the Church in the East. The theological quarrel between the Orthodox and the Monophysists, interwoven as it was with political conflict, led the emperors to strive for the attainment of domestic peace and, to avoid new frictions, they abandoned the religious persecution of the Jews. The priests occupied by their religious conflicts with the authorities, left the Jews in peace. During this period the Jews benefited also from the economic boom which the country was then experiencing and expressed this in the building of synagogues, whose remains have been preserved: at Beth Alpha, Hammath by Gadara (el-Hamma) and Gader in the north and at Jericho, Ashkelon, Gaza and others in the south. Officially, the building of synagogues was still forbidden by law, but the life of the Jews at that time was not completely circumscribed by the restrictive laws enacted against them.

The spiritual creativeness of the Jews found expression in the Agada, the literature of folklore and popular theology which had been collected over the centuries but was summarized and committed to writing mostly at this time. Together with the Agada appeared the Piyyut, a poetic literary form that combined elements of Halacha, Agada, liturgy and secular poetry of many previous generations. The creation of the Piyyut continued also into future generations, but its main force found expression in this era in which it was shaped and whence it was handed down as a permanent treasure in the spiritual life of the nation.

At the end of this period another opportunity arose that held promise for the Jews that their rule over Palestine might be restored. Early in the 7th Century, the Persians began their conquests in the East and in the year 614 reached the gates of Palestine. For hundreds of years the hope had been cherished that a Persian conquest would bring the liberation of the country and the approach of the Persians raised great Messianic

THE DECORATED FLOOR OF THE CENTRAL HALL IN THE SYNAGOGUE OF HAMMATH BY GADARA IN SYRIA; FROM THE FIFTH CENTURY.

GENERAL VIEW OF BETH SHEARIM, SHOWING THE EN-
TRANCE TO THE CATACOMBS — THE LARGEST JEWISH
CEMETERY IN THE THIRD AND FOURTH CENTURIES.

THE EXCAVATIONS AT BETH SHEARIM SHOWING THE
REMAINS OF THE BASILICA.

ENTRANCE TO HALL OF THE FIRST BETH SHEARIM CATA-
COMB. THE TABLET IN THE WALL OVER THE DOORWAY
READS, "THIS IS THE BURIAL PLACE OF RABBI YITZHAK
BAR MAKIM."

THE RUINS OF THE 3RD CENTURY SYN-
AGOGUE AT CAPERNAUM ON THE SEA
OF GALILEE.

expectations. The Jews of the Galilee welcomed the Persians with considerable help. After the subjugation of Galilee the Persians turned to Caesarea and the low hill-country and from there they came to Jerusalem and conquered it. The Persians gave Jerusalem over to Jewish rule, and placed at the head of the Jews a leader with a truly Messianic name, Nehemia ben Hushiel ben Ephraim ben Yosef. Ritual sacrifice was once more inaugurated. The Jewish rule over Jerusalem lasted for three years. In 617 the Persians changed their minds, for reasons which are not clear, and made peace with the Christians, who returned to Jerusalem and wrought bitter vengeance on the Jews. From that moment the Jews of Palestine ceased to exist as a people with even partially independent power and became a subject community, no different in this respect from all the other communities of the Diaspora.

A distinction must be made between the conditions of the Jews who resided within the Roman Empire, whose political status was always linked, in some degree, to the political status of the Jews in Palestine, and, on the other hand, the Jews of Babylonia, living under the rule of Parthians or Persians, outside the boundaries of the Roman Empire. Large Jewish communities existed in Egypt and its capital Alexandria, especially before the three year revolt by the Jews, in the time of Trajan (115-117). There were large Jewish communities in Syria and its capital Antioch, in the countries of Asia Minor and in Europe from Greece to Gaul and Spain. There had been a considerable Jewish community in Rome even before the Roman conquest of Palestine, and this continued to grow after the destruction of the Temple. The leaders of Palestinian Jewry were frequently in Rome, either as visitors to the Jewish community there or as emissaries to the Roman authorities.

The largest, and the most lastingly influential, of the Jewish communities of the Diaspora was that of Babylonia. In this ancient community there had dwelt, from the earliest days, "unlimited multitudes whose number could not be known" (Josephus). Many large cities in Babylonia, such as Nearda, Nisibis and Mahoza, were completely or almost completely Jewish. Talmudic tradition, in its references to "Diaspora", means simply Babylonia. Some of the cities with large Jewish populations had a very ancient Jewish tradition, and the Jews of Babylonia regarded themselves as citizens, of a sort, of the Land of Israel. Although Babylonian Jewry tried at times to free itself from the hegemony of Palestine, especially when the Jewish religious center in Palestine could not function because of difficult conditions imposed from outside, there was never a community of the Diaspora so consistently attached to Palestine. Many Babylonian Jews emigrated to Palestine, either to study the Law or to settle there. The Babylonians accepted the rulings of the Palestine Sanhedrin and asked the Palestinian scholars for guidance in choosing the heads of their colleges, and in other similar matters. From the 3rd Century onwards many Palestinian scholars were appointed to serve as permanent envoys of the Palestinians in Babylonia.

In the Talmud are preserved the texts of dozens of inquiries sent from Babylonia to Palestine and of the replies sent from Palestine to Babylonia. The inquirers were always the Babylonians. In periods of difficulty for Palestinian Jewry the number of refugees from Palestine who sought refuge with their brothers in Babylonia increased considerably and included many scholars who made great contributions to the enrichment of the law and the spiritual consolidation of Babylonian Jewry.

Babylonian Jewry was privileged with extensive autonomy. At its head stood the "Head of the Diaspora", who traced his lineage back to the descendants of the House of David who had been exiled to Babylonia. According to tradition, the Heads of the Diaspora had held their hereditary titles from the beginning of the Babylonian Exile, and the first of them was the exiled King Jehoiachin, but there is a gap in our knowledge about the Heads of the Diaspora until the late 2nd Century. The sound position of Babylonian Jewry, the feudal society of the Parthian Empire and the considerable eminence that they enjoyed, all contributed to give the Heads of the Diaspora a strong basis for their rule. The Head of the Diaspora was regarded as a public official of the highest status, fourth in authority after the king, in the Persian hierarchy. His powers were far-reaching in all Jewish communal affairs, including administration, civil law, criminal law and even decisions on capital punishment. With the growth of the Talmudic academies in Babylonia, the duties of the Head of the Diaspora became more limited and certain fields of jurisdiction passed into the hands of the scholars, though the scholars remained in many ways subservient to the court of the Head of the Diaspora. Many of the Heads of the Diaspora were far removed from

the world of the Law and some actively opposed the scholars and their teaching, although there were Heads of the Diaspora, especially later on in the period, who were very close to the world of scholarship and some who were noted scholars themselves. The leadership of the community was influenced by the system of local administration in Palestine, controlled by the city assembly at the head of whom stood seven elders.

The accession of the Sassanid dynasty (224) and the growth in influence of the Magi priests of the Zoroastrian religion, accompanied by a new nationalistic Persian revival, brought suffering to the Jews of Babylonia. There were religious persecutions and the right of Jewish autonomy was tampered with, but Shapur I (241-271), who restored the tradition of religious freedom brought changes for the better. Shapur himself maintained close personal ties with the Jewish scholars.

The main occupation of the Jews of Babylonia was agriculture, whether as landowners, employees or tenants of the landowners. Jews were found in every branch of agriculture, date growing, raising field crops, fishing and bird netting. Among the craftsmen and artisans there were also many Jews. In contrast to Palestine, slave-owning was accepted in the agricultural and economic life of Babylonia.

The great revival of the study of the Law in Palestine, in the days of the Patriarch Yehuda I, caused many Babylonians to migrate to Palestine to study the Law there. While some stayed, others returned to Babylon later, including the sage Abba Arikha, known by his apellation, Rab. His return, in the year 219, marks a turning point in the development of the Law and of the culture of Babylonian Jewry. He settled on his return not in the old Babylonian centers of learning but went to Sura, a large city with little tradition of learn-

JEWISH SYMBOLS IN A CATACOMB OF THE GRECO-ROMAN PERIOD.

THE MOSAIC FLOOR OF THE BETH ALPHA SYNAGOGUE
DATES FROM THE SIXTH CENTURY. THE UPPER PANEL'S
DESIGN IS OF THE HOLY ARK, FLANKED BY BIRDS, LIONS
AND CANDLESTICKS. RAMS' HORNS, PALM BRANCHES AND
INCENSE SHOVELS ARE SCATTERED THROUGHOUT THE
PICTURE.
THE CENTRAL PANEL IS DOMINATED BY A ZODIAC CIR-
CLE. THE SUNRISE IS REPRESENTED IN THE CENTER BY
A YOUTH RIDING A CHARIOT DRAWN BY FOUR HORSES.
THE CORNER FIGURES SUGGEST THE FOUR SEASONS.
ABRAHAM PREPARES FOR THE SACRIFICE OF ISAAC IN
THE LOWER PANEL.

TWO SIGNS OF THE ZODIAC—THE FISH AND THE LAMB—
DETAIL OF THE MOSAIC FLOOR OF THE ANCIENT JEWISH
SYNAGOGUE EXCAVATED AT HAMAT.

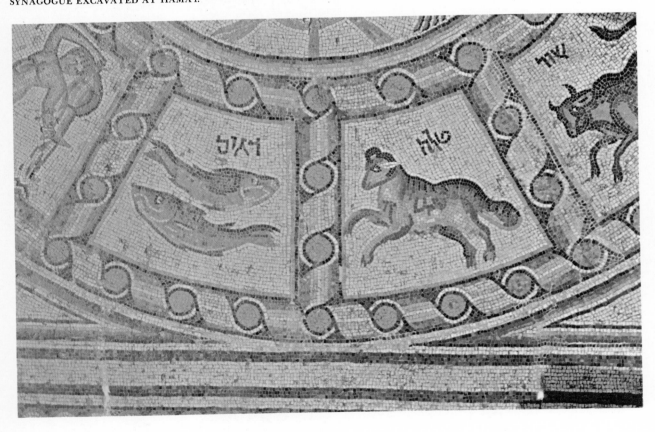

A FRESCO FOUND IN DURA EUROPOS SYNAGOGUE IN
MESOPOTAMIA SHOWS MOSES READING THE TORAH.

הדרן עלך השוכר את הפועל
וסליקא מסכתא ברחמי שמיא·

נשלמה ביום רביעי י"א לירח כסלו שנת נ"א לפרט הי"צירה
וכתבתיה לעצמי אני שלמה בר שאול נ"ע בכ"ו בגלי בוזרה·
ברוך רחמנא דסייען·

SEPHARDIC MANUSCRIPT OF THE BABYLONIAN TALMUD
SHOWING THE END OF THE TRACTATE AVODAH ZARAH
WITH A COLOPHON BY THE SCHOLAR WHO COPIED IT;
DATED TO THE YEAR 1291.

ing, and founded there a great center of the Law. In those days Nearda, which was an ancient seat of learning, developed into a great and important school. At its head stood Samuel, who had also lived in Palestine for a time, but was not as closely connected as his colleague, Rab, to the Palestinian tradition. The competition between the two schools persisted for generations with Nearda representing the Babylonian tradition and Sura the continuation of the Palestinian traditions. Many pupils were absorbed into Rab's school and his permanent pupils alone numbered 1200. During this period the "Months of Assembly" were introduced, an institution that lasted for hundreds of years in Babylonia. During two months of the year, in Adar and Elul when there was little agricultural activity, tens of thousands of people came to the schools to be taught the Law. The two schools existed in Babylonia for several centuries until the end of the Geonic period in the middle of the 11th Century. Besides the school of Nearda, which was moved to Pumbeditha after the destruction of Nearda, there were other academies which existed for varying periods of time. During the long period that Rab Ashi served as head of the school of Sura (371-427) the Babylonian Talmud was compiled, on the model of the tractates and chapters of the Mishna. Rab Ashi edited the material while teaching at the school, and his personality, initiative, and power of decision are discernible in the editing of the Talmud. In the Talmud is summed up all that the Jewish people did and lived through in the course of hundreds of years. As compared to the Mishna which summed up the Halachic material mostly in an edited form, the Talmud included material from many fields that had not been in-cluded in the Mishna, and all the important decisions and interpretations that had been added in succeeding generations. The authors of the Talmud did not limit themselves to the final decisions but included all the arguments, discussions, differing opinions, and casuistic reasoning that had been accumulated throughout the generations in solving disputes in law or logic. For this reason the contents have reached us with a full spectrum of meaning and color. Unlike the Mishna which had been edited in its entirety on one prosaic level, there are passages in the Talmud which reach great heights of religious and legal reasoning and show great brilliance of intellect. The Talmud as it has reached us does not cover all the tractates of the Mishna with its commentaries. It includes the orders of Moadim, Nashim, Nezikin, Kodashim and, from the order Zeraim only the first tractate, Berakhot (Benedictions). The Babylonian Talmud became a basic possession of the Jewish People, the source of much of its national philosophy and aspirations and its guide in practical life. Other factors that later affected Jewish life were generally recognized only to the extent that they were related to issues that had been raised in the Talmud. External realities and current events were regarded as of transient importance by many generations of Jews to whom the only true reality was found in the Talmud. Rab Ashi laid the foundation for the compilation of the Talmud, and its final editing was the work of his immediate successors towards the end of the 5th Century, a difficult period for Babylonian Jewry. The Babylonian Talmud was finally completed in the year 499 which marked a period of destruction and persecution in the days of Rabbi Josef of Pumbeditha and the last Rabbina of Sura.

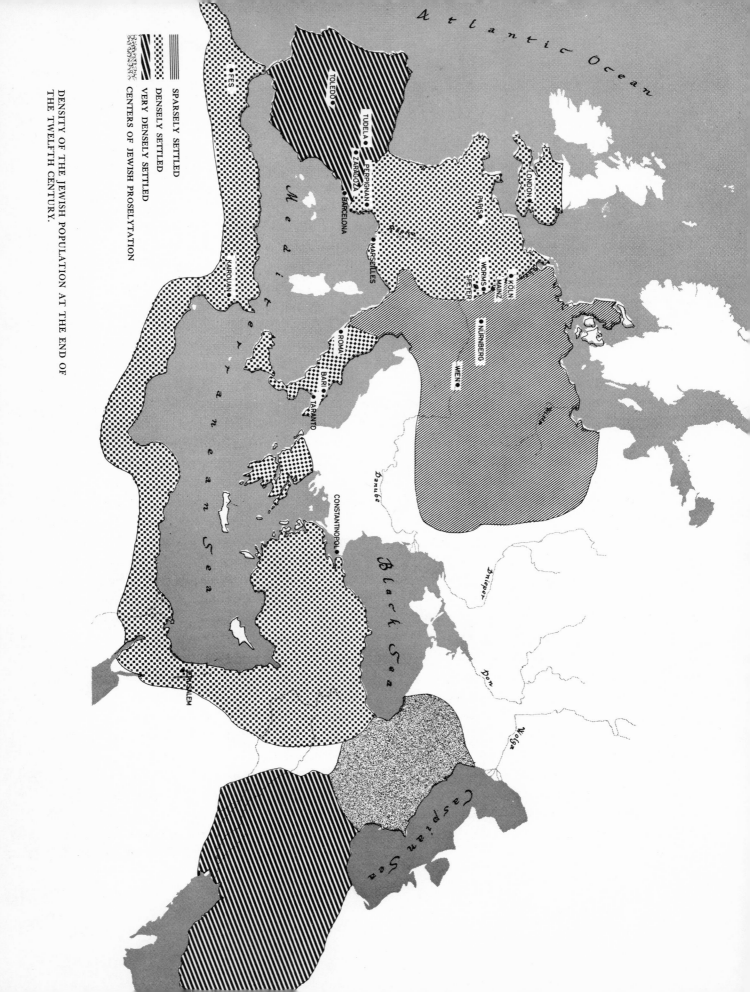

DENSITY OF THE JEWISH POPULATION AT THE END OF
THE TWELFTH CENTURY.

SPARSELY SETTLED
DENSELY SETTLED
VERY DENSELY SETTLED
CENTERS OF JEWISH PROSELYTATION

THE ILLUSTRATED HISTORY OF THE JEWS

THE JEWS IN THE
MIDDLE AGES—ENVIRONMENT

FOURTEENTH CENTURY DRAWING SHOWS A MEETING
BETWEEN THE EMPEROR HENRY VII AND THE JEWS OF
ROME. NOTE THE DISTINCTIVE "JEWISH HATS" WORN
BY MEMBERS OF THE COMMUNITY.

The history of the Jews in the Middle Ages is the history of a scattered and despised people, beleaguered in a hostile world. The nations of that world, proud yet inviting, constantly held out inducements to the Jews to cross over to their splendid abodes. The Jewish nation took upon itself to reject the monotheistic religions which had emerged from it, but which had distorted Judaism's nature in the course of winning converts. The population movements of the Jews and their ways of earning a living in the Middle Ages were very largely a means of defense in the war that the world waged against them. In this cruel war, whose motivation was mainly religious, the nations used against the Jews (as Maimonides in the 12th Century rightly observed) a combination of compulsion, persecution, persuasion and temptation. Thanks to the power of its spirit, the strength of its faith and its social cohesion, Jewry emerged from these struggles.

The Jews claimed to be bearers of the one true faith, to have been chosen by God as His beloved people. The ruling nations claimed that their faith was the true and unbroken continuation of the ancient heritage of Israel—that the divine choice of which the Jews had been deprived had been bestowed on them. The claim to be the heirs of ancient Israel's election was especially strong in Christianity, which regarded itself as the "true Israel". The Jews proclaimed their faith openly and proudly in a world in which fanaticism for the true faith was an elementary and self-evident duty. And in every kingdom it was a religion other than Judaism that was considered the one true faith.

Both Christianity and Islam preserve the memory of their early days, when Jews went forth against them as falsifiers of the truth and strayers from its path. This remembrance is particularly strong in Christianity, whose founders were Jews.

Common to both Christianity and Islam was the rule that Jews should be allowed to go on living without physical molestation, but that they should be socially degraded to insulate them from the community of believers, and legally persecuted and badgered. It was also accepted that one should try to "save the soul" of the Jew, and they did all they could, by intimidation and economic pressure, by promise of rewards and social equality, to attract the Jew to Christianity or Islam. Whoever deserted Judaism became in theory, and usually also in practice, "an ally of his persecutor"—in the words of Yehuda Halevi.

The systems of isolation and degradation by Islam and Christianity had much in common, and it is sometimes hard to decide which had the greater part in oppression. It was the Caliph Al

A MARRIAGE AGREEMENT BETWEEN THE PARENTS OF THE BRIDE AND THE GROOM; ENGLAND 1271.

EZRA PREACHING TO THE PEOPLE; FIFTEENTH CENTURY MINIATURE SHOWS THE SPANISH JEWS OF THAT TIME.

Hakim, for example, who first introduced, in the 11th Century, the "badge of shame" to distinguish Jews from believers. Pope Innocent III at the 4th Lateran Council in 1215, decreed that the "badge of shame" must be worn forever by all Jews in Christian lands.

In the "Land of Islam" the system of existence at the price of degradation was generally maintained. The circumstances of life in the Moslem kingdoms made it possible from time to time for Jews to emerge from the confines of isolation and to reach heights of dominance and influence in state and culture. The Jews in the "Land of Islam" were only one among several groups of "unbelievers and pagans". Most of these were held to be dangerous because of their possible connection with the kingdoms' enemies, but Jews were generally amenable to the government. In Islam, therefore, they did not have to suffer the fate of being the only dissenters in a unanimous world.

In the Christian countries, apart from the Iberian peninsula, the system of degradation was strongest and most consistent from the First Crusade onwards. What is more, both the Christians and the Jews themselves considered it the least harmful way of dealing with the problem in the circumstances. For in these countries there

had grown up a popular attitude to the Jews which regarded their very existence as a contradiction to the precept of extirpating evil from the midst of the believers. The simple folk transferred to the Jews all the bigotry, severity and hostility generally felt towards those who did not fit into the normal way of life, who lived differently in a society otherwise united, cemented by the same concepts of faith, the same symbols of religion and the same ways of life. The common people tended to see in the Jew a "son of Satan", a lover of evil and servant of lies, risking danger and degrading himself for the sake of the "perfidia Judaeorum".

In the countries of northwestern Europe from the 12th Century onwards (and thereafter in other countries of Christendom), because of this popular tradition, hostility to the money-lending Jew became mixed with hatred for religious reasons. The terrifying and mysterious image of the Jew at the end of the Middle Ages as it took shape in the imagination of the masses in Europe was that of an enemy of the true God, who seeks Christian blood and devours Christian wealth.

JEWS WITH "BADGES OF SHAME" ON THEIR SLEEVES ARE TAKING THE OATH BEFORE A CHRISTIAN JUDGE. THE JEW IS SWEARING WITH HIS HAND ON A HEBREW BOOK.

Shakespeare's Shylock is a dramatic rendering of this vulgar image, produced in an England that had not known a Jew for hundreds of years.

Even under Islam the Jew was occasionally the victim of violent mass outbreaks at times of social and religious unrest. Thus, for example, the outbreaks of the Almoahid Moslems in North Africa, and afterwards in Moslem Spain in the 12th Century, brought about the forced conversion of masses of Jews in these areas, the martyrdom of some and the wandering and flight of others.

But most of the religious persecutions took place in Christian countries. They both arose from and reinforced the popular attitude towards the Jews. In the Christian world religious and political passions unleashed riots against the Jews. In 1096, Crusaders on their way to the Holy Sepulchre attacked Jewish communities, proclaiming that before they redeemed the Sepulchre they would force the "descendants of the murderers of Jesus" to embrace Christianity or die. Attacks on Jews became a common feature of the Crusades.

The libels were even worse. From the middle of the 12th Century (in England first in 1144) the Jews were accused of thirsting for Christian blood, preferably that of young and innocent Christians. Various strange reasons for this libel were given during the many years that it endured: that the Jews wished to torture a Christian so as to renew the sufferings of Jesus; that they needed pure Christian blood to heal themselves or for magic spells; that they needed it to remove from themselves blemishes on their bodies and in their natures from which (unlike other men) they suffered. In common to all those is the conviction that the Jew delights in the sufferings of the pure and lusts for their blood. He is not like other men, but monstrous and false by his very nature. This is the blood libel, on whose account so many Jews were tortured in Christendom. Many died at the stake. Whole communities were slaughtered by frenzied mobs. Papal declarations that the Jews were not to be accused of this were to no avail. Nor did these declarations help the Church itself, for while its leaders denied the libel, they included some of the alleged child victims of the blood libel in the Calendar of Saints. What did it help the Jews that the Emperor Frederick II called an assembly of converts to Christianity from the countries of the West in the year 1236, and on the basis of their testimony declared that the libel was false, and forbade it to be published or repeated? It had become part of western culture. Chaucer's "Prioress' Tale", written about 90 years after the expulsion of the Jews from England, perpetuates the blood libel in a literary form. Here too it had become part of the cultural heritage of the poet, who had probably never seen a Jew.

Another common libel of 13th Century origin was the libel of the desecration of the sacrament. It spread to those countries of Christendom, especially in central Europe, where the Host was widely believed to have magic power. This magic was attributed to the Host by the people's imagination in the 13th Century, as a by-product of the declaration of the Fourth Lateran Council in 1215 by which transubstantiation became a part of Christian dogma. This was the principle that in the correct performance of the rite of the Eucharist, the wine becomes the blood of Jesus and the bread his body. The Jews were accused of paying great sums of money to wicked Christians to bring them the Christian holy bread, the Host, so that they could impale it or otherwise profane it in their houses or synagogues. According to the "logic" of this libel, the Jew himself knows and admits the miracle of transubstantiation, for otherwise why should he endanger his life in order to impale an ordinary piece of unleavened bread? But he makes use of his knowledge to wound the living god again and again when he takes bodily form. This libel too caused riots and great suffering. In western and central Europe the concept of the Jew as a Christ-hater found its most terrible and general expression in the belief of Christian peoples that the Jews had caused the great plague of 1348-9 by poisoning the wells. Hundreds of communities were exterminated because of this libel. The flea-borne plague had actually been brought to Europe from Asia by sailors and their rat-infested ships, but the true source of the infection was at that time unknown.

The libels had a cruel effect, not only in Jewish suffering, but in the distorted conception of Jews that developed among Christians. The libels themselves would not have been possible except in a world where the minority was regarded by the majority as something distorted by virtue of its very existence. This distortion was not merely "confirmed" by each new libel: it received more detail, more substance, and a more frightful form.

The church determined the general outlines of the degrading attitude towards the Jews; its preaching against them contributed—often more than was intended—towards the deterioration of the people's attitude. The popular mind could not imagine disagreement that was not the result of fundamental degeneracy—an attitude strengthened by libels and disturbances.

But the rights and obligations of the Jews in the kingdoms where they lived were in every case defined by the rulers. In Islamic lands this definition closely followed the classical attitude of Islam to "unbelievers". They had to pay a special tax and certain degrading signs were imposed upon them. In theory at least they were excluded from posts and positions of importance. Among themselves they were allowed to live in accordance with their laws and maintain their own customs.

In Christian lands, clerical influence and the vulgar attitude affected the rulers too. In addition, changes in Jewish occupations tended to improve or worsen their position at different times in various countries. For example, the status of the Jew in Christian Spain was relatively

A GROUP OF JEWS, INCLUDING OLD MEN AND WOMEN, BEING BURNT ALIVE BY THE CHRISTIANS. A WOODCUT BY WOHLGEMUTH, PUBLISHED IN NUREMBERG IN 1493.

good during the 12th-14th Centuries, though
not because of any lack of religious fanaticism
among the inhabitants. On the contrary the cru-
sading atmosphere prevailed in the kingdoms of
the Iberian Peninsula, which were fighting and
defeating the Moslems. But the situation was
good because the Jews performed a vital function
in cultural advancement and in carrying over
administrative systems at the time of the Christian conquest. In Rome a Jewish community lived
without threat of expulsion and almost without
molestation during the whole of the Middle Ages,
because there the Popes consistently upheld the
system of humiliation and isolation and prevented
the popular attitude from breaking out in
violence.

After the crisis of 1096, when people became
used to letting Jewish blood, the status of the
Jews degenerated and their position in the economy began to change. The charter tended more
and more to accentuate the kingdom's ownership
of the Jews, both for their protection and to
stress the rulers' right to exploit this ownership
and to exact many taxes from them. The heads
of the church in the 13th Century, for their part,
stressed the eternal servitude binding the Jews

A DRAWING OF THE TIME (1614) SHOWS THE SACKING
OF A JEWISH STREET IN FRANKFURT.

TWO JEWS ARE BEING TORTURED DURING AN INQUI-
SITION; THE CHIEF INQUISITIONER TOMAS DE TOR-
QUEMADA SITS IN THE TOP ROW CENTER.

for their sin in crucifying Christ. The Jews required protection, the kingdom strove to exploit
the ready cash that they possessed and there was
competition over this between the secular authorities and the Church, which intensified during
the 13th Century. Hence in the charters that the
Hohenstaufen Emperor, Frederick II, conferred in
the 1230's the Jews are "servi camerae nostrae".
This "servitude to the treasury" was formulated
more crudely and less generously by King Henry
III of England later in the same century. No Jew
might live in England unless he served the King.
In effect this servitude did not usually include
limitations on freedom of movement of Jews, nor
limitations on their right of property-holding or
inheritance. A balance was achieved: there was a
legal basis for exacting tribute from the Jews
and a special reason why the central authorities
and their officials should particularly protect
them.

In legal theory this "servitude" remained the

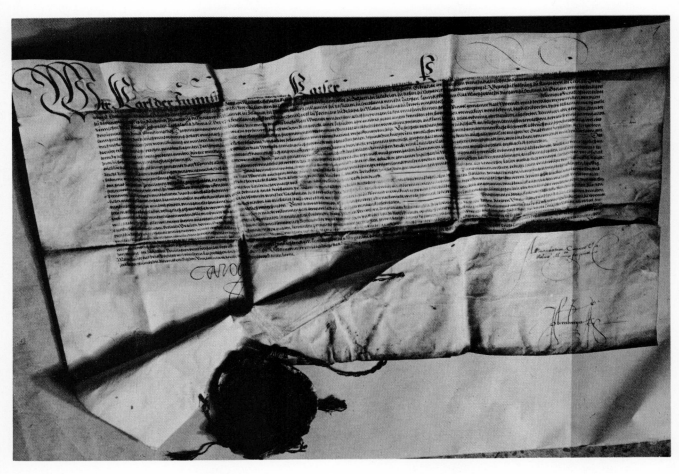

THE PROCLAMATION OF RIGHTS GRANTED TO THE JEWS
BY THE EMPEROR CHARLES V IN 1556.

DETAIL FROM A MURAL BY PAOLO UCCELLO (1396-1475)
"THE MIRACLE OF THE PROFANED HOST" IN THE
DUCAL PALACE AT URBINO. IT PORTRAYS A JEW WHO
PROFANED THE WAFER. MIRACULOUSLY, BLOOD
FLOWS FROM UNDER THE DOOR TO ATTRACT THE
ATTENTION OF THE DUKE'S SOLDIERS WHO BREAK
DOWN THE DOOR. AS THE JEW IS TAKEN AWAY TO
RECEIVE HIS PUNISHENT HIS CHILDREN, WEEPING,
TURN TOWARD THEIR MOTHER.

THE EGYPTIANS, ON HORSEBACK AND IN CHARIOTS,
PURSUE THE CHILDREN OF ISRAEL. THIS ILLUSTRA-
TION, AND SEVERAL OF THOSE FOLLOWING, ARE
TAKEN FROM A MEDIEVAL PASSOVER HAGGADA IN
WHICH THE CHARACTERS ARE ALL DRAWN WITH
BIRD-LIKE FEATURE BECAUSE OF THE BIBLICAL IN-
JUNCTION AGAINST REPRESENTING A HUMAN LIKE-
NESS.

ILLUSTRATIONS FROM TWO MEDIEVAL HAGGADOT,
BOTH SHOW ISRAELITE SLAVES, IN MEDIEVAL GARB,
BUILDING THE CITIES OF PITHOM AND RAMSES, THE
ARTISTS HAVE CONCEIVED THE BUILDINGS IN THE
STYLE FAMILIAR TO THEM.

defined status of the Jews in Christian kingdoms during the whole of the Middle Ages. This was the case in the kingdom of Poland-Lithuania, where "ownership" of those Jews who settled in the "private" cities and estates of nobles passed into the hands of the nobility.

The places of settlement of the Jews, the factors affecting their permanence in, or migration from, places and countries, their livelihood and position in the general economic sphere—all these were therefore determined to a great extent not by economic and social factors in themselves, but by the shape that these took, by their integration within or opposition to the emotional, legal and religious relationship described above.

The Roman Empire disintegrated, as is known, at an increasing rate from the 4th Century onwards. The European nations usually consider the end of the 5th Century as the beginning of the Middle Ages in their history—a beginning marked by political disintegration and the cutting of communications. In 632, when the fast-spreading Arab conquest began, most of the regions formerly held by the Roman Empire on the Mediterranean coasts united with the vast Moslem areas. Consequently, the Middle Ages start in our chronology with the unification of more than 90% of the Jewish people in the 7th Century, under one regime within the "Islamic land". Communications in the Caliphate, during the first years of its existence, were easy and safe for those times.

During the Middle Ages a considerable portion of the Jewish people moved north of the Alpine and Apennine ranges, and during the later Middle Ages the Jews spread out and established notable communities in central and eastern Europe, until their expansion was halted at a line extending approximately from modern Leningrad to modern Bucharest. This process was halted in the east not because of any weakening of impetus but be-

cause of the 15th Century prohibition imposed by the Russian Kingdom upon Jewish settlement within its borders. The western border of Russia became the eastern boundary of Jewish settlement. During that period the old places of settlement of the Jews along the shores of the Mediterranean and in the countries of the Fertile Crescent were still their main areas of concentration.

Jewish settlement came to an end in certain places and countries as the result of persecution and expulsion. The general expulsion from England took place in 1290, the expulsions from Spain and Portugal in 1492 and 1497 respectively, and there were hundreds of expulsions from small principalities and cities in the German Empire during the 14th-16th Centuries.

After the expulsion from Spain, Jews turned to the Ottoman Empire, essentially because of its moderate attitude towards them. Jewish settlement in considerable numbers in the Kingdom of Poland-Lithuania came about because of persecution in western and central Europe, but this settlement developed and became stabilized there because of favorable economic circumstances. In a number of lands Jews played the part of colonizers. At the end of the 11th Century Jews were considered a desirable element in the population of the cities of the Rhine area. The Jews were builders of urban settlements and the bearers of urban culture and economy in Christian Spain from the 12th Century onwards. In Poland-Lithuania they were an important urban element together with the German colonists in the building of the main cities of the kingdom. And from the 16th Century onwards they fulfilled a function of primary importance in establishing new cities on the initiative of the nobility, and in the development of agriculture and commerce in the southeastern areas of the kingdom — the modern Ukraine.

The big Jewish population concentrations were a) the ancient areas of settlement from the coasts of Africa to the eastern borders of modern Iraq, b) Christian Spain, from the 12th Century to the end of the 15th Century, c) the expanses of Poland-Lithuania, particularly from the 16th Century, d) the Medieval Empire, including Northern France, a sparsely populated area of Jews, as compared to the former, but rich in Jewish creativity.

For internal religious and social reasons and because of the religious and legal compulsion of those in whose kingdoms the Jews lived, a special "Jewish street" usually came into existence wherever a considerable number of Jews lived. Ancient settlement traditions from the east carried over the legacy of self-isolation of a national, religious and occupational group in its own quarter. The theory and order of Jewish life, in this respect, integrated with the antagonistic attitude of the surroundings. The Jews had their street— an area in the city where they could live their lives according to their laws and around their institutions—the synagogue, the "Mikveh" and so on. Their street was also their point of concentration and defense in times of danger. To the non-Jews—particularly to the Christians—around them, the separation of the Jews was desirable, both to prevent their influencing the populace and to ensure that they were recognizable in their degradation and in their occupations.

The vast majority of the Jews in the Middle Ages were city-dwellers. In the "Islamic land" the Jews were engaged in all the occupations to be found in the city. Legal limitations occasionally inhibited these activities, and precluded them from one calling or another; but not for long. Among them there were always many tradesmen, shop-keepers and peddlers; there were also big merchants. In the 10th Century we hear of rich merchants, "bankers of the Caliph" in Baghdad, who financed the needs of the kingdom with monies that probably accrued in large measure from loans received from other Jewish merchants. It has recently become clear from documents discovered in Egypt that the Jews conducted active and varied trade in the Indian Ocean up to and including the 12th Century. We know too of prominent Jewish physicians at the courts of ministers and kings; such were Hasdai Ibn Shaprut in Moslem Spain in the 10th Century and Maimonides in Egypt.

In the Christian states matters were more liable to change. In Byzantium the Jews' economic structure was similar to that in Islamic lands, but the upper strata were lacking, particularly the court physicians. In Western Europe from the 7th to the 10th Century the Jews were the main international traders between Western Europe and the "Islamic land"; they even reached the lands of spices in the Far East. The goods that Jewish merchants brought back from the East were luxuries for the highest ranks of society; and economic contact with the Jews was made in a spirit of appreciation for these merchants and their services. From the 11th Century a change for the worse became apparent. Italian cities began to have trade relations with Islam, and they pushed the Jews out. Religious hatred and disturbances—from the end of this century onwards —undermined the security of the Jewish merchant on the road. The Christian city in Western Europe was also consolidated—from the 12th Century onwards—on definite Christian principles, which left no source of livelihood in trade or craft for anyone who was not a Christian. As a result of all this, the Jews in Western Europe (England, France, Germany) were squeezed out of international commerce and were not permitted to find a foothold locally.

AN IDEALIZED RURAL SCENE AS IMAGINED BY ITALIAN
JEWS AT THE END OF THE FIFTEENTH CENTURY. AN
ILLUSTRATION TO THE BOOK OF JOB.

A MEDIEVAL RUBRIC SHOWING JEWS IN TYPICAL DRESS
INCLUDING ONE, AT RIGHT, IN THE CONICAL "JEWISH
HAT". THE DRAWING REPRESENTS THE BRINGING OF
THE TIDINGS TO ZACHARIAH.

SAMUEL ANOINTING DAVID. A MEDIEVAL CHRISTIAN
ILLUSTRATION FROM FRANCE.

JEWS PRESENTING A SPANISH TRANSLATION OF THE
OLD TESTAMENT TO THE COMMANDER OF THE CATH-
OLIC ORDER OF CALATRAVA, 1443. A CHRISTIAN ILLUS-
TRATION FROM SPAIN.

AT LEFT, ABRAHAM WEARING A "JEWISH HAT" AD-
MINISTERS THE OATH TO ELIEZER; AT RIGHT, ELIEZER
AND REBECCA AT THE WELL. AN ILLUSTRATION FROM
A CHRISTIAN BIBLE CODEX.

There was, however, one essential service the Christian was forbidden to provide for his fellow-Christians: lending money at interest. It is well known that the Torah forbids co-religionists to lend to each other at interest. The Jew possessed ready money, but was increasingly prevented from investing it in commerce. Christian capital —insofar as it existed and insofar as its owner was prepared (secretly or openly) to subvert the prohibition of the church concerning loans at interest—was tied up in the city and its business and was directed towards loans for urban commerce and small industry or for large-scale military and political enterprises. Hence the Jew became a moneylender in the cities of western Europe, lending at interest to those requiring loans for consumption purposes—to cover debts, for example, that had accumulated because of excessive spending or as a result of domestic accidents and legal proceedings. The Jewish moneylender thus fulfilled the function of a small bank granting frequent, urgent and indeed vital loans. The Jew generally lent on the basis of both a promissory note and some security. The rate of interest was of necessity high, for ready cash was in great demand and hard to come by in those days. The economic necessity and social value of Jewish moneylenders in the cities of North-west and Central Europe is reflected in the fact that in most places where they were expelled for religious reasons and because of popular hatred of usurers, they were invited back because their loans were needed. Christians maintained that Christian moneylenders who took their place were harder on borrowers than the Jews.

In Spain and Portugal, until their complete expulsion in 1492 and 1497, the Jews maintained their urban way of life in all its diversity even after the Christians reconquered the Peninsula. Moreover, the cultural superiority and adminis-

trative experience of the prominent Jewish families lent them status in the free professions, in financial administration, in the taxation of the kingdom, and even in the determination of its policy. All this made them part and parcel of ruling circles in the Christian kingdoms.

From the 13th Century, Jews from Germany reached the Kingdom of Poland (paired with the "Grand Duchy of Lithuania" from the beginning of the 16th Century) as immigrants. The first charters show that they came in the beginning as money-lenders. However, in the economic

IN THIS FIFTEENTH CENTURY MINIATURE FROM SPAIN NEHEMIAH (IN "JEWISH HAT") FREES THE SLAVES.

circumstances of the relatively new kingdom, the Jews were allowed to turn to commerce in the cities too, despite the bitter opposition of the burghers. This bitterness was sharply expressed at the end of the 15th and the beginning of the 16th Centuries. Moreover, during the 16th and 17th Century the Jews became agents and administrators of the estates of the Polish nobility in the east of the kingdom as renters of the estates. These functions placed Jews in a position of

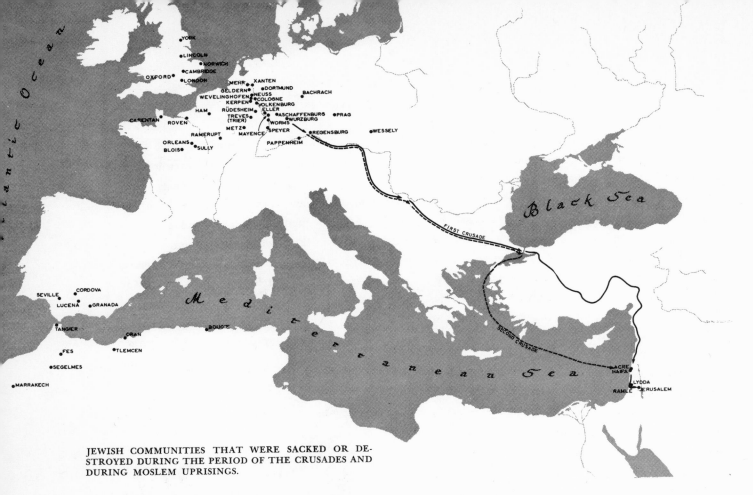

JEWISH COMMUNITIES THAT WERE SACKED OR DE-
STROYED DURING THE PERIOD OF THE CRUSADES AND
DURING MOSLEM UPRISINGS.

authority over much of the export trade in grain, forest products and cattle which in those days flourished between Poland and the West. They also acquired an important position in Poland's trade with Turkey. During the 16th and 17th Centuries the Jews of Poland and Lithuania were often the majority in the "private" cities established by Polish nobles on their own land and under their tutelage. There they were in complete control of commerce. The business of renting out estates of the nobles, and sometimes the revenue of the kingdom and its mines, provided a livelihood for many Jews. They were sub-agents of branches of landholdings or officials of their richer brethren. Commerce, the administration of rural landholdings, and to a certain extent also trades, lent a rich and variegated character to economic life and society of the Jews of Poland-Lithuania.

Even in the German Empire itself—in the principalities and the almost independent cities—

changes took place in the livelihood of the Jews. From the 15th Century onwards, they began to earn their livelihood by peddling and being middle-men between the city and the village, side by side with money-lending. From the end of the 16th Century the Jews began to penetrate gradually into the trade in precious metals and gems. This came about through their initiative and with the aid of the connections of the Spanish-Jewish exiles who settled in German cities, in the Low Countries, and in England. Their links with the Jews of Poland-Lithuania helped them to penetrate into the field of military supply and trade with eastern Europe.

The sources of livelihood of the Jews of the Middle Ages were urban, changing from place to place and from one period to another, in accordance with the economic opportunities open to members of a minority group, and in accordance with the attitude of rulers and people towards members of another faith.

THE JEWS IN THE
MIDDLE AGES—SOCIETY

THE SEAL OF THE AUGSBURG JEWISH COMMUNITY HAS
A "JEWISH HAT" BETWEEN THE TWIN HEADS OF THE
EAGLE.

THE JEWS IN THE MIDDLE AGES—SOCIETY

By the Middle Ages the Jewish people were already experienced in self-rule. They had no independent state of their own, but possessed well-tried methods of their own voluntary organisation, within the autonomy allowed (in greater or lesser degree) by the foreign kingdoms. Under the rule of the Patriarchs and the Sanhedrin in Eretz Israel, the nation had learned to establish law courts for itself and to carry on relations with foreign rulers. Jews, dispersed in many and far-flung countries, felt that their center was in Eretz Israel and its leadership, a feeling fostered by emissaries from the Holy Land. In Sassanid Babylon, Exilarchs, judges and sages of the academies led the people, represented them to the outside world, and taught the nation for hundreds of years.

Thanks to this tradition, and the nation's circumstances of life in the Middle Ages, this self-rule worked during the whole period. The Jews refused to bring law-suits between Jews before an alien court and judges not of their own people. In the Middle Ages it was accepted that law and justice are of God. The Jews therefore regarded appearing before judges not of their own faith as recognition of the gods of those judges, i.e. something approximating to idol-worship. Their approach blended well with the corporate structure of the kingdoms of the Middle Ages, which had different laws and judges for the different classes and corporations of feudal society. In particular it suited the aspirations of the western cities of the Middle Ages to be judged within their walls and according to their own laws, by their own judges.

(*Top*) GENERAL VIEW OF TOLEDO, SPAIN.
(*Center*) TOLEDO STREET, ONCE PART OF THE JEWISH QUARTER.
(*Bottom*) THE FOURTEENTH CENTURY HOUSE OF RABBI SHMUEL HALEVI IN TOLEDO. IT IS FORTIFIED AND WINDOWLESS.

The internal objectives of the Jews were well suited too to their isolated position in the Christian world, and as one of the "infidel" communities of the Islamic world. Kingdoms that regarded themselves as bearers of the law and sword of Christianity or Islam could not judge their inhabitants by other than religious law. And this law in every case would have involved the destruction of Judaism, had the Jews been judged in their own life according to its precepts.

In their own communal life the Jews used not only persuasive spiritual influence, but also coercion in the form of fines and sometimes even imprisonment and the death penalty, with the help of the rulers. Above all they coerced through the ban (the "Herem"). The Herem was considered both a curse that cut a person off from his Creator, bringing down on his head the retribution of God's wrath, and a means of isolating the transgressor from his fellow-Jews. For this reason the ban both punished the known sinner and deterred the one who hid his sins. The fact that this was an effective weapon, when a person so isolated in Israel could easily find refuge by leaving the Jewish and entering the Christian camp, shows the reverence and cohesion of even transgressors in the community.

The very right of the Jews as a group to life was continually denied in Christianity. In Islam and Christian Spain they were accused of trying to transgress the officially prescribed limits of degradation. Christendom continually threatened them with fire, sword and libel from the latter part of the 11th Century. This complicated life necessitated negotiations with the rulers from time to time in order to define the legal status of the Jewish communities, to rescue communities and individuals from libels and false trials, to determine the amount of tithes imposed upon the Jews, methods of collection and so on. All this meant that the Jewish community was forced to carry on a "foreign policy" within the particular kingdom in which it was situated. (The Ashkenazim called this "Shtadlanut"). Sometimes the external representation of the Jews was entrusted to Jews of ancient aristocratic families with a defined status. (See below regarding the Exilarchs). Elsewhere individuals who had close connections with the rulers through economic and social service to them, became heads of the Jewish community largely owing to their willingness to use their position in the foreign society in order to intercede on behalf of their people and defend them. Jewish aspirations also fitted the situation in the medieval state, with its very weak administrative machinery and its limited ability to assess the income and possession of the citizens and tax them efficiently. The State was always forced to farm out the collection to individuals and groups who paid in advance, extending privileges to individuals and groups in exchange for the willingness to undertake the burden of finance or defense. Jewish "shtadlanut" was not therefore exceptional in character — the farming-out of taxes by communities or countries was part of the order of things.

Charters were granted to the Jews as the result of negotiations between the rulers and the "shtadlanim" — the representatives of the Jews. Negotiations of this nature preceded, except in cases of violent extortion, the imposition of taxes. The extent to which the medieval state was prepared to allow the Jewish community to be self-contained in its own sphere, handing over its members to the Jewish leadership, emerges clearly from the fact that in Christian Spain explicit permission was given to Jews to execute informers — in exchange for a payment stipulated in the writ of privileges. On the other hand, the independent leadership of the Jews regarded itself as so dependent upon the kingdom that in the 12th Century in France, the Sages, at the conclusion of the regulations against informers, requested the following: "We the undersigned beg those close to the ruler to coerce through the power of the Gentiles anyone who transgresses one of these our ordinances." And in the 13th Century the communities in the Rhine region decided that "Whosoever transgresses any of these ordinances shall be under the excommunication of all the communities, and if he persists in his obduracy for a month it shall be permissible to hand over his property to the king or other rulers." The Polish king in 1551 authorizes the Jews of a large area of his kingdom, "to unanimously choose as a rabbi whom they desire." This is a kind of merging of the two trends: dependence on the government and recognition of the community by the government. The king gave to the rabbi so chosen "full authority to judge, to investigate, to decree and to sentence without appeal, this in relation to all Jews in the region of his magistracy, to impose punishment and bans according to the law and religion of Moses." And, by way of strengthening the authority of Jewish leadership: "Those Jews themselves declared before us: If anyone dare . . . to oppose him . . . or show irreverence towards the punishment and bans which the rabbi placed upon him . . . and the other leaders . . . do not determine to release him from them within a month, he shall be handed to us in order to suffer the death penalty, and all his possessions shall be confiscated by our treasury."

The Jewish people therefore cooperated with the authorities within the corporate framework of the medieval kingdoms. But it regarded itself as the bearer of authority and order in its own street, through the medium of its institutions, and in accordance with the laws of its Torah.

It recognized the kingdom only to the extent that was necessary. The kingdom, for its part, recognized the autonomy of the Jewish community and was prepared to help it impose its authority on the Jews. The aims of the Jewish community found common cause with the corporative objectives of the kingdoms of the Middle Ages, benefited from them and were influenced by them.

The Jews always regarded their community as "the company of the Lord on the earth." The function of the autonomous bodies was to lead the nation in its dispersion, so that it would do the will of the Creator and reach the time of redemption healthy in body and spirit.

These aims and methods of activity found different institutional expression at various times and in various lands during the Middle Ages. The Moslem Caliphate long included in its borders the majority of the Jews. The necessity for this Caliphate to recognize a central leadership of the various Christian cults within its sphere established an overall framework for a central leadership of the Jews too. The ancient institution of "Exilarchs", who were counted as descendants of the royal House of David, achieved new power and splendor. At the outset they possessed representative authority and sole leadership over the Jews of the land of Islam. For generation after generation a son of this family was elected to the seat of his predecessor, and he was the one whom the Caliph recognized as the head of the Jewish community. Because of quarrels among the Christians, the Caliph in 825 allowed every ten "heretics" to choose their own head. The esteem in which the Exilarch was held by the people became especially apparent then, for until the 13th Century the honor and position of this family was maintained, and the Exilarch had the authority of a leader fluctuating somewhat according to the influence of other leaders of the community. In the 10th Century we hear of the ceremonial crowning of the Exilarch in Baghdad, a ceremony in which every step, every movement and every line of prayer added to the honor and glory of the descendant of the House of David. From the 10th Century too we hear of the property that the Exilarch possessed, of the taxes and revenue due to him. The tradition relates the respect and esteem in which he was held, in the streets of the city and in the royal court. Even in 12th Century Egypt, Maimonides rose to his feet when the Exilarch's letter was read aloud.

But from the very outset, the Exilarch was not the only leader of Jewry. At his side there were always the two yeshivot — Sura and Pumbeditha — which retained their identity and their special status even after they had both moved to Baghdad. These yeshivot were what we might call high academies for the determination of the correct text and true explanation of the holy writings in Israel, and particularly of the Talmud; and they were also the centre of the study of the Torah for all the dispersions of Israel. At the same time they constituted the high court before whom one appealed, the court whence legal judgement went forth to all parts of the Diaspora. The posts in the academy and the high court of justice were held by a small and well-defined circle of sages, who came from families of sages, and generally passed on the legacy of their place and status in the yeshivah to their sons. The standing of a person in the yeshivah was apparent from the row in which he sat. Status and seniority were most important in these institutions, permeated as they were with

(Top) THE RASHI SYNAGOGUE AT WORMS.
(Center) TWELFTH CENTURY SICILIAN SYNAGOGUE.
(Bottom) THE ERFURT SYNAGOGUE, BUILT IN 1357.

(Top) SILVER TORAH-SCROLL ORNAMENT, NOW OWNED BY THE PALMA DE MAJORCA CATHEDRAL.
(Bottom) FOURTEENTH CENTURY CARPET WOVEN IN THE DESIGN OF A HOLY ARK.

tradition. Their function as centers of learning was fulfilled both by the discussions and consultations of the resident sages, and also by teaching and instruction in a number of institutions affiliated to them. For example, instruction was given to the "bnei tarbitza" — hundreds of young people who came to sit at the sages' feet and learn and in the mishnaic schools the sons of the sages were taught the fundamentals of the oral law. At 'yarkhei kalah" — gatherings twice a year of a month's duration — thousands of Jews came to the yeshivot to learn the law orally in the company of the sages.

The yeshivah acted both as an academy and as a high court, giving responsa in reply to the questions asked by Jews in all parts of the Diaspora. These questions concerned problems of exegesis and theory as well as practical issues. They were discussed by the sages at the time of the "yarkhei kalah", and the replies were sent off, signed by the Gaon in the name of "the court of the yeshivah", to the communities. Judges were also appointed in the name of the yeshivah, to judge and lead the communities that were under its jurisdiction; such a judge was appointed not only to pass judgement, but also to supervise the religious observances of the local people.

At the head of every yeshivah was the Gaon (the name is the abbreviated form of the full name: Head of the Yeshivah of Gaon Jacob). Aristocratic descent was important in choice of the Gaon. Among the families of the sages there were six "families of Geonim" from whom the Geonim were chosen. The Gaon was not merely the spokesman and leader of the yeshivah — he was its ruler. He signed the responsa clarified in the course of discussions by the rows of sages. He appointed the other office-bearers in the yeshivot (there were many titles and functions there). He appointed the judges in the name of the yeshivah.

The leadership of the overwhelming majority of the nation during the 8th to 11th Centuries was therefore in the hands of the authoritative educational institutions. Descent, strict hierarchy, external splendor and social ceremony served there as instruments to maintain the tradition of nobility of the priesthood, of the preeminence of the sages, of the leadership of Patriarchs, dating back to before the times of the Second Temple and shortly thereafter. This aristocracy of families of sages regarded their yeshivot as "the Holy Chair of the Torah"; and even in the 12th Century, a Gaon maintained that the name yeshivah was taken from the expression: "Moses sat (yashav) to judge the people", and he defined its function as that of supervising the nation that it "should not err or turn aside" from the way of the Torah.

Between these institutions of leadership there was bound to be some tension. But what characterizes the hierarchies and the genealogies is their unity in leading the people and in relation to the outside world, despite all tensions. This leadership made the Talmud the nation's book of life. Beside the yeshivot and Geonim of Babylon, during most of the time there were also yeshivot and Geonim in Eretz Israel. But the latter never attained the central position or influence of the centers that were situated in the capital of the Caliphate.

When the Moslem Caliphate began to disintegrate, local authorities began to gain influence in the kingdoms that arose on its ruins. In various places we hear of "negidim" who rule the Jews of these lands. The nagid is usually a man close to the court by virtue of economic or professional service, who has been given supreme control over the Jews of his land. Thus there arose in Moslem Egypt the family of negidim descend-

ants of Rambam; the courtier and army commander Rabi Shmuel Nagrella and his son Yehosef were negidim over the Jews of the kingdom where they functioned in the 11th Century, by virtue of their services to the kings.

Gradually one also hears the voice of the leadership of local communities. Documents of the 11th Century from the Mediterranean region bear witness to the fact that these combined at times of spiritual and social crises, and set up their own leaders. We hear in the 12th Century in Egypt of communities that organized in opposition to those appointed by the central authority. The communities developed methods to divide the burden of taxes among their members. As a result of the breakdown of central authority the local communal leadership increasingly took its

16TH CENTURY WOODCUT SHOWING A DISPUTE BETWEEN JEWS AND CHRISTIAN CLERGYMEN.

place. In Christian Spain in the 12th Century, the local community was already formed with its own institutions and leaders. It had judges of its own and an official the "albedinus", a kind of public prosecutor and policeman in one. In the kingdom of Castile, the Jewish leaders were called elders ("viejos"), trustees ("secretario"), and "mukadamin".

In communal leadership the exclusive rule of members of aristocratic families, wealthy and powerful, gradually broadened to include the lower classes in public institutions and decisions. The tension that accompanied transitions of this sort was most obvious in Christian Spain. There the community was often the battlefield between a few distinguished families, whose sons, because of the splendid past of these families and their own education and closeness to the court, claimed the proprietory right to lead the nation, and between 'commoner' Jews who opposed this aristocracy. The latter demanded for themselves a share in the leadership, and even condemned, from certain points of view, the way of life and outlook of the Jewish aristocracy. In the ordinances of the Toledo community of the year 1305, there was a stipulation that every ordinance had to be signed by eight men from eight distinguished families. However, in the community of Barcelona, at the turn of the 13th, 14th Centuries, the lower levels of the population succeeded in attaining, after a struggle, the creation of a council (consilium), a committee that supplemented the distinguished leaders of the community, and limited their influence to some extent.

As a result of this tension and the changes which it caused, differing arrangements were made from place to place in Spanish communities. Rashba* in 1264 summed this up as follows: "The custom of the communties in these matters is not the same everywhere—since there are places

in which all matters are conducted by their elders and their councils; and there are others where even the majority are not entitled to do anything without the advice of the whole community and its unanimous agreement. There are places where they appoint certain people for limited periods of time, the community conducting its affairs according to the decisions of these appointees in all general matters, they being the custodians. I see that you (members of the community of Saragossa) are accustomed to appoint over yourselves leaders called 'mukadamin'."

In the Rhineland and in France and Germany we already find in the 12th Century that the community ordains that its territory as a sphere of jurisdiction is to be considered an independent, closed, legal entity, and anyone entering it is bound to appear before its court and obey its decisions. In the same century we also hear that the communities proclaim the "settlement ordinance" or the "settlement ban", forbidding Jews from other places to settle in the community without explicit permission from its members. These arrangements are specifically urban. In the 13th Century the Jewish community was well founded in institutions and procedures. Rav Meir ben Baruch of Rothenburg stipulated in the same century the following procedure for the running of the community, detailing its head and office-bearers: "One must gather the tax-paying householders . . . everyone stating his opinion impartially and for the good of the city (community), and the majority will rule . . . to elect and decide about the heads . . . the cantors . . . the benefit of charity . . . to build . . . to demolish the synagogue, to buy a house to conduct weddings and other festive occasions . . . to arrange and rearrange all the requirements of the community . . . The majority, or the appointees of the majority as heads over them, have the right of coercion

*Rabbi Shelomo ben Adreth

(over the minority)." In documents of the 12th Century mention is made of the "mehuganim", i.e. the better people, a majority of whom is sufficient to lead the community: a designation and status corresponding to that of meliores among Christian citizenry. This consideration for the upper strata in the community was not as extreme in northwestern Europe as in the southwest, and aroused less opposition there.

The institutions of the community developed along these lines in Spain until the expulsion of 1492. The exiles tended to form communities centered around their synagogue in the lands of refuge, and did not generally become part of the local Italian community or that of the Balkans for example, except where they predominated culturally and the local people adapted their customs and institutions to the Spanish style, as happened in many places.

In northwestern Europe the development continued on the above mentioned lines, and at the close of the Middle Ages the local communities of Poland-Lithuania were also established and consolidated. This late offshoot of the Ashkenazim also had its well established and clearly designated leaders of the community and its institutions. In large communities there were cases where they functioned according to the principle of the "parnass hachodesh", who leads the community in 'his' month. But the community of Poland-Lithuania showed occasional signs of social tension, as in Spain. The common factors of population growth, varieties of occupations and differences in wealth among the Jews had similar effects in the communties of the Iberian Peninsula and of eastern Europe.

During all those centuries in which the independent Jewish leadership withdrew and Jewish autonomy to a large extent enclosed itself within the walls of the city, consciousness of the fact that the communities were but cells of one united people was not lost. We have already heard of the negidim who led the Jews of whole kingdoms by force of their personalities and their status in the Gentile world. Afterwards we hear, in Castile of "el Rav", "Rab de la Corte", who was the leader of all communities, and came from the circle of the Jewish courtiers. In Castile there was also a single and permanent organization of all the communities that convened gatherings at fixed times. In 1432 the Rab de la Corte Don Avraham Benveniste gathered together the representatives of the communities, who promulgated many regulations affecting all spheres of life. In Aragon a number of small communities united around a large community for purposes of taxation and other common matters. This unity of small communities under the aegis of the large community was called a "collecta". The persecutions of 1348 nevertheless led to the gathering in Barcelona (1354) of representatives of the communities in this kingdom too, so that "all the communities should become one association, possessing one treasury—lest our position be undermined and our appearance spoiled". In 1390 Rav Hasdai Crescas was appointed by the king as sole judge on informers in all of Aragon, and he was subsequently in charge, on behalf of both the government and the communities, of the rehabilitation of the communities damaged in the disturbances of 1391.

Even in northwestern Europe attempts were made at centralized leadership. The sages served as the focal point of communal unity and leadership: personalities like Rabbenu Gershom Meor Hagolah (the Light of the Exile) in the first half of the 11th Century, Rashi in France at the end of the century, his grandson Rabbenu Yaakov Tam in the 12th Century, Rabbenu Meir bar Baruch of Rothenburg in the 13th Century, all promulgated ordinances, published commentaries, wrote to various communities and regions with appeals and instructions, and their authority was accepted in their generation and afterwards, by virtue of their greatness in the study of the Law. Their authority was such that ordinances that they had not promulgated were subsequently attributed to them, because it appeared fitting and natural that their authority should confirm them.

In the course of generations, certain defined institutions were determined, within which and by force of which great sages of the Torah exerted influence. Rabbenu Tam promulgated his ordinances as the head of a gathering of sages; Rav Meir bar Baruch was appointed Chief Rabbi, by the government. In England the Presbyters of the Jews, "Bishops of the Jews", were appointed by the king over all the communities. Already at the end of the 11th Century we hear of councils of heads of communities from the Rhineland at Cologne at the time of the great fairs there. In the 13th Century these councils became a source of influence over all German Jewry; their ordinances are known as "takanot shum" (after the initials of the three main communities in Hebrew:

Spiers, Worms and Mayence). Gatherings of this kind continued also in the 14th and 15th Centuries.

In permanence, scope and regularity the central leadership of Polish-Lithuanian Jewry resembles the central leadership of Babylon, although based upon very different organizational foundations and social principles. Its greatest period is from the second half of the 16th Century and throughout the 17th Century. In Poland-Lithuania of those days, the small communities that were known as "the districts" were subjected to a main community—an arrangement that is reminiscent of the "collecta" of Aragon. In Lithuania the scope of authority of the main communities—there they were known as communities of the chief Beth Din—was greater than in Poland. The communities used to gather for consultations of "lands" that were parallel to a large extent to the historic and administrative division of the districts of Poland. They would gather at the places of regional fairs and at their times.

(Top) INTERIOR OF EL TRANSITO SYNAGOGUE IN TOLEDO, BUILT BY RABBI SHMUEL HALEVI IN THE FOURTEENTH CENTURY.
(Bottom) INTERIOR OF A FORMER SYNAGOGUE, NOW THE CHURCH OF SANTA MARIA LA BLANCA IN TOLEDO.

Already in 1551, the Jews of the western province —"Greater Poland"—attained the right to choose a chief rabbi for themselves. This tendency to centralized rule increased. It fitted into the organization by districts of representatives of the communities and was based on the central fairs of Poland as a whole. From the last decades of the 16th Century we hear of rabbis who were considered—in the eyes of the government—as having authority over the whole of Poland, of Jewish representatives and their heads known to be of great influence. At the same fairs there were sages who were accepted as "judges of the land" over the traders who met there from all the communities. From the year 1581 an ordinance has survived stating in its preamble that "the heads and leaders of the four lands agreed" at the Fair of Lublin and enacted it. Henceforth we hear regularly of the existence of a "Council of Lands" supplemented by a supreme Beth Din of Polish Jewry composed of the elder delegates of the lands and their main communities and the sages of the whole of Poland. The Council gathered regularly at the Lublin Fairs, in the center of the kingdom, and the Fair of Jaroslav in the east. A record book (pinkas) has remained, beginning from 1623, and proving the existence of a separate central institution of Lithuanian Jewry—the Council of the Grand Duchy of Lithuania—and its court. This structure of communities of lands, central councils, or, in Lithuania, communities of main courts, the Council of the Duchy, was entirely based on the local community as a basic cell.

In Italy too there were attempts in the late Middle Ages to establish central institutions. In Germany a central gathering of sages and heads of communities came together in 1603 in order to set up a permanent organization for the collection of taxes and for the promulgation of overall regulations. Communal associations of the isolated lands of Germany occasionally existed over considerable periods of time. As from 1650, ordinances of the Councils of the Jews in Bohemia-Moravia are also known.

To sum up, the aspiration to centralized authority was never abandoned. In Castile it existed in orderly fashion until 1492; in Aragon it found some expression in the uniting of a number of communities around a large community (the collecta).

The Jews ruled themselves throughout the Middle Ages, and lived their lives in their communities according to their own law. This achievement of continuous existence and of autonomous rule helped the nation to maintain its form and na-

ILLUSTRATION FROM A FOURTEENTH CENTURY SPANISH PASSOVER HAGGADA, SHOWING A SCENE IN A SYNAGOGUE.

tional and humanitarian way of life, in spite of the forces that besieged it. The demands of the kingdom were regarded by the Jews sometimes as the imposition of the justified and true burden and law of the kingdom, and sometimes as an evil decree. But only Jews could (in their own opinion) formulate ordinances and sit in moral and legal judgment on other Jews. The Gentile state remained foreign even when it strengthened Jewish self-rule or appointed it.

In the period of rule of the Geonim and the exilarchs a national way of life took shape, according to the forms of Talmudic law and the study and understanding of the Talmud was diffused throughout the diaspora. Because of this, a 'class' of sages emerged in the course of time and academies were established that were not of the members of the families of the sages, and not from the academies of Babylon. To a large extent the decline of the Babylonian center and the rise of other territorial centers is the story of the very success of this first center in the spreading of the Torah, and the provision of an example for the whole of Jewry.

The leadership of the negidim regarded itself as defending the fairly high status of the Jews, achieved by them in Moslem Spain and envied by the Gentiles partly because of hatred for the Jew who was close to the court. The negidim enforced the law of the Talmud with a firm hand in the Jewish communities. The winning of charters and the unceasing attempts to maintain them and to punish those who harm the Jews is to be put to the credit of the Jewish leadership in the Christian lands as a whole.

Even the ordering of family structure and life was determined to a certain extent by the communal leadership. In the days of the Talmud a movement in favor of monogamy in the Jewish family was already heard of in Judaism. In Egypt

for example, in the 12th Century, a condition was written in the "ketuboth" (marriage contracts) and maintained by the courts, precluding the husband from marrying a woman in addition to his wife or from buying a female slave for himself without the agreement of the first wife. However, only in northwestern Europe was the leadership successful in changing, fundamentally and permanently, the character of the Jewish family. This was done by a series of ordinances, bans and prohibitions attributed to Rabbenu Gershom Meor Hagolah. It was stipulated that it was forbidden for a man to marry a second wife; only if the first be of unsound mind and cannot be divorced and there is no possibility of maintaining normal family life—only then may the husband take a second wife if he obtains the "permission of a hundred rabbis" of three lands. This permission will be granted only after he has deposited the sum due to the first wife under the marriage contract and arranged for her support. The most revolutionary change is that which precludes the husband from divorcing his wife without her consent. The Jewish family was converted in this fashion from a social institution in which a husband kept his wives according to his whims, into a legal partnership between a couple bound by the will of both.

In the Jewish society of Christian Spain, the social aims of the various strata clashed. In 1281, Rav Todros suggested that the redemption from Galuth depends upon correct ordinances to a large extent, upon the appointment of people "to the market and other places" so that they should supervise the behavior of individuals; one must watch their talk as well as care for proper weights and measures. He attacked the members of the upper classes, particularly "in relation to the Moslem females," where the loose practices on the part of the masters in relation to the female

flexibility of reaction to the changes and dangers in the occupational sphere are apparent. From the effort to stabilize the livelihoods of Jews in western Europe, there developed a custom by which no Jew might compete with his fellow-Jew in his connections with a Gentile client who was already in contact with the former. This custom is in accord with the general spirit of the Middle Ages, which attempted to limit competition, and particularly opposed this among members of the same corporation. In those countries, and at the time when money-lending was the chief occupation of the Jews, rules were promulgated to prevent the receipt of goods in security where there was a suspicion that they were stolen.

slaves were obnoxious to him. The demand for reforms and regulations stemmed from the call to repentance which Rav Jonah Ghirondi preached in the 13th Century in his sermons and writings.

The communal leaders also dealt with economic matters. From the economic ordinances promulgated in various lands at different times during the Middle Ages, the constant awareness and

JEWISH GRAVESTONES FROM MEDIEVAL EUROPE.
(Top) LEON, SPAIN, 1094.
(Right) GERMANY, 14TH CENTURY.
(Bottom) VENOSA, 822.
THE CROSS WAS CUT IN THE TOMBSTONE ON TOP OF THE MENORAH BY OTHER HANDS AT A LATER PERIOD. THE INSCRIPTION READS: HERE RESTS JOSEPH SON OF — —, WHO DIED AT THE AGE OF THIRTY-FIVE, FOUR THOUSAND FIVE HUNDRED AND EIGHTY-TWO YEARS AFTER THE CREATION OF THE WORLD, SEVEN HUNDRED AND FIFTY-THREE YEARS AFTER THE DESTRUCTION OF THE HOLY TEMPLE, MAY IT BE REBUILT IN OUR DAYS AND IN THE DAYS OF ALL ISRAEL, AMEN.

When the occupations of Jews in Poland-Lithuania expanded and became diversified, the main innovation was, as has been stated, their occupation as agents of the nobles, in rental of land-holdings or other branches of the economy.

The Jewish leadership regarded itself bound to prevent competition in the new branches of occupations too, to bring this form of livelihood into conformity with the law, and to arrange it in such a way that it would prevent hardship,

from the point of view of the Gentiles. A series of ordinances of the councils of various lands tried to regulate the problem of the employment of serfs on the Sabbath by Jewish agents. One of the ordinances suggested to the Jewish agent that he forgo the work of the serfs on the Sabbath at his own expense. For "where the Gentiles are serfs in the hand of the Jews, the Jews must maintain the precepts of the Torah and of the sages, and they must not kick, God forbid, with the riches given them at him who gave them this affluence. Let them endeavor to glorify the name of the Lord and let them take care that it be not desecrated by them." In order to prevent competition in the renting of landholdings — called "arenda" — an ordinance was promulgated: if a Jew rented a manor or a portion of it, for a period of three years, no other Jew was permitted to compete for this "arenda" during the lifetime of the first. There was another sphere of renting

where the Jewish community leadership was divided on the question of maintaining it or giving it up. These were the "great arendas" of the kingdom: customs, mines and taxes. In 1581 the Council of Land of Poland prohibited this type of arenda because it aroused the ire of the Polish nobility who wanted it for themselves. In 1623 the Council of Lithuania decided to encourage it in regard to custom stations "which is basically for the good of all . . . when the hand of Israel is strong . . . because of the customs which it holds . . . would that it should be so. In all the places of settlement of the Jews the customs should be in the hands of the Jews . . . so that they should have the upper hand." Within the space of 43 years two radically opposed decisions were reached by the Councils of Poland and Lithuania on a matter where economics and the social power and danger that result therefrom were intertwined

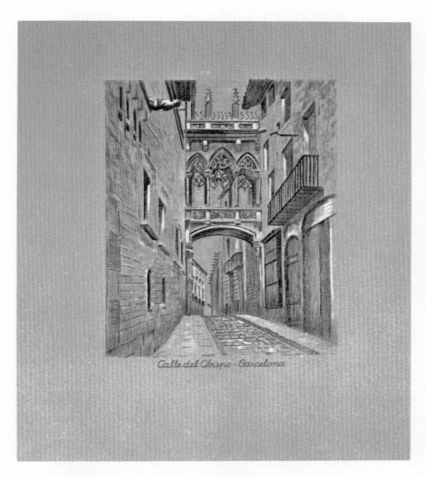

Calle del Obispo - Barcelona

STREET IN THE JEWISH QUARTER OF BARCELONA.

A CANTOR, WITH BIRD-LIKE FEATURES, WRAPPED IN A FRINGED PRAYER SHAWL, READS IN THE SYNAGOGUE. AN ILLUSTRATION TO THE SONGS OF PRAISE IN THE HAGGADA.

PREPARING THE MATZOT FOR THE PASSOVER. *(From right to left)*: MIXING THE DOUGH, PERFORATING THE UNLEAVENED BREAD, PASSING THE MATZAH TO THE RABBI (IN "JEWISH HAT") FOR INSPECTION.

PASSOVER CELEBRANTS AT THE SEDER TABLE; FROM
A 15TH CENTURY HAGGADA FROM DARMSTADT. THE
FIGURES AROUND THE BORDER ARE ALL SEEN STUDY-
ING FROM BOOKS.

JEWISH WORSHIPPERS IN THE SYNAGOGUE. AN ILLUS-
TRATION FROM A MEDIEVAL MISHNA.

A WORSHIPPER, WRAPPED IN A PRAYER SHAWL, HOLDS
HIGH A TORAH SCROLL (IN AN EMBROIDERED COVER)
IN FRONT OF THE HOLY ARK WHICH IS DECORATED
IN GOTHIC STYLE. AN ILLUSTRATION FROM THE
ROTHSCHILD CODEX, AN ILLUSTRATED PRAYER BOOK
FROM NORTHERN ITALY, 15TH CENTURY, NOW IN THE
BEZALEL MUSEUM.

THE ROSH-HASHANA (NEW YEAR) KIDDUSH PRAYER. A
PAGE FROM THE ROTHSCHILD MANUSCRIPT; NORTHERN
ITALY (15TH CENTURY).

THE JEWS IN THE
MIDDLE AGES—CULTURE

INSCRIPTION IN ARABIC AND HEBREW READS "BLESSED
BE THY COMING AND THY GOING," FOUND IN SPAIN
IT DATES FROM THE ARAB CONQUEST.

THE JEWS IN THE MIDDLE AGES—CULTURE

In the Middle Ages only the Jewish people had direct ethnic, social and religious continuity with the past heritage from the ancient world. The surrounding nations and religions — Christian and Moslem — were a combination of new ethnic factors, developed from cultures that were not their own. A good deal of the dominant nations' adopted heritage, moreover, came from Judaism. The Jews were thus at the same time both closely related to them and utterly foreign to them.

Judaism of the Middle Ages is a creative cultural force, fighting both an offensive and a defensive battle. From the first it had inherited a tradition of opposition, the outlook of a nation alone in a pagan world. In its own eyes Judaism kept the glowing ember of divine truth and Torah from being quenched in the surrounding sea of falsehood. In the eyes of Christians and Moslems too, there was power here. The very fact that they persecuted the Jews, disputed with them, tried to degrade and isolate them, proved that they recognized in Judaism a social and spiritual force.

The Jews' attitude to their inheritance was one of veneration for divine law, which had been handed down for generations and had accumulated layer upon layer with time. The older the layer the greater its sanctity and authority in the eyes of succeeding generations. Hence the fundamental importance of exegesis as the root of both conservation and change in the legal code and theory of medieval Jewry. The Torah, the earlier and later Prophets, the Mishnah, the Talmud and the Midrashim (and in the course of the Middle Ages, the writings of medieval sages) — all these the Jews tried to understand for the sake of their spiritual salvation and their individual and social life in Jewish society. Every change or influence that was introduced, from within or without, consciously or unconsciously, was used to explain former layers of tradition, or served as the basis

for preferring one Jewish authority or trend to another. Medieval scholars hide real originality under the constant appeal to ancient authorities: formal acceptance of the authority of older writings and generations is of the essence of medieval thought, Jewish, Christian and Moslem. When systems of thought like the Aristotelian-Arabic philosophy, penetrated from outside, they were given a place in Jewish culture by exegesis. When mystic symbols made their way in, they were filled with content and woven into the structure of ancient Jewish symbolism by the same method.

During the Middle Ages, the study of the Torah was not merely considered important and meritorious spiritually. Knowledge of it was the foundation of social esteem and family honor. Holiness and splendor together surrounded its study and its student. Generations and methods might come and go: the lofty status of the Torah remained.

In the Babylonian yeshivot, over the centuries, authenticated commentaries on the Talmud evolved, as well as authoritative practical decisions. Matters were discussed orally in the course of study and put down in writing when a question was sent from a Jewish place of dispersion outside. A question of this kind would be placed before the whole yeshivah, and the Gaon would give an authoritative reply in the name of the rest of the yeshivah. The "responsa" of the Geonim, which we possess today in their thousands, are only part of the creative work of the Babylonian yeshivot.

Anan ben David opposed the domination of the Talmud effected by the Geonim in the 8th Century. Karaism, which began with him, had many shades. In the 10th Century, one of its branches was very active — the "Shoshanim" in Jerusalem. These were extreme Jewish rationalists, who regarded the Bible (as understood by the individual intellect) as the sole basis of their lives and faith. They especially stressed the crisis engendered by the destruction of Jerusalem and demanded mourning for her. The majority of Jews, however, followed the Geonim and accepted the rulings of the yeshivot and their studies.

In the course of time, study and knowledge became widespread. In Spain during the 11th Century, R. Shmuel Hanagid describes — albeit with some disfavor — the high voices heard coming from the "Beth Midrash", where "they read from the Talmudic tractate and section ... and behold the Rabbi, and the pupils nodding their heads back and forth ... and the Rabbi explains at great length and extracts from them a letter and a word." The bodily movements, the raised voice, the teacher's method and the pupils' discussions in the "Beth Midrash" aroused the ire of the courtiers. They were destined to be found wherever Jews studied Torah in the Middle Ages.

During the 12th Century in northern France, special ceremonies were held in which the baby was brought as if by magical touch and adjuration to hold a pen when he grew up, to read a book, to love the Torah. "It is a custom after the 'milah', at the nearest date wished, to gather ten people, and take a manuscript codex of the Pentateuch. The tiny one is in the cradle, and they put the book upon him and say: May he keep what is written in this book ... An ink pot and pen are placed in his hand, in order that he should grow to be a skilled writer in the law of the Lord. And when a person introduces his son to the study of the Torah, the letters are written for him on a board; they wash him and dress him in clean clothes, and three white loaves of fine flour are kneaded ... three eggs are cooked for him, and they bring him apples and various fruit. And they ask an eminent sage to take him to the school; he takes him under his prayer-shawl and

delivers him up to the synagogue. They feed him white bread in honey, the eggs and the fruit, and read the letters to him. Afterwards (the board) is covered with honey and they say to him: lap up ... and when they begin to teach him, first they entice him and eventually strap his back ... And they accustom him to sway his body when he studies." This type of general education of all men, and this sort of love of study was to be found in medieval Christianity only in the monasteries. From this point of view the Jews of the Middle Ages were "a kingdom of priests" in Europe. A learned monk, one of Peter Abelard's scholars, writes in the 12th Century that unlike the Christians, who teach their children so that they may be priests and monks, "the Jews —

TWO JEWS DISCUSSING A SCHOLARLY TEXT. SKETCH BY PETER BRUEGHEL.

out of zeal for God and love of the law — put as many sons as they have to letters, that each may understand God's law. A Jew, no matter how poor, if he had ten sons, would put them all to letters, not in order to profit thereby, as the Christians do, but for the sake of understanding the Torah of God, and not only his sons, but also his daughters." This high level of education was therefore common to Jewish centers of culture. There were, however, variations in the content of this education.

Jewry in the Islamic world was very receptive to the culture of the environment. Arabic, in the east, was the language of biblical and talmudic commentary and exposition of the law. Concepts and systems of Greek-Arabic philosophy were included in the beliefs of the Jews living there at that time. Those in the upper strata of Jews earned a rich livelihood and rose in social status partly thanks to their achievements in and contributions to general culture. Jewish poetry that developed there is characterized by the structural forms borrowed from Arabic poetry. Its subjects are friendship, love and wine, side by side with penitence, prayer and dirges — a mirror of the forms of Arab poetry. The speculative literature is influenced consciously and unconsciously by Arab philosophers, by translations from the Greek, and by the problems that pervaded Islamic thought.

This openness and receptiveness was maintained and even extended here and there, when Christianity began to conquer Spain from the Moslems. Jewish notables acquired status at the courts of Christian rulers, in the cities and in educated circles. This was largely due to the fact that they emulated the culture of the Islamic world, its content and systems, and taught them to the Christians. Provence, the southern province of France, belongs to the Spanish-Jewish

CELEBRATING A JEWISH FESTIVAL, AN ILLUSTRATION FROM MEDIEVAL SPAIN.

culture. The Jews imbibed the culture of their environment, and Jewish struggles and expression arise to a large extent from the impetus produced by this contact. This is the specific characteristic of the culture of Sephardic Jewry.

Much internal tension was engendered by this. The tendencies described above produced a reaction that was mystic in spirit and ascetic in social outlook. This reaction gathered force from the 13th Century onwards; it demanded an uncompromisingly fervent religious world-view, in a frame of reference of mystical symbolism, and sought a way of escape from the influence of non-Jewish culture and manners.

After the expulsion in 1492, Sephardic culture was carried, in all its spiritual wealth and internal conflict, to North Africa, Palestine, Asia Minor, the Balkans, Italy and the Netherlands, and from there (in the 17th Century) to England and north-west Germany and even to the American continent. In these places the mutual penetrations of Spanish-Jewish culture and the culture of the Ashkenazi Jews began.

The roots of Ashkenazi culture were in the Jewry of southern Italy, which had received the greater part of its Torah learning from Palestine and Byzantine Jewry. From the very beginning the Ashkenazi Jews could derive little from the Christians around them: they differed from them in faith and customs, and were richer than they in cultural tradition and thought. Subsequently the cultures of Jews and Christians in those areas developed on parallel lines of ascetic tendencies and moral austerity. The two were arrayed side by side, related in the foundation of the culture developed in the same cities and permeated by a religious atmosphere that was at the same time very similar in character and very different and opposed in fundamental belief and practice. Radical differences and a basic affinity operated here simultaneously.

This Ashkenazi Jewry considered the proper content of its education to be the Jewish cultural heritage only. The language of written exegesis, of sermons in writing and legal responsa, was Hebrew — but mixed with words taken from the local language (e.g., French and German) to explain difficult expressions in Hebrew. Its poetry was entirely religious, in the form of ancient liturgical poetry. Its writings were overwhelmingly concerned with and based upon the Bible and the Talmud. Love of the Torah and fear of God contributed here to a special profundity of penetration into and permeation with the spirit of the ancient sources and great enthusiasm in divine worship. From the first Ashkenazi center — that of western Europe — this culture spread to Poland-Lithuania. There it was the culture of a variegated society enjoying freer contact with the Gentile population. In central and northern Italy, where the Ashkenazi culture was also planted, the occupational variegations were small in comparison with Poland but the contact with non-Jewish culture was great and very fruitful. Thus, at the waning of the Middle Ages, two shades of Ashkenazi culture might be discerned — the Polish and the Italian — each of which resembled more or less the problems and content of Sephar-

dic culture. The development in Italy formed a kind of Sephardi-Ashkenazi cultural mosaic.

The physician, translator, author and merchant Yehuda Ibn Tibbon, who was born in Granada in Moslem Spain, about 1120 and wandered northwards to Lunel in Provence, left a last will and testament which reflects the manner of life and ideals of the upper circle that moulded the character of Sephardic culture. The will was intended for his son Shmuel, who translated the writings of Maimonides from Arabic into Hebrew. Arabic style and calligraphy were important in his view: "For the foremost men of our nation never attained high distinction except through their proficiency in writing." For that reason he even explains the need "to read the weekly portion of the Pentateuch in Arabic, because this will improve your Arabic vocabulary and will be of advantage in translating, if one wishes to translate." He has an ingrained cultural sense and esteem for fine form and social status: "As far as your means allow, honor yourself and your house . . . in decent dress . . . spare from your belly and put on your back." A goodly portion of this last will and testament is devoted to detailed instructions concerning punctiliousness in handwriting, writing materials and form of letters: "for the beauty of a composition depends on the writing and the beauty of the writing on pen, paper and ink; and all these beauties of the written composition are an index to the writer's worth." In the prestige that has accrued to his son thanks to the father's position, he includes that "you were honored by me, the princes, the bishops, priests and the monks." He commands his son, the doctor: "be good and pleasant unto people . . . and if you take payment from the rich, heal the poor for nothing. And the Lord will reward you . . . you will be honored . . . among Jews and Gentiles. Your good name will go forth far and wide." The content of the studies of the honored Jewish doctor was "in the study of your Torah and the science of medicine." The tenderness in family relationships — including the wife — the composed moderation in social relationships that he advocates, are also reflected in his attitude to his library which he compares to a garden: "Consider your books your companions. Let your cases and shelves be your pleasuregrounds and gardens. Bask in their paradise and gather their roses ... And if your soul be sated and weary, change from garden to garden, from furrow to furrow and from prospect to prospect, for then will your desire be renewed and your soul be pleased." Esthetic pleasure and mental freshness come to him from the many shades and differences of his cultural treasure. This will, concludes Yehuda in the same spirit, is "a small cloud rising from the sea of intellect and learning, carried by the breeze of wisdom and understanding." Rationalism and aristocracy are here united.

In the same 12th Century, Abraham Ibn Daud (Rabad) in his "Seder Kabbalah" praises the courtier Yehuda Ibn Ezra as a redeemer and savior (thanks to his services to the Christian king) of the Jews who fled northwards from the Moslem lands. In his view, the Jewish society, protected and led by the upper circle, that served Christian society, is inwardly and outwardly sound. But these are the days of the Crusades. War has become a way of serving God. Israel has no sword. The doctor and poet Yehuda ben Shmuel Halevi (1085-1145) feels the danger of living between two armed camps: "While they fight their battle, we will be the victims." "Between the armies of Seir (Christendom) and Kedar (Islam) my host will be lost, and Israel has no men of war." He also feels that the fighters of Islam and Christendom are both sincere in their desire to worship their Creator with the sword. As a result of this historic instinct (and influenced by the religious philosophy of the Moslem, Ibn Ghazali) Yehuda Halevi develops in the Book of Kuzari (written in Arabic) the idea that "Israel among the nations is like the heart among the limbs, healthier than all and sicklier than all," for it is a chosen people and in a central position. He probes deep into the question of the nation's attitude to its exile and concludes that it is an attitude "halfway between compulsion and voluntary acceptance." The Jew does not really and actively welcome suffering, but neither does he make use of the door opened by the other religions to come over to them and attain equality "by the uttering of a simple word", and become "a friend of the oppressor". He considers Israel 'chosen' in that the mark of its creator is stamped upon it in the gift of prophecy, given to Israel alone, to be fulfilled in the chosen land of Eretz Israel, through its behavior in the chosen way — the way of the Torah.

In his system of thought these factors are intertwined: concern with the dangers of Israel's position in the world of the Crusades, the need to explain to the Jew the meaning of his suffering and degradation, and the way of his choice and redemption; and biological concepts drawn from medieval science and medicine. The definition of Israel's chosen character is derived by him from the very fact of Israel's suffering and degradation.

All the knowledge available to a Jew in the 12th Century, the Jewish Sephardic culture and the general culture of the Islamic lands, come together in the works and personality of Rabbi Moshe ben Maimon (Maimonides or Rambam, 1135-1204). Born in Cordova in Moslem Spain, he fled at the age of 13, with his family, from the religious bigotry of the Moslems who ruled there and forcibly tried to convert them. He studied Torah, medicine and philosophy during his wanderings in North Africa, whence he reached Palestine. He subsequently settled in Egypt and earned a living as Vizier's physician.

In the spheres of philosophy, medicine, mishnaic and talmudic exegesis, Maimonides was truly creative. He composed letters intended for whole communities and for his pupils (a number of which are full-scale literary works in content, form and length), many halakhic responsa, and the great Jewish legal code. Most of his writings are in Arabic; but his sole large Hebrew composition, the code "Mishneh Torah", is an exemplary linguistic work.

Maimonides' system of thought is revolutionary and at the same time sums up all Jewish tradition. In "Mishneh Torah" (according to his own introduction) "the laws of the Torah are all in clear language and concise form, so that the oral law may be completely familiar to all, without difficulty and without argument and answer — not 'one (sage) says thus and another says thus' — in order that no-one will require another book to know a law of the laws of Israel . . . I therefore called this composition 'Mishneh Torah' — for a person who reads this will know the whole Oral Law. And he will not need to read any other book." Generation upon generation of later scholars, adherents and opponents alike, have agreed that his words were correct: "This composition comprises the whole Oral Law, including the ordinances, the customs and the decrees promulgated from the days of Moses until the compilation of the Gemarah, according to the exegesis of the Geonim in all the works that they wrote after the Gemarah." One word in Maimonides' code sometimes summarizes and crystallizes dozens of ancient sources. This code was a revolutionary experiment. Its aim and its

achievements were to extract from the gigantic sea of the Talmud (which debates and associates, giving the opinion of the outnumbered individual as well as the prevailing opinion) a systematic code of laws, methodically stated, erasing the debate and deleting the associations. Maimonides was the first and greatest of Jewish codifiers. Although succeeding generations refused to give up the sources and retained the whole oral Torah for practical use (even adding to Maimonides' code annotations of the sources and discussions from which he had drawn), the codifying trend continued throughout the Middle Ages.

In philosophy, Maimonides' Arabic "Guide to the Perplexed" formulated an all-embracing philosophical-religious metaphysical system that profoundly influenced Judaism. Its basis was religious rationalism; it merged the fundamentals of Jewish faith and tradition with philosophical method and achievement. He objected violently to the mystic-symbolic approach, which he held to be idolatry. He opposed every "embodiment" (hagshama), i.e., anything that gave the slightest hint of human form or behavior to the Divine. He repudiated all "shituf", i.e., anything ascribing positive titles and attributes to the Divine Being, apart from unity and eternity. Expressions in the Torah, the prophetic writings and the Talmud that appeared to stray in this direction, he explained as parables, whose content one must understand, but which one dare not explain according to their linguistic "shell". As early as the 10th Century Sa'adia Gaon (in his Arabic book "Emunot Vede'ot") and Shmuel ben Hophni were thinking on similar lines.

Maimonides' code of law also includes the fundamentals of his philosophical outlook, particularly in "Sefer Hamada", which introduces it. It was Maimonides who formulated the "Thirteen Principles", which to this day are the binding credo of Judaism for the majority of Jews. His conception of life sees man and society from the aristocratic point of view. In his famous Parable of the Palace in "Guide to the Perplexed", he portrays the venerable sages, who found the entrance to the Divine palace, as the only worthy persons before God. The rest of humanity is created to serve them. Prophecy and messianism are dependent for this realization upon the prior attainment of this complete wisdom.

This intellectual criterion automatically disqualified a certain messiah who revealed himself in Yemen, and Maimonides warned the Jews there against this man in his "Letter to Yemen". He wished to see the nation in its exile led by great scholars and sages like himself, who do not profit from the community they lead. His nobility and intellect compelled him to serve the whole nation — in explaining the law, in philosophical leadership, in day-to-day instruction — while doing exhausting work as a physician.

The roots of the struggle over Maimonides' teaching lie in his greatness. Many Jews in subsequent generations utterly negated religious rationalism, opposed the merging of Aristotle and the Law of Moses, and declared that the essence of Judaism is the mysticism Maimonides rejected. During the 13th and 14th Centuries, in Spain and Provence (with tendrils in a number of other lands) a conflict developed between the "rationalists" — followers of Maimonides — and his opponents. This was a struggle over the fundamentals of faith and the content of Jewish education. The anti-rationalist camp united, basing itself on the "Cabbalah", the world of Jewish mysticism that springs from ancient roots and lore. Beginning in 12th Century Provence, in small, closed circles of mystics, it branched out in a series of works by these Cabbalists and the Spanish Cabbalists of the 13th and 14th Centuries. The latter

ascribed some of their compositions to the " Tannaim" and the ancients. The focal point of this creativity was "the Book of Splendor" (Sefer Hazohar) ascribed to the Tanna Shimon bar Yochai. The Cabbalists regard God, the creation, and the fate in a mystic-symbolic light which negates the rationalist method of explanation. One of the sages of Spanish Jewry, the biblical commentator Rabbi Moshe ben Nachman*, who publicly disputed with the Christians in Barcelona in 1263, expressed this mood well when he said: "Man has no share in the teachings of Moses our teacher until we totally and completely believe that all happenings and doings in the world are all miracles, being neither natural nor part of the fixed ways of the world, either in relation to the community or the individual."

Ashkenazi Jewry engaged in exegesis even more than Sephardic Jewry; its venerated leaders expressed the problems of their generation and proposed solutions thereto in a system that makes even the works of the greatest of them part of one collective whole. In the poetry of Rabbi Shimon bar Yizhak, in the work of Rabbenu Gershom, "the Light of the Exile" as he was called, Ashkenazi Jewry in the 10th and 11th Centuries achieved its own well-defined form. Study of the Torah was its foundation; guided and directed by an acute sense of the perils of existence — the existence of a community of fervent believers within a world of equally fervent hostile belief. Rabbi Shimon poetically describes the society of knights who bear arms and brightly blazoned shields and dwell in their castles, comparing it with the community of Israel which has nothing to protect it but its Father in Heaven. In another poem he compares the manner of life and ideals of the great learned sages with that of simple householders in the community. The former are recognizable by their expert-

*(Ramban)

JEWS, LONGING FOR THE RETURN TO THE HOLY
LAND, POINT TO A VISIONARY JERUSALEM, BUILT IN
MEDIEVAL CHRISTIAN STYLE.

ILLUSTRATIONS FROM THE HAGGADA. AT THE TOP
THE SHEKHINAH, THE DIVINE PRESENCE, HOVERS
OVER THE KNEELING FIGURES OF AARON (IN JEWISH
HAT) AND MOSES. ALONG THE BOTTOM THE ANGEL
OF GOD STAYS THE FALLING SWORD AS ABRAHAM
PREPARES TO SACRIFICE ISAAC. BEHIND ABRAHAM IS
THE RAM, CAUGHT BY HIS HORNS IN THE THICKET.

THE CROSSING OF THE RED SEA. AN ANGEL HOVERS
OVER THE ISRAELITES WHO ARE HEADED BY MOSES,
WIELDING HIS STAFF. FROM THE "MACHZOR RIDJIN",
LORRAINE, 15TH CENTURY.

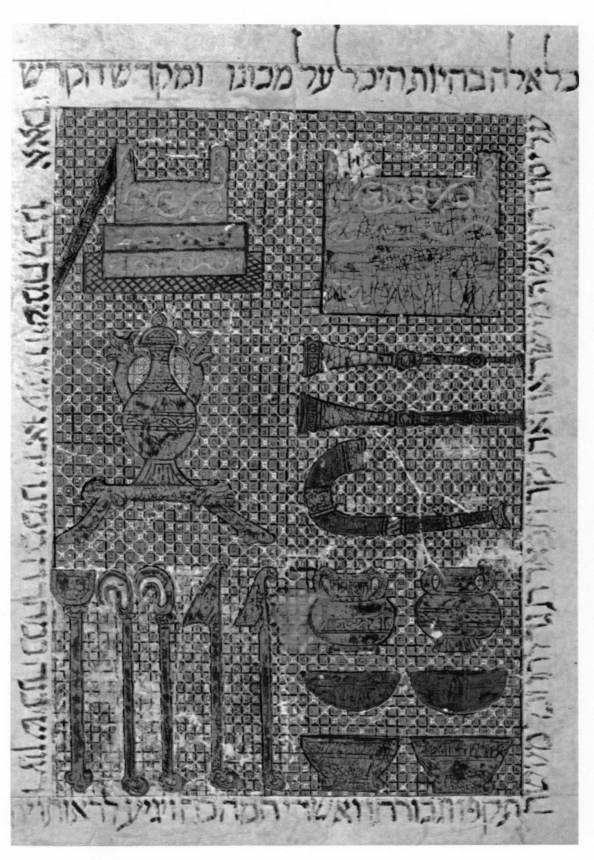

ILLUMINATED PAGE FROM A MANUSCRIPT BIBLE, PROVENCE, 1301. SHOWN ARE CEREMONIAL VESSELS FROM THE TEMPLE INCLUDING TWO ALTARS *(top)* AND TRUMPETS *(center right)*.

OPENING VERSE OF THE FIRST PSALM WITH COMMENTARY, FROM A 15TH CENTURY PSALTER. THE ILLUSTRATIONS SHOW SCENES FROM THE LIFE OF DAVID.

THE MESSIAH, RIDING A WHITE ASS, AT THE GATE OF THE CITY. BEFORE HIM GOES A HERALD BLOWING A TRUMPET.

A SCRIBE COMPARES HIS COPY WITH THE ORIGINAL
MANUSCRIPT. FROM THE ROTHSCHILD MANUSCRIPT AT
THE BEZALEL MUSEUM, JERUSALEM.

TITLE PAGES FROM TWO WORKS BY MAIMONEDES;
ITALIAN MANUSCRIPTS FROM THE LATE 15TH CEN-
TURY. THE DRAWINGS SHOW KNIGHTS ENGAGED IN
A TOURNAMENT *(left)* AND ASTRONOMERS TAKING
READINGS ON THE STARS *(right)*.

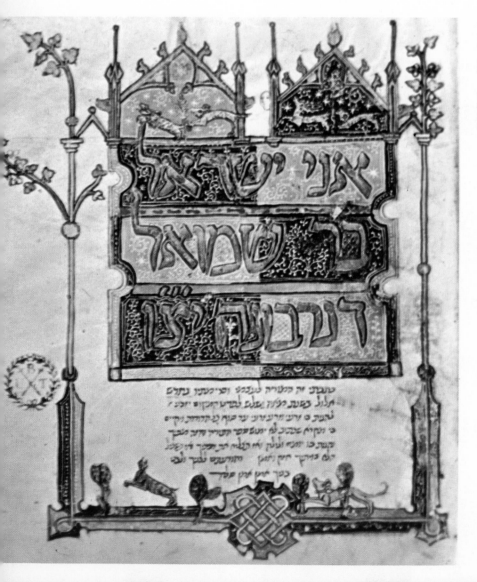

CLOSING PAGE OF A FOURTEENTH CENTURY MANU-
SCRIPT CODEX. THE SCRIBE, ISRAEL SON OF SAMUEL
OF NARBONNE, GIVES THE DATE OF COMPLETION OF
HIS TASK AS ELUL 4103 (AUGUST 1343)

ness in the whole Torah, by their service to the nation — not given for gain — by their nightly diligence in study, by their legal decisions and the personal example that they set. For the rest of the people the ideal behavior is: honesty in economic dealings and meticulous observance of both minor and major precepts, permeated by the awareness that they are members of the chosen people, careful in reciting prayers and accustomed to give charity. These sets of obligations and values and this fine distinction between two strata according to their education and religiousness, were destined to be the guiding light of Ashkenazi Jewry during the whole of the Middle Ages. In the works of Rabbenu Gershom we see a Jewish society educating its children from the Bible and Talmud and possessing books; studying them was not out of the ordinary. One must not forget the significance of this in those days when books meant manuscripts and the work of scribes was very costly.

Rabbi Shlomo ben Yizhak of Troyes in France (Rashi, 1040-1105) summarized in his exegetical works to the Bible and Talmud, in his responsa and poetry, the achievements, problems and struggles of the generations preceding him. These commentaries so facilitated the understanding of the source that they were accepted by all the dispersions of Israel — even by the Sephardim — as the basis for the study of the Bible and Talmud.

Towards the end of Rashi's lifetime, Ashkenazi Jewry was subjected to the disturbances of the First Crusade (the holocaust of 1096). The members of these congregations reacted to the challenge by acceptance of martyrdom (Kiddush Hashem). This martyrdom was conceived as a war for the honor of the Lord, even to the point of sacrificing one's life in the battle for the faith against Christianity, (according to a description of these happenings written in the first half of the 12th Century). If possible, Jews should die sword in hand, as they tried to do in Mayence; if not, the Jewish fighter turns his sword on his children, his wife and himself. The Lord has commanded His people to be brave and true and open in the declaration of their faith. Therefore it is a meritorious deed to be killed, as long as one does not surrender and abandon one's faith. This is the sacrifice and holocaust of the heroic generation chosen by the Lord to do His will. They preferred family suicide to being killed by the enemy because they feared that the Christians would force the children into Christianity. Martyrdom became a guiding principle in the life of Ashkenazi Jewry during the Middle Ages. It penetrated and influenced both Spanish Jewry and modern Jewry. Thus the Jews upheld the principle of no surrender in the face of sword and suffering — in a manner both splendid and terrible.

In the 12th Century their creativity did not cease despite their suffering. In 1196 the pious Eliezer of Worms described his home life in a dirge on the murder of his wife and children. In the house of the sage, the learning of the father and his sermons were the focus. The

CHRISTIAN SCULPTURE SHOWING THE LEGEND OF LEMECH.

mother concerned herself with him and his pupils, looked after the sick and helped impecunious brides. The pious one laments the loss of the beauty, songs, games and embroidery of the daughters, which were some of the pleasures of his life. The grandchildren of Rashi developed, in their yeshivot the "tosafot" — the system of examining the concepts of the Talmud through penetrating discussions — as was the case in the Talmud itself. In fact, the "tosafot" are, from the point of view of scope and the spiritual energy invested in them, the Talmud of France and Germany.

A HYMN OF PRAISE BY THE ELEVENTH CENTURY SPANISH RABBI YEHUDA HALEVI. A PHYSICIAN, YEHUDA HALEVI WAS CONSIDERED SPANISH JEWRY'S GREATEST POET.

The problems and forces of this Jewry found expression in the movement of the "Pious of Ashkenaz" (Hassidei Ashkenaz). This movement arose during the 12th-13th Century in Germany and spread also to France. These pious men were a small and tightly-knit circle; they made extreme demands on themselves and wished to lead the people through the force of personal example. Therefore their teaching contains a number of concepts and practices which were intended in one way for the Hassid and in different ways for the rest of the Jews. The pious must be ascetic in the extreme; the rest of the nation much less so. Property was regarded by them as a "deposit" which the Creator placed in the care of the rich that they should distribute it among the poor. They vehemently opposed formal and equal division of taxes; they demanded individual consideration for the situation of the person. They demanded contributions to charity not for the sake of social honor but because charity is good in itself.

This movement, like Christian religious movements of the same period, contained elements of extreme orthodoxy combined with revolutionary innovation. They maintained that the law of the Torah (Din Torah) was given in certain instances as a kind of concession to and compromise with the social conventions, whereas the pious must behave in accordance with "the law of heaven" (Din Shamaim) which means the true essence of things without consideration for that which is acceptable to society. They valued asceticism, recommended it particularly as a measured repentance (Tshuvath hammishkal), in which the body and soul are mortified by self-affliction in payment for the pleasure they derive from sin. The rules for prayer were demanding; the pious must count every letter and the various shades of meaning of every word, whereas in the prayers of ordinary people they were satisfied with the general intent and even allowed them to forego the fixed formulation of the prayer. The influence of these pious men was great. They were in the forefront of those who slew themselves for the "sanctification of the Name", and their outlook helped to direct and guide the leaders of congregations and sages for hundreds of years afterwards.

The expectation of a Messiah who would come any day was part of the Jewish belief and atmosphere of life during the Middle Ages. In times of general ferment and change it became a stormy and revolutionary factor in society. The belief in the Messiah includes the renewal of the kingdom of Israel and the ingathering of its exiles, the resurrection of the dead, the reform of the world as the Kingdom of God, and the destruction of evil in the world before the coming of the Messiah by a great cataclysm. It was to be a time of revenge and repayment to evildoers, a time of "wars of Gog and Magog", the revelation of the chosen Israel to all the nations of the world which would then acknowledge the truth and be saved too.

During the period of the rise of Islam — the 7th and 8th Century — messiahs appeared bringing tidings of miraculous redemption, including in their message the war of Israel, sword in hand. During the Crusades at the end of the 11th and during the 12th Centuries there were no less than ten messianic movements headed by messiahs, prophets and even a prophetess. The holy simplicity of national faith took every promise seriously. The Jews of Baghdad waited one night on the roof-tops for angels to carry them to Jerusalem, as they were told by the seers. After the expulsion from Spain in 1492 the ferment increased. Prophets and prophecies foretold redemption and revenge for the forced converts. The appearance of David Hareubeni in the 1520's is to be seen in this context. He maintained that he was the son of a Jewish royal family governing strong Jewish tribes on the "second front" against Is-

CLOTHING WORN BY JEWS IN MEDIEVAL GERMANY.

lam. Aided by his strong and colorful imagination he conducted diplomatic negotiations with the Pope and kings. He succeeded in awakening the saintly figure of Shlomo Molcho the Portuguese Converso who circumcised himself and from then onwards adhered to Judaism. Shlomo Molcho had a complete and fervent belief in his mission and the truth of his prophecy and was burnt as a martyr.

The love of Eretz Israel and belief in its holiness caused pilgrimages to the Holy Land and settlement in it throughout the Middle Ages. In the Islamic lands the practice of a pilgrimage to Jerusalem or another feasible place in Eretz Israel never ceased. In the 12th Century Yehuda Halevi made this the obligation of the individual: to settle in Eretz Israel is the right way to observe the precepts in the promised land. Benjamin of Tudela the Sephardi and Petahya of Regensburg

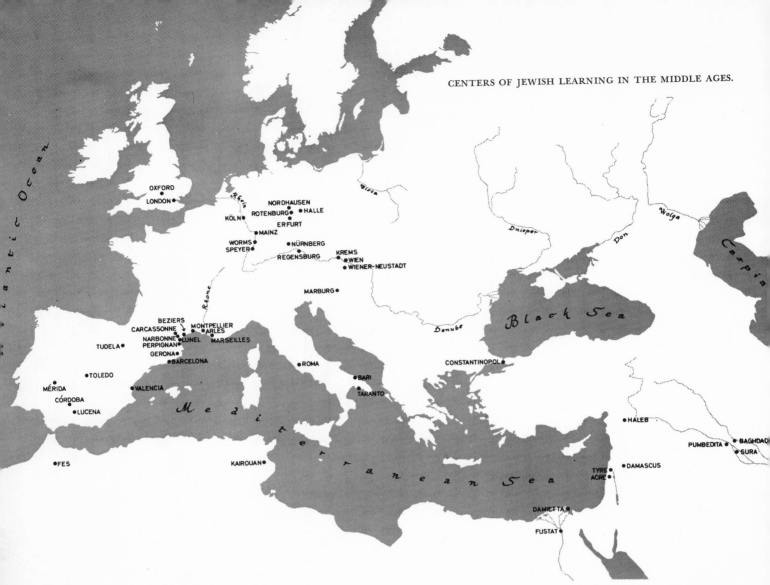

the Ashkenazi told at the end of the century, of the land and of their journeys there and back. During the 13th Century groups of sages "went up" from western Europe. At the end of the 15th Century pilgrimages grew more frequent, and during the 16th and 17th Centuries they increased, particularly among the Spanish exiles and those fleeing from forced conversion.

Jewish creativity during the Middle Ages was vital and alive, whatever form it took: in rationalism and mysticism, in religious law and homiletic exposition, in synthetic summary and in commentary on original sources, in the building of spiritual life in the exile and in looking forward to Eretz Israel and the redemption. This Jewry carried on the tradition of previous generations and added strong, broad tiers of thought and poetry. It fashioned two shades of culture — of Sepharad and Ashkenaz — in a savagely hostile world.

THE ILLUSTRATED HISTORY OF THE JEWS

THE JEWISH RENAISSANCE

THE JEWISH QUARTER IN PRAGUE.

THE JEWISH RENAISSANCE

Despite the subjugation of the Jews in medieval Christian Europe, they continued to hold their ground both economically and spiritually. But as cities developed and the burgher class grew strong, as the cultural level of Christian Europe rose, the more developed states began to expel their Jews. Between the 13th and the 15th Centuries, the Jews were expelled from England, France, Spain, Portugal and Southern Italy. In most of the German cities whole Jewish communities were exterminated by mass murders and burnings at the stake, and only in isolated towns did Jewish communities remain.

These murders and expulsions determined the direction of movement of Jews at the end of the Middle Ages: from west to east. Few remained in the towns and villages of central Europe; most of them became concentrated in the Kingdom of Poland-Lithuania, and in the Ottoman countries of the Near East and North Africa. They established themselves in these new countries where they fulfilled those same economic functions that had become superfluous for the burghers and rulers of the more developed lands of Europe.

However, those very factors in European society that had brought about the expulsion of Jews from these lands, such as the growth of the cities, the expansion of commerce and industry and the strengthening of centralized authority, also undermined the foundations of medieval society itself. During the 16th and 17th Centuries they paved the way for new developments in political structure and economy, for innovations in religion and cultural ideas. The discovery of new territories with their natural resources opened up new fields of economic activity, beyond the authority of the old merchant guilds and closed trade associations. The rulers, concentrating increasing authority in their hands, were no longer prepared to share this with any class or group. Kings and princes refused to be classed merely as the secular branch of the religious authority which alone, according to the concepts of the heads of the Church, was charged with the task of enforcing Christian ideals. Instead the kings regarded themselves as the bearers of a divine authority; they looked upon the state as a lofty concept in its own right, entitled to enforce even religious beliefs upon its subjects. All this was associated with the desire for religious reformation, with religious wars and secular cultural ideals. In sum, political rulers were trying to shake off church intervention in their affairs while society was seething in an atmosphere of religious reformation, religious wars and the introduction of a new secular culture.

MENASSEH BEN ISRAEL OF AMSTERDAM, RABBI AND LEADER OF WESTERN JEWRY IN THE SEVENTEENTH CENTURY, WHO NEGOTIATED FOR THE RETURN OF JEWS TO ENGLAND.

Against this background, the role of the Jews in European life once more increased. Groups of refugees from Spain and Portugal established themselves during the 16th and 17th Centuries, in the commercial centers and ports of the Atlantic Ocean and the Mediterranean, either in the guise of Christians ("New Christians" — Marranos) or openly as Jews. They became merchants of great substance and significance. In Antwerp and Amsterdam, in Bordeaux and London, in Hamburg and Leghorn, Jewish families developed important commercial companies, maintaining the contact between their cities and the ports of the Iberian Peninsula, of the Levant and of the centers of commerce in India and America. Their trade in diamonds, spices and sugar had many ramifications in the auxiliary industries estab-

(Above) EXPULSION OF JEWS FROM FRANKFURT IN 1614. *(Below)* EXODUS OF JEWS FROM VIENNA, AFTER EXPULSION BY EMPEROR LEOPOLD I, 1670.

lished by the merchants such as diamond polishing and silk weaving. They established sugar cane plantations in Brazil and the Caribbean Islands and opened up mines; they supplied European goods to North African states and the cities of the Levant; they even bought pirate spoil, and ransomed captives. Their contribution to commercial empires of the European states was not insignificant, and the rule of France in Canada, for example, was based in no small measure upon the fleet of one of these Jewish families from Borddeaux.

These communities of Spanish Jews in Holland, France, England and their colonies were numerically small, even in the 18th Century. The number of Jews in the various lands of Germany was larger. When tens, and eventually hundreds, of these states began to develop as separate political units, particularly after the Thirty Years War of 1618-1648, and to create armies and the framework of centralized government, it became apparent that many difficulties confronted them. Large states and small principalities in Germany needed financial assistance as well as the food and equipment to establish armies; and they lacked people experienced in financial matters. This was where the role of "Court Jew" was created. They served as contractors, agents and advisers to the

rulers in the management of their private treasuries as well as those of the state and armies. These "Court Jews" utilized their connections with the Jews of Poland to supply the various armies with food, fodder and horses, and as a result were able to influence the Polish nobles to support the election of the Prince of Saxony to the throne of Poland. Among the "Court Jews" were some who helped to strengthen the influence of the House of Habsburg over a number of German principalities and helped to gain for the ruler of Hanover the title of "Kurfuerst" (Prince-elector). Süs Oppenheimer, known as "Jew Süs", tried to strengthen the authority of the Prince of Württemberg at the expense of the Estates. The attempt was made on his own initiative and under his direction, but his opponents were too strong and his career was brought to an untimely end on the scaffold.

The "Court Jews" in Germany were a very limited group. Behind them were their Jewish agents, clerks and assistants, whose existence and status depended upon the success and standing of the "Court Jew". The latter were not always successful in maintaining their positions; they were susceptible to changes in the mood of the prince, and to the strong resistance of the various classes who were opposed to the centralizing aims of the ruler especially when these were furthered through the help of the Jews. Many of the Jews of Germany were merchants in grain, wine and cattle, or moved among the villages as peddlers. In this respect their sources of livelihood were similar to those of the majority of the Jews in Poland, few of whom were rich land-holders or agents of overlords, but were mostly servants of the rich agents, inn-keepers, craftsmen in the small villages, produce merchants or peddlers.

Already during the 17th and 18th Centuries the split in the sources of livelihood of the Jews of

SEVENTEENTH CENTURY SKETCH OF JEWS IN A POLISH MARKETPLACE.

Europe was apparent. In the west their livelihood was based on maritime commerce and on the large urban centers, whereas in central Europe it came mainly from the economy of the State and the treasury of the ruler. In the east they earned a living mainly from the manor and the village. This split was widened after the French Revolution when there was a rise in the number of Jews of Germany whose source of employment was of a specifically urban nature. In Europe important banks arose, which, as contractors of government loans and through investments in railways and the financing of industries, attained great economic influence in European society. A sharpening of economic disparity occurred between those Jews who took an active part in the new and dynamic capitalist development, raising their own standard of living in the process, and those Jews who lived in the backward agricultural lands, whose high birthrate sharpened the competition for the few traditional sources of livelihood, thereby increasing their poverty. In the 18th Century there was still a common economic interest between the eastern and western European Jews, but later this common interest faded and then vanished. The Jews of Europe were split into two: western Jewry, whose economic position became steadily better, and eastern Jewry whose economic basis was increasingly weakened.

European society in the Middle Ages was built in a fixed pattern, each class and each corporation possessing separate legal status. The separate organization of the Jewish community under own laws under charters granted by kings and rulers, thus fitted well into the general framework. But the strong religious and social hostility to the Jews created in the popular mind a frightening image of the Jew. Towards the end of the Middle Ages this image was a threatening figure associated with the devil, enticing the population into his clutches by usury, and thirsting for the blood of Christian children.

The ferment of the Reformation in the 16th Century brought renewed religious awakening and after the efforts of a number of reformers to attract the Jews to their religion had proved futile, they too indulged in poisonous propaganda against the Jews. The efforts of the Catholic Church to fight the Reformation intensified religious intolerance in general and most markedly against the Jews. At this time the custom of establishing ghettos spread and the separation of Jews from Christians was more stringently enforced. More and more prohibitions were enacted, preventing Jews from keeping Christian servants, from staying at Christian inns, and above all, excluding them from various sources of livelihood so that, for example in Rome, dealing in rags became their sole source of income.

Even those rulers who did not strictly enforce the church prohibitions were influenced by anti-Jewish propaganda. Many rulers of European countries during the 17th and even 18th Centuries, believed that the Jews were exploiting the states where they lived. As a result there developed an attitude of confirmed suspicion towards the stranger whom they assumed to be harmful. Even those rulers who employed Jews in their service were not completely at ease and regarded it as a temporary, necessary evil. This attitude was explicit in the legal position of the Jews in many countries. Fear of the Jew by the local population expressed itself in the desire to limit the number of Jews. In almost all of the German states, Jews were forbidden to settle unless they paid the ruler a "tolerance fee". Even the "tolerated" Jew could pass his right of settlement only to his eldest son so that all his other children were obliged to acquire their own "toleration". The absolute rulers tended, because of the nature of their rule, to go into the most detailed definitions of the status of Jews, and the authorities kept a watchful eye on Jewish doings. Even the "poll-tax" which every Jew was obliged to pay on

entry to any town, and which was imposed only on Jews and animals, was not primarily intended to increase income but to impose strict supervision on the movement of Jews.

The attitude of the subjects was even more severe than that of the rulers. The clergy called for the expulsion of the Jews from Christian countries, and warned rulers that it was a great sin to take Jews into their service. Mobs in the cities despoiled and assaulted the Jews (in 1614 at Frankfurt on Main; in 1664 at Lwow, etc.). The lesser nobility in Poland was jealous of the Jews, who were the agents of the landed aristocracy. But the opposition of burghers was particularly virulent. In England, when the British Government introduced a bill in 1753, permitting Jews who had lived in the country for a certain period of time to be naturalized, a wave of opposition arose among the members of the London guilds. Mobs attacked Members of Parliament who voted for the Bill, which was named the "Jew Bill" by its opponents. Public resentment was so great that the government was forced to repeal the Bill in the same year. The merchant guilds and trade guilds of every city were on guard against the danger that the Jew might dare to get a foothold in a source of livelihood similar to that of the burghers, and because of their opposition the Jews were limited to a few degrading branches of work.

Only a few voices were heard in opposition to discrimination against Jews, and those not before the 17th Century. Among them were elements who hoped to attract the Jews to the Christian faith through a more lenient attitude. There were also writers who proposed general tolerance in questions of religion, and aspired to the separation of civil status from religious adherence. These called not merely for the legal equality of all Christian denominations, but also for the free right of Jews to worship God in their own way. Economists and political thinkers had more influence than the few fighters for abstract tolerance, for they pointed to the economic benefit that Jews could bring to the state. Jewish authors had been the first to argue this (Sinho Luzzatto, Manasseh Ben Israel), and their works, written in European languages, had found a sympathetic ear. The mercantilist ideas popular at the time also served as a favorable background against which to explain that the capital of the Jews, and their initiative and experience in commercial matters, could bring benefit to the national economy. Nevertheless conceptions such as these concerning the Jews had few adherents, even in the 18th Century, and exerted no influence on the legal status of the Jews, or on the attitude of Christian society to them in practice. In the second half of the 18th century, a few enlightened rulers and their intimate circles began to alter their relationship to the Jews in principle. The "Edict of Tolerance" (Toleranzpatent) which Joseph II conferred upon the Jews of Vienna in 1782, states that it is his desire that the Jews too should enjoy the "general welfare" and human rights, and the widening of the spheres of employment of the Jews is emphasized. Above all the Edict proclaims the desire to spread European enlightenment among the Jews, to establish schools for their children to teach them the language of the country. Similar ideas were expressed at the same time by an important Prus-

(1) A SILVER MEDALLION MINTED IN AMSTERDAM IN 1734 FOR RABBI ELAZAR BEN SHMUEL, RABBI OF THE AMSTERDAM ASHKENAZI COMMUNITY. HE WAS BORN IN CRACOW, POLAND IN 1665 AND DIED IN 1741 AT SAFED.
(2) JOSEPH SUS OPPENHEIMER ("JEW SUS") WAS BORN IN HEIDELBERG IN 1698 AND EXECUTED FORTY YEARS LATER IN STUTTGART. HE WAS THE "COURT JEW" OF THE PRINCE OF WURTENBERG.
(3) SILVER MEDALLION ISSUED TO COMMEMORATE THE EXECUTION OF "JEW SUS".
(4) ANTI-SEMITIC COIN BLAMING THE JEW FOR THE GRAIN SHORTAGE AND HIGH PRICES IN GERMANY. ISSUED IN 1694.

sian official, Ch. W. Dohm, who suggested reforming the structure and manner of life of the Jews by spreading education among them and changing their occupations. As a prior condition of all this he demanded their legal equality with other citizens. However, before these suggestions could make any impression, the French Revolution broke out. In its wake a far more radical suggestion was enunciated; the complete legal emancipation of the Jews, placing them on an equal footing with all other citizens without any conditions or reservations whatever.

While the problem of the legal emancipation of the Jews was being discussed in western Europe, while the concept of religious tolerance and the desire to bring together Jews and Christians was fast gaining ground in central Europe, the position of east European Jewry was radically different. The economic lines of demarcation were becoming progressively sharper and so were the political lines. The Russian Empire, after the partition of Poland at the end of the 18th Century, became the state with the largest Jewish population in Europe. For a while the Russian rulers took up the ideas of "enlightened absolutism", but soon they began to reduce the legal status of the Jews. Limitations on the free movement of Jews were imposed, particularly at the end of the 18th Century. They were precluded from settling beyond the areas of Poland that had been annexed to Russia (the "Pale of Settlement"), they were commanded to leave the villages and settle in the towns even within the

JEWISH PEDDLERS PROCLAIMING THEIR WARES IN 18TH CENTURY HAMBURG.

"Pale of Settlement" itself, and the taxes imposed upon them were double those of other subjects. During the 19th Century a wide range of discriminatory laws against the Jews was enacted. In a period when the Jews of the west were realizing their greatest aspiration of equal rights, the Jews of the east despaired of securing any improvement in their situation.

The corporate structure of society in the Middle Ages had given the Jews the possibility of consolidating themselves and of creating a special closed society of their own, living according to their laws and in their own special tradition, but supported externally by the rulers. In the period of transition from the Middle Ages, when centralist tendencies in European states grew stronger, complaints against the partial Jewish autonomy began to be raised. Lawyers and politicians claimed that the right of Jews to maintain special courts of their own made the Jewish community a state within a state, and they demanded that the Jews too should be brought under the

general jurisdiction of the temporal state.

In particular those groups in western and central Europe who were striving for religious tolerance on the basis of the separation of church and state, were demanding the abrogation of the authority of the Jewish community over its members. In their opinion, the Jewish community, like any other religious corporation, could have no jurisdiction in social and economic matters; its authority covered only matters of religion and worship. All other matters must come under the sole authority of the state and its institutions. The community must therefore change its form, from an autonomous body, controlling almost all spheres of life for its members, into a public association, devoid of authority, concerning itself with synagogues and worship.

This opinion demanded of the Jews that they give up their ancient and deep-rooted institutions, which would be detrimental to their religious way of life since in certain important spheres, such as marital law, inheritance and Sabbath observance, Jewish religious precepts had an obvious economic and social effect. Nevertheless, in certain Jewish circles in the 18th Century this view found support and the firm hand of the community towards its members strengthened this attitude.

Despite the integration of the Jews of the Sephardic (Spanish) communities in the important urban centers of Europe with their neighbors by acquiring their language and culture, and despite the fact that some Jewish notables, such as the Texeira family in Hamburg in the 17th Century, behaved like the higher aristocracy, the Spanish communities punctiliously safeguarded the community structure that had emerged in their country of origin and even their particular language, Spanish or Portuguese. Not only did they safeguard their pure origin, but they regarded themselves as a special "nation", refraining from assimilation even with other Jewish groups. Moreover the structure of their community was rigid and oligarchic. The Community Board (Ma'amad) was not elected; the outgoing member had the privilege of nominating his successor.

A number of members of those communities where ideals of tolerance had spread, merged with their environment. The authorities in many places were not inclined to give support, or sometimes even recognition, to the community organization. Because of this some Jews reached the conclusion that there was no point in bearing the heavy yoke of communal authority and began to discard it; some even left the Jewish community completely.

The tendency to break away from the community existed in the Germanic lands too. There too it was particularly the wealthy who began to assimilate to their social environment. Here however the communal structure was not as rigid and firm as among the Spanish communities. In

Germanic countries these tendencies gained ground especially because of the relative weakness of the Jewish communities. Very few communities were as fortunate as those of Frankfurt or Prague, which had enjoyed almost continuous existence from the Middle Ages, and were possessed of a consolidated tradition of internal life. Most of the communities had been re-established in the 16th and in the 17th Centuries, some of them in the wake of the "Court Jews" who had come to serve the rulers. The settlement of any Jew in a place was generally conditional upon the payment of a "tolerance fee". This legal position made the Jew more dependent upon the ruler than upon the members of his community. Therefore, when the new tendencies became apparent among the Germans in the 18th Century, there was no one who could exercise authority over the rebels in the community. When people of this type wanted to introduce reforms or changes in the educational system or in other spheres of life, there was almost no one to oppose them — provided, of course, that the authorities had no objection.

In the east the position was radically different. Not only did each Polish community exercise authority over its members, but there was a national representation, "The Council of Four Lands", which promulgated regulations for the whole Jewish community throughout the country. There was hardly a sphere in which the Jewish leadership in Poland did not supervise the activities of the individual; source of livelihood, travel, manner of life and the study of the Torah. The Jewish individual needed the community and depended upon it at every stage of his life.

Social ferment was not lacking in the Polish communities, especially in the 18th Century. Preachers expressed criticism of the leadership, societies of tradesmen sought ways and means to rid themselves of the supervision of the community, and small communities tried to rebel against the authority of the bigger and stronger ones. There were those who turned to the authorities and suggested reforms in the communal order or even its complete dissolution. But these were not able to weaken, to any considerable extent, the status of the autonomous Jewish leadership or to weaken the link between the Jewish individual and the community. In 1764, the Polish regime withdrew its recognition from the "Council of the Four Lands" as the national representative of the Jews, and cancelled the central tax levied by it. However, this failed to affect the community as the basic organizational unit of the Jews, and the provincial councils, the board of

GERMAN JEWS IN FESTIVAL CLOTHING.

representatives of the various Jewish communities in each province of Poland, continued to exist thereafter.

The partition of Poland, which brought the majority of the Jews under the rule of Russia, did not change this situation. The Russian regime continued to recognize the community and even in certain spheres extended its authority beyond that which had been granted to the internal Jewish autonomy in the Polish state. Only the Hassidic movement, which began to develop in Poland during the second half of the 18th Century, created its own specific social groups (Hassidic congregations) whose activities were outside the sphere of the community and beyond its reach. For the first time in hundreds of years, Jewish organizational forms were created that were not based upon the community and its functions. The Hassid was able to live part of his life in this new framework. Consequently the authority of the community in relation to the individual, and the dependence of the individual upon it, were also reduced.

The variety in organizational forms that the Hassidic movement brought about did not weaken the communal organization: in certain respects it even strengthened it. This movement dampened the effect of the social ferment of the previous period, and by relying upon the authority of the Hassidic leader, the Tzadik, succeeded in extending its authority even in those spheres where the authority of the previous communal leadership had been undermined. It provided an impetus to a new discussion of the problems of Jewish tradition, and it created, both within its own camp and within the camp of its opponents, the Mitnagdim, a new leadership, more popular among the Jews than the previous one. This leadership succeeded, over a long period, in repelling the penetration of the "Haskalah" (Enlightenment) and

DECLARATION
des
GENERAL-
Juden-
PRIVILEGII,
de 1750.
in Ansehung des,
denen Juden
gestatteten
Handels, mit Häusern.

De Dato Berlin, den 4. Julii 1763.

MINDEN,
Gedruckt von Johan Augustin Enax, Königlich-Preußischen
privilegirten Hof-Buchdrucker.

A DECREE FROM BERLIN DATED 1763, LIMITING THE RIGHTS OF JEWS IN COMMERCE AND REAL ESTATE.

the influence of the outside environment, which were brought to the Jewish community both by the authorities and by groups of "Maskilim" (proponents of the Haskalah) from within. In this sphere too, the division between east and west was revealed: internal Jewish autonomy became weaker in the west and even stronger in the east.

The condition of life of the Jews and their organizational structure found expression in their cultural activities. Towards the end of the Middle Ages, Jewish religious tradition became codified. The endeavor to codify the religious law of the Jews and their way of life in a systematic form, which had been attempted on a number of occasions since the days of Maimonides, was accepted by almost all the Jewish Diaspora in the "Shulhan Aruch", the code of Rabbi Joseph Caro (1488-1575). Rabbi Joseph Caro, who came from the exiles of Spain living in the east, summarized in his work the essence of the Halachic tradition and the practices of Sephardi Jews. In Poland, which, in the 16th Century became the most important center for the study of the Torah, Rabbi Moshe Isserlis added to the "Shulhan Aruch" his "Mapah" which included the Ashkenazi practices. Codification, which had always elicited protests in previous periods, aroused opposition in Poland too, but towards the 17th Century there could no longer be found anyone to question the authority of the "Shulhan Aruch", and great Halachic scholars were busy writing commentaries upon it.

The traditional Law, as summarized in the "Shulhan Aruch" was not merely the fruit of a protracted study of the law in previous generations. It was created against the background of hundreds of years of conflict of opinion within Jewry concerning the essential nature of Jewish faith, the significance of the existence of the Jewish people and the meaning of its long exile. After many attempts to compromise between the basic assumptions of religious tradition and the rational philosophic thought developed during

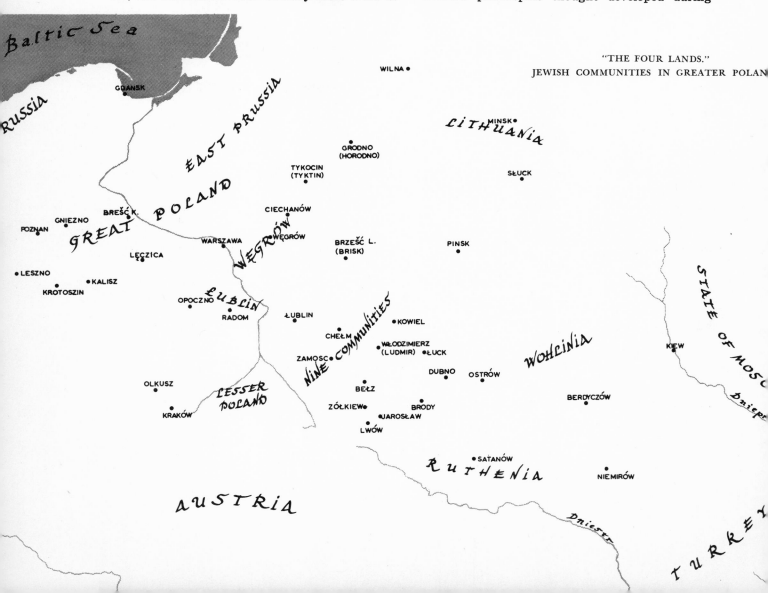

"THE FOUR LANDS."
JEWISH COMMUNITIES IN GREATER POLAN

THE PETITION REQUESTING PERMISSION FOR THE AD-
MISSION OF JEWS TO ENGLAND, ADDRESSED TO OLIVER
CROMWELL, LORD PROTECTOR OF THE COMMON-
WEALTH, BY A GROUP OF JEWS HEADED BY MENASSEH
BEN ISRAEL; 1655.

EXPULSION OF THE JEWS OF PRAGUE UNDER THE
ORDERS OF EMPRESS MARIA THERESA OF AUSTRIA.
1745.

BURIAL SOCIETY BEAKERS MADE IN THE EIGHTEENTH
CENTURY AND USED ON THE SEVENTH OF ADAR, THE
TRADITIONAL DATE OF MOSES' DEATH. ABOVE: FROM
EISENSTADT; RIGHT: FROM PRAGUE.

ENGRAVING ON A MARRIAGE CERTIFICATE OF PORTU-
GUESE JEWS IN HOLLAND-ROTTERDAM, 1648.

A JEWISH WEDDING SCENE INCLUDING THE RABBI, THE
BRIDE AND GROOM AND THE CANOPY POLE BEARERS.
THE EMBROIDERED SCROLL-COVER ON THE TORAH WAS
MADE IN GERMANY IN 1737.

THE RASHI SYNAGOGUE IN WORMS AS IMAGINED BY JEWS
IN MOHILEV IN THE EIGHTEENTH CENTURY.

JEWISH STREET IN MARBURG.

the Middle Ages, parallel attempts appeared to provide answers to these questions through the mystic symbols embedded in tradition through Cabbalistic construction. In particular, a group of Cabbalists was formed in Safed in the 16th Century, around Rabbi Isaac Luria (Ha-Ari). This group and its teacher sought means of utilising the hidden powers in the deeds of the mystic Cabbalist in order to influence the upper world by the process of Restoration ("Tikkun"), thereby hastening the Redemption. The quick spread of Cabbalistic ideas and its magic practices among groups of learned men, can be explained on the basis of the "active factor", the belief of the Cabbalists that they could influence the process of history by practising the system. Many Cabbalists, if not all, in those generations saw a parallel mystic meaning for every single precept contained in the "Shulhan Aruch".

The spread of these beliefs prepared the ground for the transformation of the yearnings for Redemption into active ferment. The stage was set for the appearance of figures promising a quick solution. Most celebrated of these was Shabbetai Zvi, who proclaimed himself "King Messiah" during the 1660's, prophesying the year 1666 as the Year of Redemption. His appearance aroused messianic hopes throughout the Jewish Diaspora, and few indeed were those who had no faith in him. He assumed the mantle of royalty, abolished the fasts of mourning for the destruction of the Temple, and turned them into festivals of joy. Many great communities accepted his messages. From all the dispersions envoys were sent to his court. The messianic awakening was accompanied by an awakening of personal charity and repentance. When Shabbetai Zvi was imprisoned and especially when he embraced Islam, the messianic faith in him was dashed, but the searchings for mystic means of bringing about the Redemption continued. Some small secret sects continued to believe in Shabbetai Zvi as the true Messiah.

Mystic yearning for redemption, emanating from faith in tradition, was still the accepted way in matters of faith and belief in all Jewish settlements during the whole of the 17th Century. However, at the beginning of that century there

TEXT OF THE EDICT AGAINST "THE TRANSGRESSORS OF LAWS", FROM THE MEMORIAL BOOK OF THE KONICE COMMUNITY IN MORAVIA.

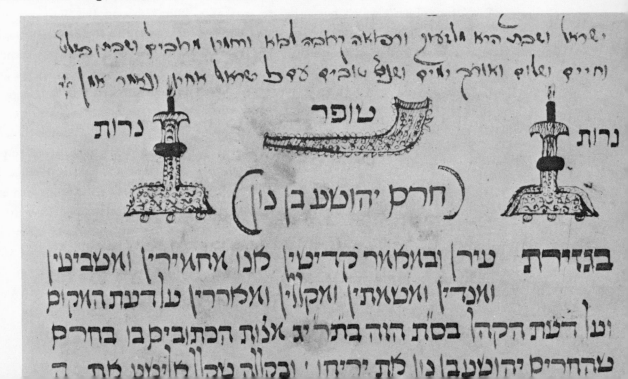

had already appeared individuals and groups who levelled rational criticism at the basis of Jewish religious tradition. They based this on the Jewish philosophical concepts of the Middle Ages and rejected the idea of Divine Providence, obedience to the Commandments of the Law, etc. The most extreme and logical exposition of these views appeared in the "Tractatus Theologico-Politicus" of Baruch Spinoza.

On the other hand, there were groups faithful to tradition in western Europe, who had found an affinity with the culture of their environment and whose exponents created a literature in European languages which was basically "apologetic" and intended to explain and justify to the enlightened person the separate existence of the Jews in the midst of European Society. They described Jewish traditions as well as the customs and messianic aspirations of the Jews, in terms familiar to the enlightened circles of those times. These efforts were partially successful. They were attuned to the thought of 17th Century European theologians, jurists and philosophers, and particularly to those concerned with these problems as a result of the spread of the concept of "Natural Law", which purported to give an overall explanation of the legal and social developments of all groups of people.

HERALDIC DESIGNS ASSUMED BY JEWISH TRADERS IN EIGHTEENTH CENTURY ENGLAND, WHO HAD BEEN APPOINTED OFFICIAL SUPPLIERS TO MEMBERS OF THE ROYAL FAMILY.

Once again, the position in central Europe differed from that in eastern Europe. In the Germanic lands of the 18th Century, rationalistic enlightenment engendered an interest in the position of the Jews and their culture, but as this enlightenment was hostile to tradition, its discussions were extremely critical. After the hesitant beginnings of the first generation of "Maskilim" among the Jews of Germany, centered around Moses Mendelssohn, their disciples associated themselves with this trend of thought. The attempts of the first groups of Jewish "Maskilim" to revive the Hebrew language and culture from its pure biblical sources, were short-lived and early in the 19th Century the "Maskilim" ceased almost entirely to write and to publish in Hebrew in western and central Europe.

Only in eastern Europe was cultural creativity maintained. Hassidism created its own popular tradition. Its opponents brought about a revival and spread of the study of the Torah. In the sphere of spiritual creativity too, there was a parting of the ways between the development of

A CARICATURE SHOWING JEWISH PUGILISTS IN ENGLAND, 1814. JEWS WERE PROMINENT AMONG THE PRIZE FIGHTERS AT THAT PERIOD.

the Jews of the West and those of the East.

Despite this the history of the Jews from the Middle Ages until modern times is not a tale of splintered and scattered groups sharing a common historic past, but that of one people spread over many lands. The forecast of certain Jewish thinkers that the processes which had begun in the 18th Century would turn the Jews into members of a religious denomination scattered in various nations, without a common national cohesion, was disproved. It is true that the more the Jews found an affinity with the culture of the countries in which they lived, the more they became integrated and earned equal rights, the closer grew their ties with their countries of residence and their identification with them and many Jews came to regard themselves primarily as citizens of the nation in which they lived who happened to be of Jewish persuasion. Some also came to believe that the Jewish communities were not linked with each other except by the bonds of solidarity natural to separate congregations of one religious denomination.

As events proved, contact between various Jewish communities did not merely exist — it even developed stronger. Despite the tremendous geographical spread of Jewish communities from the 16th and 17th Centuries onwards, their contact with each other was not weakened. When the governor of the Dutch colony of New Amsterdam (subsequently New York) persecuted the Jews arriving there in 1655, the Jews of Amsterdam protested strongly in their defence. When the Jews of Poznan were accused in the Blood Libel of 1736, various Jewish communities, Vienna among the first, came to the assistance of the persecuted. In 1744-1745, when the Empress Maria Theresa decreed the expulsion of Jews from Prague and the whole of Bohemia, Jews in several countries came to the assistance of their brethren. Utilizing their connections with various rulers they organized diplomatic pressure on the Empress so that she would cancel the order of expulsion.

When Damascus Jews were accused in the Blood Libel of 1840, a tremendous reaction was evoked

EIGHTEENTH CENTURY JEWISH WEDDING IN GERMANY.

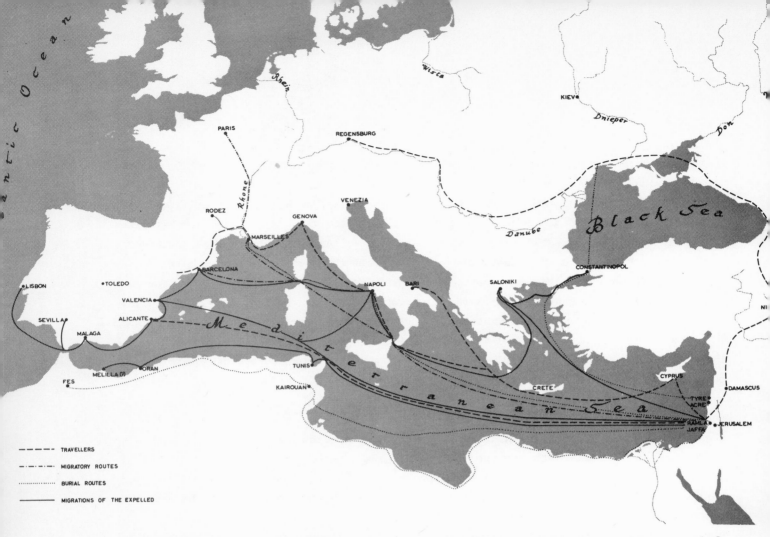

ROUTES OF PILGRIMAGE AND IMMIGRATION TO THE LAND OF ISRAEL.

in most of the Jewish communities of Europe. A delegation went east comprising Montefiore from England, Cremieux from France and Munk from Germany, representing a common Jewish interest for the suffering of their fellow Jews in the East who had a natural claim on their brethren for succour.

Despite their integration into the life of the countries of their residence, the Jews remained different from the people among whom they lived, both in their peculiar economic structure and in their spiritual character and manner of life. Despite differing conditions, there was a marked similarity between the members of one Jewish community and those of any other. The difficulties of integration into the environment aroused feelings of affinity among Jewish communities and emphasized the traditional tendency of Jews against assimilation with the existing conditions. Hence the multiplicity of reformers and revolutionaries among the Jews, who were striving to integrate into European society. This characteristic, too, encumbered the process of integration and aroused anger and suspicion on the part of the society around them. The struggle for integration itself perpetuated the seperate existence of Jews as Jews.

THE RISE OF
EUROPEAN JEWRY

A SILVER SPICE-BOX IN SIXTEENTH CENTURY STYLE
USED IN THE "HAVDALAH" CEREMONY AT THE CLOSE
OF THE SABBATH. MADE IN HAMBURG IN THE EIGH-
TEENTH CENTURY.

In the 18th Century the Jews of Europe were organised in their own communities whose legal status had been defined by the political and religious traditions that had developed during the Middle Ages. In the course of this century, though, the European states became influenced by unifying tendencies and there was opposition to the existence of separatist corporations or any barriers intervening between the ruler and his subjects. Leading philosophers of the times had formulated a universal political and social theory, which emphasized the affinity of all men and minimized the differences between them. Of special concern for some of the philosophers were the differences originating in religion.

Enlightened Europeans believed that their imperfect society was destined to give place to a reformed society built on rational principles. They inspired a belief among the enlightened of the Jews, the "Maskilim", that they could become integrated as equals in the surrounding society, achieving complete equality of rights and duties. However, while these emancipatory opinions were slowly spreading, the outbreak of the French Revolution converted the philosophical question of equality for the Jews into a practical question, capable of rapid solution by political means.

In theory, this problem was solved when the French National Assembly endorsed the principles of the revolution in the "Declaration of the Rights of Man", by which all religious discrimination was forbidden. However, when the Assembly began to discuss the practical aspects of civil rights, it became clear that many of the members were not prepared to extend the full rights to the Jews. The representatives of the clergy claimed that the Jews were not merely a religious sect but a separate and distinct nation, and could consequently not be counted as members of the French nation or be full citizens in a French state. The proponents of equality explained this by saying that only past persecution had kept the Jews as a separate group but that it was their earnest desire now to become members of the French nation in all respects. In this they were the most extreme negators of separate Jewish nationality; as one of their enthusiasts proclaimed: "If the Jews wished to remain as a nation within the nation, they would have to be expelled completely from the state."

For almost two years the National Assembly prevaricated over the law of equality, and only in September 1791 was it passed. In accordance with this law, every Jew in France became a citizen with full rights and it was widely assumed that the end had come of the Jewish community as a separatist unit. The victorious revolutionary army carried the principle of equality for Jews, together with the other ideals of the revolution, to all the countries it conquered. The Jews of Italy and of certain German cities received the French conquerors with enthusiasm.

The Batavian National Assembly of Holland

PAGE FROM THE DIARY OF THE JEWISH DELEGATION FROM BORDEAUX TO THE FRENCH NATIONAL ASSEMBLY IN THE FIGHT FOR JEWISH EMANCIPATION, 1791.

also passed a law assuring the legal equality of the Jews in 1796. At the end of the 18th Century the Jews of Germany appealed to the Assembly of the rulers of the Germanic lands to proclaim their equality. It appeared as if the great aspiration of the Jewish "Maskilim" had been realized, and realized with relative ease.

However it very quickly became apparent that European society was still far from willing to accept the Jews as an equal in its midst. In Alsace the strong opposition to the Jews provoked riots. In Germany many pamphlets were published that were antagonistic to the Jews and rejected their demands. And when Napoleon established himself as Emperor of France, he too began to regard the Jews with suspicion. In 1808 he published a decree against the Jews, the "Decret Infame", that imposed severe restrictions on the economic activities of the Jews in various spheres and limited their civil rights. In Prussia a decree of equal rights was actually published in 1812; however it contained certain reservations in relation to Jews, and this was the last attempt in the direction of emancipation during this period. With the collapse of the French regime in western Europe after the defeat of Napoleon, most countries abolished their laws of equality.

Only in France and Holland did the emancipation of the Jews continue after the fall of Napoleon. In Prussia the decree of equality was not in actual fact abolished but it was stripped of all meaning. In other parts of Germany the anti-Jewish manifestations increased and in certain places brought on actual riots, the most notorious of which were connected with the Hep-Hep movement of 1819. Even many liberals maintained that the Jews should not be accorded equal rights as long as they refused to give up the precepts of their religion which differentiated them from others. The great hopes of many Jews that radicals and liberals would supplant the reactionary

THE ARREST OF A JEWISH PEDDLER BY NAPOLEON'S SOLDIERS IN 1812.

policies of the monarchist regimes were not realized even in the series of revolutions of 1848. Not only did the revolutions fail, and the absolute rulers continue to discriminate against Jews, but in many places the revolutions themselves were accompanied by physical attacks on Jews. Disappointed, considerable numbers of Jewish radicals migrated to the United States.

Legal equality for Jews became established fact only after the European states had adopted the forms of representative government based upon general elections. When the right of determination in political matters became the inalienable right of all citizens it was no longer legally possible to discriminate against minority groups. In England, the country that had been in the vanguard of these developments, the Jews had attained the right to vote in parliamentary elections

(Top) TITLE PAGE OF THE EDICT OF EMANCIPATION FOR THE JEWS OF PRUSSIA, MARCH 11, 1812.
(Below) COVER OF THE REGISTER (PINKAS) OF THE ALTONA COMMUNITY NEAR HAMBURG, 1698.

and to serve in various posts as early as the first half of the 19th Century but reactionary elements were able for many years to deny the Jews right to take the seats in parliament to which they had been elected, by insisting that members of parliament had to swear a Christian oath on assuming office. This limitation was removed only in 1858. In Austria-Hungary the equality of Jews before the law was one of the many political changes of 1867, after the military defeat of the empire at the hands of Prussia. In unified Germany the decree of equality was granted in 1869.

After the principle of equality of all citizens, irrespective of their nationality or religion, had been enacted in most western and central European states, it became acceptable, at least in theory, to most of European society. When the Congress of Powers discussed the status of the Balkan countries in Berlin in 1878, it forced the Balkan states to accept this principle. Most agreed to it, but Rumania, which wished to avoid it, continued legal discrimination against the Jews by declaring that all Jews were aliens who had only recently arrived and that there was no obligation to confer citizenship upon them. This attitude continued in Rumania until after World War I.

The legal position of the Jews of Russia, which included Poland, Lithuania and Bessarabia until World War I, was most difficult. The division of the inhabitants according to estates was maintained. The constitutional provisions concerning the Jews of Russia, dating back to 1804, had proclaimed their equality before the law, but there was no universal law dealing with all the citizens of the state, and different practices obtained in relation to each group. The regime set itself the aim of assimilating the Jews within the Russian population by forcible means, primarily by conversion to Christianity. This was the main objective underlying the law for compulsory military service which was imposed on the Jews in 1827, under which Jewish children were taken from their families when between the ages of eight and twelve years old, and organised in special "Cantonist" units for a military education. Within this framework the children were forced, through persuasion and torture, to apostasize. Some of the

EARLY EIGHTEENTH CENTURY ETCHINGS OF A JEWISH WEDDING IN GERMANY. *Above:* THE VEILED BRIDE IS BROUGHT TO THE CANOPY. *Below:* THE CEREMONY TAKES PLACE OUTSIDE THE SYNAGOGUE. THE WEDDINGS WERE CONDUCTED UNDER THE STARRED CANOPY.

youths simulated conversion, others preferred to sacrifice their lives and suffered religious martyrdom. These methods achieved, if anything, the opposite of their aim and served only to stiffen Jewish unity. The Cantonist system existed in Russia until the liberalization measures of the mid-1850's. The atmosphere that resulted, automatically doomed to failure the rest of the methods that the Russian regime had adopted in its struggle against the "prejudices" of the Jews. Few Jewish children attended the special government schools that were established for them in the 1840's. The withdrawal by the government of its recognition of the autonomous powers of the Jewish community resulted in semi-clandestine activity by the Jewish organizations. The proposal to place most of the Jews of Russia outside the

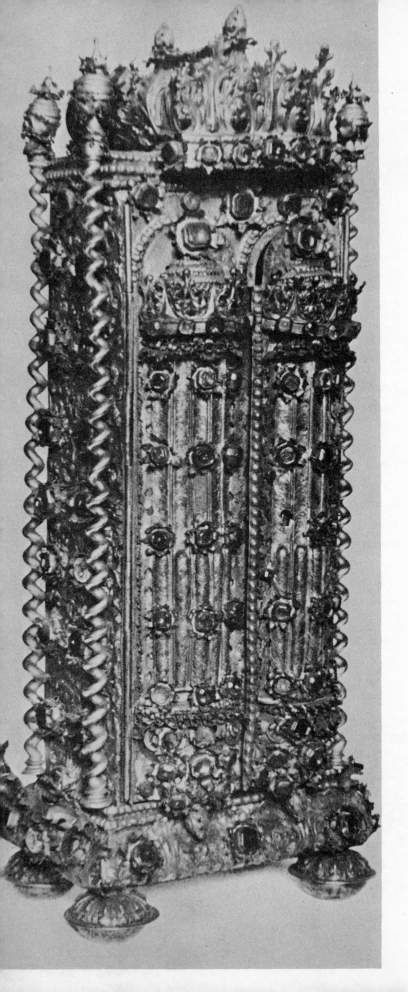

law in many respects by labeling them as "unnecessary", offended even the majority of Russian officials by its cruelty, and was completely abandoned at the death of its proponent, Nicholas I, in 1855.

When Alexander II ascended to the throne certain restrictions were lifted from limited groups of Jews. The wealthy, the better educated, and the skilled craftsmen were given the right to leave the "Pale of Settlement" and live in inner Russia. The number of young Jews who received their education in the Russian language and began to integrate into the life of Russian society also increased. Some of them joined the revolutionary movement in Russia. However, after the murder of Alexander II by revolutionaries, in 1881, power was assumed by a group of courtiers, who believed that the only solution to Russia's problems lay in the bolstering of Czarist autocracy. They regarded the Jews as aliens who could not be absorbed, and set themselves the task of countering "the harm that the Jews were causing the main body of inhabitants". This period was characterized by further deterioration of the legal position of the Jews and increasing discrimination against them. At times of social upheaval, such as during the period leading to the 1905 revolution, pogroms against the Jews were organized with government support in dozens of towns and villages causing the deaths of many Jews. The hatred of the Jews by the Russian government and considerable sections of the Russian people continued till the outbreak of the Russian revolution in 1917.

Generally speaking, the Jews of most western European countries achieved legal equality during the first half of the 19th Century, and those of central Europe during the second half of the cen-

PORTABLE HOLY ARK MADE OF SILVER AND INLAID WITH GOLD AND JEWELS, VIENNA, 1707.

tury; in eastern Europe legal discrimination continued even after World War I.

The 19th Century was a period of tremendous numerical growth for European Jewry. At the beginning of the century less than two million Jews had lived in Europe; by the middle of the century there were more than four million, and by the beginning of the 20th century their number had grown to almost nine million, of whom five million were living in Russia and two million in the Austro-Hungarian Empire. Their increase was more than twice that of the general population, not so much because of a higher birthrate, but because of the lower mortality among Jews. The rate of natural increase was even greater than these figures would indicate, but already during the first half of the century the mass emigration of Jews from Europe had begun, increasing in momentum after the intensified persecution of Russian Jews in the early 1880's. During the years 1904-1908 the annual rate of migration of Jews to the United States was over 100,000, and in 1906-1907 the rate was 150,000 per year. Altogether, more than three million Jews emigrated from Europe before World War I.

There were political, demographic and economic reasons for this mass emigration. It was natural that Russia and Rumania should be the two countries from which the main emigration came. In both countries the Jews despaired of attaining equal rights, and it had become inescapably clear that the policy of these governments and the attitude of a considerable proportion of their population were of overt hostility to the Jews. Emigration represented a flight from oppression to emancipation, from pogroms to security and personal freedom. But in addition to the political factor, other factors were at work. Under a hostile regime, not only was natural increase unaccompanied by a suitable increase in the tra-

ditional sources of livelihood, but these sources were progressively curtailed. This situation caused heightened competition among the Jews, and the swift impoverishment of the poorer classes, and in Russia also of the middle classes. In Galicia, which was part of the Austro-Hungarian empire that had guaranteed equal rights, similar pressure was felt in the growing population. Therefore a proportionately much larger number of Jews emigrated than did the other nationalities of Russia and Austria. Furthermore, although emigration for economic reasons was common among all the peoples of Europe, Jewish emigration had a distinct and peculiar nature. It included a much greater proportion of tradesmen (most of the other emigrants from eastern Europe being farmers, who migrated to find work as agricultural workers), the percentage of families emigrating together was higher and the proportion of emigrants returning to their former homes was considerably smaller.

AN 18TH CENTURY HANUKA MENORAH MADE OF BRASS, FROM POLAND. THE POSITION OF THE "SHAMASH" LIGHTS AT EITHER END AND THE BIRD DECORATIONS ARE TYPICAL OF EAST EUROPEAN DESIGN.

All these developments took place against a background of profound changes in the economic activity of the Jews in Europe during the 19th Century. In eastern Europe the Jews were progressively uprooted from the rural economy. The importance of the manor in the national economy declined. From among the farmers a powerful stratum developed that began to gain a foothold in commerce, thereby restricting the traditional function of the Jews as the middlemen between the city and the village. The considerable number of Jews who had earned a livelihood as innkeepers during the 18th Century was reduced to a negligible number by the end of the 19th Century, but the number of Jews engaged in marketing agricultural produce was still great.

During the 19th Century, the number of Jewish craftsmen increased. However, because the market for their products did not expand to the same extent, the competition between the craftsmen intensified, their earnings dropped, and most of them lived on the verge of poverty. A not inconsiderable proportion of Jewish wage-earners turned to cartage, to unskilled labor and to domestic work. Starting in the 1870's a distinct Jewish proletariat was forming in eastern Europe, working in the tobacco, food and clothing industries, but with the greater proportion still comprising craftsmen and their apprentices. Some, lacking a permanent source of income, required the assistance of the community and the number of destitute Jews rose steeply. The industrial development in the countries of eastern Europe removed many of the traditional sources of livelihood for the Jews, and as they found no others to replace them, a great deal of hardship was suffered by the Jewish masses.

For the rich Jews, on the other hand, this was a period of growing economic activity. In Galicia there were a number of wealthy Jewish property owners. In Russia, as in all European countries with the exception of England, Jews played an important part in the financing of railways; they helped establish the sugar and clothing industries, and were active in banking, in river transportation, in export trade and in the marketing of oil and precious metals. The contrast between the wealthy few and the poverty-stricken masses grew rapidly wider.

In central and western Europe the situation was different. In the first half of the 19th Century a number of Jewish banks, with the House of

(Top) SEVENTEETH CENTURY ENGRAVING OF THE PORTUGUESE SYNAGOGUE IN AMSTERDAM.
(Bottom) THE NEW SYNAGOGUE IN STRASSBURG.

Rothschild at their head, were leading contractors for government loans, and prominent in the financing of railways and in the promotion of industries. Their relative decline began only during the second half of the century. During the 1860's and 1870's the Jewish banker Bleichroder served as financial adviser to Bismarck, Baron Hirsch was building railways in the Balkans, the Pereire brothers were modernizing Paris, and above all the name of Rothschild still symbolised tremendous financial power; but the swift spread of the system of share-holding in banking and industry gradually lessened the importance of Jewish family banks in the economy.

At the same time the status of the lower economic strata of Jews was rising. The dwindling of the influence of the merchant guilds and the trade associations provided openings in inter-city trade for many Jews. Jews became businessmen and shopkeepers in the cities in ever growing numbers, and the Jewish peddler, so ubiquitous in the past, disappeared almost completely. Jews also were active in industry, particularly the new chemical and electrical industries. The number of Jewish professionals grew, as did the number of Jews in journalism, literature, the theater and academic

life. The disparity between the various strata in the Jewish communities began to shrink, and most of them became members of the established middle class.

The migration of Jews from east to west affected this process. Many Jews from the district of Poznan migrated to Breslau and to Berlin, and those from Galicia and other territories of Austria moved to Vienna. A considerable number of emigrants whose ultimate destination had been the United States never got that far, and many settled in the East End of London, which became a predominantly Jewish quarter. As a result of this migration large Jewish centers with tens and even hundreds of thousands of Jews were established in the main cities of Europe. This concentration in important economic and political centers and the integration of Jews in the professions brought them a growing influence in public affairs and in cultural and economic life. It also increased there a widespread fear of Jews, who were popularly seen as "penetrating everywhere" and "pushing to the head of the line", and encouraged a ready acceptance of propaganda against the "predominant position of the Jew". The migrants from eastern Europe created a new unsettled class. The number of tradesmen among them was large, and London became a point of concentration of Jew-

(Above) THE ALT-NEU SYNAGOGUE AND JEWISH COMMUNAL OFFICES BUILT IN THE SIXTEENTH CENTURY IN PRAGUE.
(Below) THE NEW SYNAGOGUE (NINETEENTH CENTURY) IN BERLIN, INTERIOR AND EXTERIOR VIEWS.

ish workers. A new division between Jews came into prominence. Here it took the form of an antagonism between the better educated, more cultured Jew of the west, and the Jew from the east who spoke Yiddish and was considered uneducated, Hebrew education and knowledge of the Torah not ranking as evidence of culture among Jews of the west.

The changes in the legal status of the Jews, in their places of settlement and the sources of their livelihood strongly influenced their relationships with surrounding society. Those Jews who saw no further significance in their association with Judaism and strove to imitate the people among whom they lived and to assimilate with them completely, increased in number. Some considered that the easiest way to achieve their aim

A STREET IN THE JEWISH QUARTER OF CRACOW.

was to give up their religion. A small minority was converted to Christianity out of genuine religious conviction but the majority did so to obtain what Heine called "an entrance ticket into Christian society". Christians and Jews both had reservations in regard to these converts and held them to be lacking in moral principles.

The number of Jews who based their hopes on political changes was greater. They assumed that as the order of society changed, all those factors, that had prevented the complete integration of Jews with their surroundings, would vanish. They opposed the concept of separate organizations for Jews in the struggle for civic betterment and equated the problem of the Jews with the solution of the general problems of the society in which they lived. Gabriel Rieser (1806-1863) associated the eventual equality of Jews with the unification of Germany, just as other Jewish statesmen had identified it with the success of liberalism or socialism. At the end of the 19th Century, when the Jewish socialist movement arose, it saw the way to achieve its aims in the victory of European socialism.

The shortest path to the complete integration of Jews in their environment was seen as cultural assimilation, primarily the supplanting of Hebrew and Yiddish by the language of the country. This caused the neglect of Torah study, the weakening of Jewish institutions of learning such as the "heder" and the "yeshivah", and an increasing number of Jews was educated in general schools and institutions of higher education. This process advanced at such a pace in central and western Europe that by the second half of the 19th Century, there remained hardly any knowledge of the Hebrew language among the masses. Jewish literary creativity expressed itself in the vernacular and was Jewish only in that it was written by Jews, and that it dealt with problems affecting the Jews. Many Jews were writing in European languages on subjects that had no connection with Jews or Judaism and others composed music or engaged in the fine arts, as authors, composers and artists of their homeland and not specifically as Jews. Although there had been similar manifestations in earlier periods of the history of the Jews, there was a distinction between these and that of the 19th Century. In the past, Jewish authors had tried to attain a synthesis between the beliefs and opinions accepted by Judaism and the influences that stemmed from the environment. During the 19th and 20th Century, however, most of them voluntarily relinquished their historic heritage and sometimes even despised it and only from the end of the 19th Century were there experiments to create a new synthesis between Jewish and European culture. Most of the Jews of western and central Europe saw in their cultural assimilation the absolute proof of their loyalty to their various European states.

The reaction of European society to the aspiration of the Jews towards integration and submersion was not uniform. During the first stage, when the number of Jews wishing to be assimilated was limited and the powerful culture was able to ascribe to itself the function of instruction and direction, it evinced a preparedness to do so. The society into which the Jews wished to be integrated was still composed of a small number of educated people who honestly aspired towards the realization of the principles of universal equality. The position began to change when the number of Jews seeking integration increased, and when they rose on the social ladder as a result of emancipation. Their importance in affairs of state, and the activities of many of them in the reform and revolutionary movements, turned them from pupils into teachers in many fields. This process increased the criticism of the Jews and the ex-

pressions of anger at their behavior, to the extent of renewed anti-Jewish resentment among many classes of the European populations.

Judeophobia has accompanied the Jewish people during most of its history. Modern anti-Semitism, which in Europe assumed the character of a public movement from the 1880's on, has characteristics of its own. Its main complaint is not against the acts of Jews such as "their religious perfidy", or their "economic exploitation", but against their "nature" and their very existence. Most of the anti-Semites attribute negative qualities to the "Semitic race" of the Jew and see in this something opposed to the "Aryan race" of the nations of Europe. As racial stigmata, according to the anti-Semites, cannot be altered, the Jews can never

A STREET IN PRAGUE'S JEWISH QUARTER.

integrate among European nations, and will always retain their "poisonous influence". Hence they call for the expulsion of the Jew from European countries in every possible way. Although organized anti-Semitic parties were always in a small minority until World War I, various aspects of their propaganda were readily absorbed by the masses, who continued to see certain peculiarities in the Jews, in the manner of their life, their occupation and their spiritual attitudes, that had not been eliminated despite emancipation and assimilation. Moreover, the attempts of certain individuals and groups to show their emancipation from the burden of their Jewishness in an extreme and demonstrative fashion, increased suspicion towards them.

Few Jews chose to assimilate through conversion. In addition to the suspicion and revulsion

that become the lot of the convert who takes this step for other than purely religious reasons, there is also a certain self-denigration and inner hypocrisy, for one who abandons Judaism for motives of gain cannot thereby appreciate the dogmatic truth of Christianity. Most of the Jewish intelligentsia was therefore faced with the problem of blending its Judaism with the aspirations to integrations, the problem of how to be a Jew and also a German or a Frenchman or a Russian at the same time.

This problem prompted some the "Maskilim" to suggest reforms in the Jewish religion, primarily by eliminating its ethnic-national content from the "purely religious" aspect contained in Jewish law, which was to be maintained. The reformers in Germany at the beginning of the 19th Century began by changing the external form of Jewish worship, to make it more acceptable to the

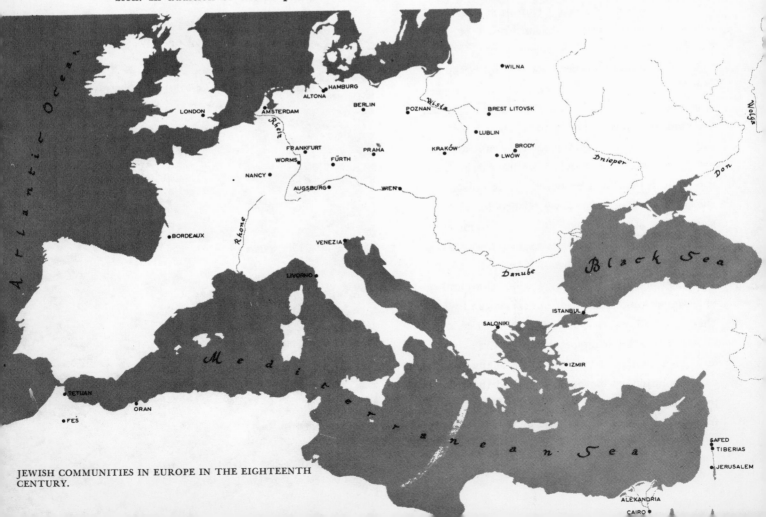

JEWISH COMMUNITIES IN EUROPE IN THE EIGHTEENTH
CENTURY.

THE TORAH, A SERIES OF ENGRAVINGS BY G. EICHLER, 1748. WRITING THE SCROLL *(top left)*; THE TORAH, IN EMBROIDERED VESTMENTS AND DECORATIVE CROWN ON THE LECTERN *(top right)*; THE TORAH IS BROUGHT TO THE SYNAGOGUE FOR THE FIRST TIME. A CANOPY IS HELD OVER THE TORAH BY A PROCESSION OF WORSHIPPERS.

FRENCH ENGRAVING BY B. PICART, 1725, SHOWING THE SCROLL BEING HOISTED AFTER THE TORAH READING OF THE SABBATH SERVICE.

EARLY 18TH CENTURY DUTCH ENGRAVING SHOWING THE SYNAGOGUE ON THE FESTIVAL OF PURIM. THE WOMEN ARE SHOWN IN SPECIAL SECTIONS BEHIND METAL GRILLES AT THE SIDE. OF SPECIAL INTEREST TO THE ARTIST WERE THE YOUTHS, BANGING ON BENCHES WITH THEIR HAMMERS, WHENEVER THE NAME OF HAMAN WAS HEARD DURING THE READING OF THE BOOK OF ESTHER.

THE SUKKA (TABERNACLE); A MID-18TH CENTURY ENGRAVING BY G. EICHLER. THE ELABORATE SUKKA AT THE LEFT IS IN THE HOME OF A WEALTHY FAMILY. IT IS CONTRASTED WITH THE SIMPLER SUKKA AT RIGHT, MADE BY REMOVING SOME TILES FROM AN ATTIC AND COVERING THE HOLE WITH FOLIAGE, IN WHICH A PIOUS JEW BOTH EATS AND SLEEPS THROUGHOUT THE FESTIVAL.

ROSH HASHANAH, THE FESTIVAL OF NEW YEAR. THE ENGRAVING BY G. EICHLER IS FROM GERMANY, MID 18TH CENTURY. AT THE TOP IS THE SERVICE IN THE SYNAGOGUE AND SHOWS THE SHOFAR BEING BLOWN *(from the pulpit, top right);* THE RITUAL IMMERSION BEFORE THE FESTIVAL AND THE CUSTOM OF EMPTY-ING THE POCKETS INTO A STREAM DURING THE TASHLICH PRAYER ON THE FIRST DAY OF THE FESTI-VAL, ARE SHOWN IN THE SMALLER PANELS.

THE ELABORATE ARON KODESH (HOLY ARK) WITH TENS OF TORAH SCROLLS, IN THE PORTUGUESE SYNA-GOGUE AT AMSTERDAM. THE EIGHTEENTH CENTURY ENGRAVING SHOWS A SCENE DURING THE FESTIVAL OF SIMHAT TORAH (THE REJOICING OF THE LAW).

THE CIRCUMCISION CEREMONY AMONG 18TH CENTURY
PORTUGUESE JEWS IN AMSTERDAM. THE ARTIST
SHOWS THE MOTHER, SURROUNDED BY OTHER JEWISH
WOMEN, IN A SEPARATE CHAMBER AT UPPER RIGHT,
"JEWISH WOMEN NOT TAKING PART AT THIS CERE-
MONY. THOSE SHOWN HERE ARE CHRISTIANS".

RABBINICAL COURT DURING THE GRANTING OF A
BILL OF DIVORCEMENT. FROM AN ENGRAVING BY
P. E. KIRCHNER, NUREMBERG 1726.

LITHOGRAPH MARKING THE ARRIVAL OF THE FIRST TRAIN IN THE BRNO STATION IN 1839. THE RAILWAY WAS FINANCED BY THE ROTHSCHILD FAMILY.

European of that period. However, within a short time, this became an attempt to "purify" Judaism, by eliminating from prayer books any mention of the return to Zion, and by distinguishing between those precepts that were, in the opinion of the reformers, the basic source of Judaism and those that were the fruits of later developments. To this

BENJAMIN DISRAELI, A CONVERTED JEW WHO BECAME PRIME MINISTER OF ENGLAND.

end, conventions of reform-minded rabbis were called in Germany during the 1840's, to create an institution with authority to decide on these issues but the participants failed to reach acceptable decisions. Out of these groups there developed a study into the history of Israel and its literature, which was called the "Science of Judaism", which laid a basis for the investigation of Jewish history and of its spiritual creation, in a series of monumental scholarly works.

However, it was not the result of the research that motivated the religious reformers, who had known what they sought before any research had begun. Their primary aim was to prove to the surrounding society that Judaism was only a religious denomination like other denominations and adherence to it did not constitute a contradiction to loyalty to one of the European nations. The fundamental truths of Judaism are eternal, according to the 19th Century reformers, whereas its precepts can vary in accordance with changes in historic conditions. The religious reform movement grew considerably from the 1860's in Germany, Hungary and in the United States. Its growth influenced the community structure of the Jews in many lands and the process of emancipation became associated with the abolition of the obligation of belonging to the Jewish community. The communal organization gradually lost its obligatory character and became a voluntary organization, with authority only over those who wished to belong to it. During the early stages the religious reformers endeavored to elicit the support of the secular authorities to enforce their views on the whole Jewish community, while those faithful to the traditional Jewish framework requested that every religious trend be allowed to organize itself independently. During the 1870's the extremely orthodox Jews, particularly those in Germany, led by Rabbi Samson Raphael Hirsch, fought successfully for the right of every Jew to leave the established community and set up a new one which suited him better. This tendency towards separation was one of the characteristics of the German orthodox revival.

In the course of this process, a trend towards Jewish sectionalization occurred, but on the other hand there was another tendency towards centralized organizations serving the various religious trends. This development increased the need for national and international organizations of all Jews, overriding religious differences. By 1860 the "Alliance Israèlite Universelle" had been organized in France with the objective of fighting against anti-Jewish discrimination in every country while spreading education among the Jews of the East. The Alliance fought against discrimination against the Jews in North Africa, in Switzerland and in Rumania; it submitted a memorandum to the representatives of the powers at the Congress of Berlin in 1878, proposing a declara-

SEDER PLATE COVER OF THE EARLY NINETEENTH CENTURY, FROM GERMANY.

tion of equal rights as an agreed international principle. Similar Jewish organizations arose in other countries too. When the pogroms against the Jews of Russia began in 1881, a committee to assist the victims was organized in England, and highly placed Jews from all countries gathered to discuss the problems posed by the growing migration. In Germany a committee was set up to assist the migrants, which in the course of time expanded the sphere of its activities. In 1891 Baron Hirsch founded the Jewish Colonization Association, whose objective was to transfer the Jews of Russia to agricultural settlement in the Argentine and elsewhere. While the links between the various religious trends were weakening as a result of mutual antagonism, new overall Jewish associations were being organized, whose aims were philanthropic, to render assistance to persecuted Jews in various lands, to the migrants, and to needy Jewish communities.

The integration of western and central European Jews into the culture and life of their countries brought about a situation where the main cultural creativity of the Jews became indistinguishable from that of the majority community; and while Jews such as Marx, Freud and Einstein made their mark on the spiritual and intellectual life of Europe, it is difficult to discern the specific Jewish basis of their cultural contributions. On the other hand, in eastern Europe, independent Jewish creativity continued. The "Maskilim" in eastern Europe laid the foundations of a new Hebrew and Jewish literature which, within a relatively short period, saw the appearance of writers of the stature of Bialik, Tchernichovsky and Frishman, writing in Hebrew, and Mendele Mocher S'farim, Shalom Alechem and Y. L. Peretz in Yiddish.

During the 19th Century, Hassidism continued to influence large sections of the Jewish people.

Hassidic lore and legend continued to develop and to find its literary expression. At the end of the 19th Century it began to influence modern authors writing in Hebrew, Yiddish and in European languages and Hassidic liturgy influenced the works of Jewish composers during this period. In those areas where Hassidism did not penetrate, particularly in Lithuania, the study of the Torah flourished, attaining an influence and profundity hardly paralleled even during the golden period of Talmud study. The yeshivot of Lithuania became the new creative sources of the bond between the Jew and the Talmudic tradition of the past, and their fame spread to all the dispersions of Israel. The students of these yeshivot were among

(Top) PREPARING FOR THE FEAST OF PASSOVER, NUREMBERG, 1734.
(Bottom) THE PASSOVER SEDER, ENGRAVING BY PICART (1663-1733).

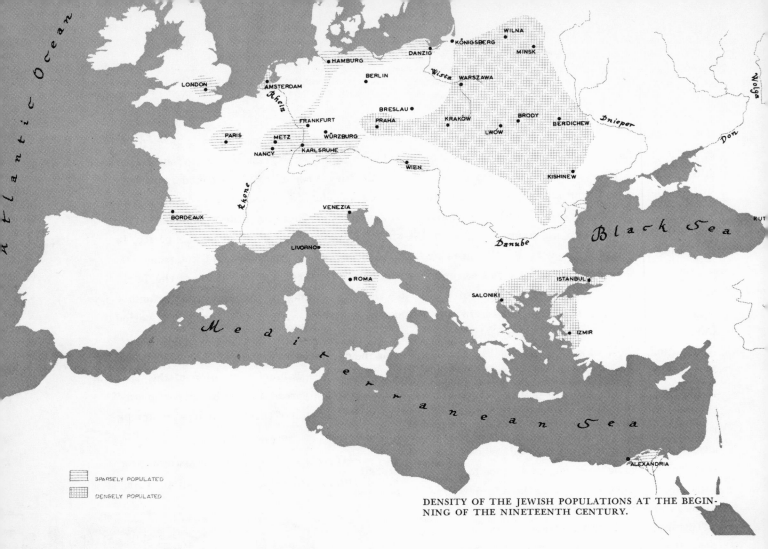

SPARSELY POPULATED

DENSELY POPULATED

DENSITY OF THE JEWISH POPULATIONS AT THE BEGIN-
NING OF THE NINETEENTH CENTURY.

the first readers of the new Hebrew literature, they were the first to embrace the modern idea of a physical return to Zion; they were also among the first Jewish socialists.

The Jewish atmosphere, the special manner of life and the Jewish spiritual tradition influenced also Jewish writers who did not write in Hebrew or Yiddish. There had always been periods in most European countries in which Jews wrote on Jewish subjects for Jewish readers in the vernacular. Now though there were also creative artists, writers and composers who departed from this Jewish inspiration and their Jewish background is not apparent in most cases.

The specifically Jewish creativity during the 19th Century and the beginning of the 20th was diversified and significant but the contribution of Jewish creativity and tradition, as one of the sources of general European cultural creativity during this period was tremendous. It can be compared only to that early period when the religious tradition and moral and social expression made its mark upon the people of Europe, during the first centuries after the appearance of Christianity. At the end of the 18th Century very few Jews had associated themselves with European culture; by the end of the 19th Century many Jews were helping to mould its form.

THE ILLUSTRATED HISTORY OF THE JEWS

NATIONAL AND SOCIAL MOVEMENTS

EMBLEM OF THE FIRST ZIONIST CONGRESS HELD IN
BASLE 1897.

THE NATIONAL AND SOCIAL MOVEMENTS

Jewish thought and life in modern times have been marked by the tendency towards change. The historic heritage of the Jews and the conditions under which they have lived in the dispersion, have always urged on the majority a striving for redemption. Among other nations, the reformers were either upper-class visionaries or belonged to the class of the underprivileged; among the Jews, everyone without exception regarded the present as fraught with evil. The lot of the Jews grew worse as the national consciousness of European nations was heightened with the increasing trend towards centralized authority. Denunciations of the Jewish autonomy grew more frequent, and the alien feeling of the Jew increased.

The Jewish people was wearied of its bitter and endless exile and longed for redemption. The longing, nurtured in Cabbalistic circles, burst forth in a messianic mass movement in the 17th Century among the followers of Shabbetai Zvi that blended mystic religious ideas with a rational political plan. It fused the personality of the "King Messiah" of the Halachists and visionaries of previous generations with the purely medieval concept of the statesman-commander.

The apostasy of Shabbetai Zvi brought disillusionment. The hopes and enthusiasm engendered by the false messiah were all wiped out. Yet a few refused to accept reality and sought a sublime hidden reason for the defection of the 'messiah'. Secret groups continued here and there, to turn to Shabbetai Zvi in their prayers and to regard him as divinely inspired. They acted as if the hoped-for redemption had begun, and as if the meticulous observance of the Torah in the period of exile was no longer necessary. Their various leaders were regarded as reincarnations of Shabbetai Zvi, and a schism developed between them and the rest of Judaism.

The secret groups, combining religious fervor with antinomistic and nihilistic tendencies, were bound to degenrate and die and only the appearance of a vigorous leader could prolong their existence. Such a leader was Jacob Frank, a native of Podolia in Poland, who had spent his youth in Turkey associating with Sabbatian circles and learning the essence of their faith. His mystic lore was essentially negative anud oversimplified. Had it not been proved, he reasoned, that all the many profound theories had failed to help the Jews so far. He therefore introduced a number of new political ideas. According to him, Poland and not Eretz Israel was the promised land; he hoped to attain his objectives by raising a large army and exploiting the propitious hour of an outbreak of war between the states.

The dynamic personality of Frank influenced

MOSES MENDELSSOHN, CONSIDERED TO HAVE BEEN THE FATHER OF THE ENLIGHTENMENT MOVEMENT AMONG GERMAN JEWS IN THE SECOND HALF OF THE EIGHTEENTH CENTURY.

certain groups in various villages of Podolia, especially among the poorer class. However, when the secret meetings, often accompanied by sexual orgies, were discovered, the Jewish community began to persecute the Frankists and to excommunicate them. The Frankists sought the protection of the clergy, and made wild accusations against the rest of the Jews, including the blood libel. The clergy forced the Frankists to embrace Christianity, but as the church did not believe

the sincerity of their conversion, Frank was separated from his followers, and imprisoned. Years later he settled in Offenbach and adherents from various places came to him. His daughter Eve eventually took over the direction of the movement together with him, and after his death she became its leader. All traces of the Frankists did not disappear till the middle of the 19th Century.

From the same region of Podolia in Poland, a new religious movement grew around the middle of the 18th Century. This was Hassidism. Unlike Sabbatianism it enjoyed tremendous popularity among the people; it adhered to the fundamentals of Jewish tradition and was even stricter in the observance of some of the laws.

Israel Baal Shem Tov, the founder of the movement, was an unassuming person. While still young he had won renown as a healer and an exorcizer of evil spirits. During the fourth decade

not only fails to attract mercy to the world; he actually increases the severity of judgment, for, by contrast with the light of his righteousness, the rest of Israel is then seen as greater sinners. Hence the "tzadik", the righteous man, must descend from his own level to that of the sinners in order to raise them up and act as the channel of influence from the upper world, bringing the lower world closer to the upper. The tzadik must regard himself as the intermediary between the upper world and the whole of Israel.

Whether the need for a new leadership with strong spiritual authority brought about the

of his life his mission began. He saw mystic visions and felt himself in touch with Heaven and its powers. A group was formed around him which began to work to hasten the redemption of Israel and to protect it from persecution and tribulation.

During this period there were other groups that occupied themselves with the secret Cabbalistic wisdom, but the followers of the Baal Shem Tov were essentially different in method and doctrine. Most of the Cabbalists wished for "Tikkun", the correction of the cosmic aberrations that had caused the Shekhina, the Divine Presence to be absent from the Jewish People and had caused dispersion of the Jews. They thought to achieve this by mystic influence attained through a life of asceticism and contemplation. The more they separated themselves from sinners and evildoers, the more would their influence grow. The Baal Shem Tov and his disciples, on the other hand, saw as their ideal the service of God through their day-to-day life. The essence of their doctrine lay in regarding the whole of Israel as one unit, and the way to redemption by its elevation to the appropriate spiritual level. For the Hassidim, one who lives an ascetic life in isolation

GRAVESTONE OF RABBI YEHEZKIEL LANDAU OF PRAGUE,
A STRONG OPPONENT OF THE ENLIGHTENMENT AND
HASSIDISM AND AUTHOR OF THE BOOK "HANODAH
BEYEHUDA."

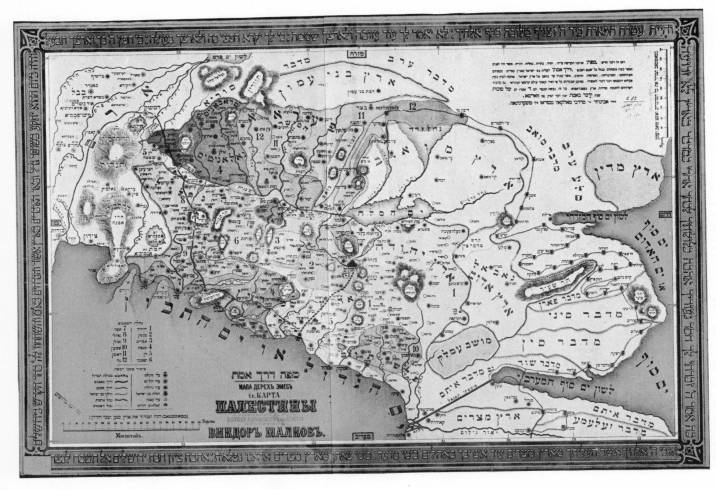

MAP OF THE LAND OF ISRAEL DRAWN IN WARSAW IN
1891 HAS BOTH BIBLICAL AND NEW SETTLEMENT NAMES.

KINNERETH, ONE OF THE SETTLEMENTS FOUNDED WITH
THE ASSISTANCE OF BARON EDMUND DE ROTHSCHILD.

POSTCARD SENT BY DR. HERZL FROM PALESTINE TO HIS
SECRETARY, DR. ISIDOR SCHALIT IN VIENNA.

formation of a religious doctrine of this nature, or whether the new religious doctrine, having been strongly established, required the activity of the tzadik as a leader of the community, is hard to decide. At all events, Hassidism brought about a far-reaching change in the religious and social outlook of its generation. The tzadik became the instructor and leader of the Jewish community because of the firm faith of the community in his connection with the upper world. The Baal Shem Tov and Jacob Joseph, his faithful pupil, who is known as Baal Toledoth after the title of his book, "Toledoth Jacob Joseph", may have aspired towards a tzadik who would be the one leader of a whole generation, but this hope did not materialize. After the death of the Baal Shem Tov in 1760, Rabbi Dov Ber, the Maggid from Mezzeritz, inherited his place as leader of the new movement. Even in his lifetime his pupils established groups of their own Hassidic communities. They directed their followers along the new religious path and also cared for their daily problems. The Hassid came to the rebbe, as the Hassidic leader came to be called, to explain his problems and receive the rebbe's blessing. Sinners would abandon their practices for fear of the power of the rabbi's curse.

After the death of Rabbi Dov Ber in 1772, and the violent opposition to the Hassidic movement by Rabbi Elijah, the Gaon of Vilna, there was no longer any single authoritative leader of the Hassidim. Under the threat of excommunication, the specific objective of which had been to separate and isolate the Hassidic sect from the rest of Judaism, the power of Hassidism became centered in its houses of prayer. There, Hassidism fostered a special form of Sephardic liturgy according to the order of prayers of Ha-Ari, and a characteristic social atmosphere. The Hassidism did not abandon their customs or ideas, nor were they isolated from the rest of Jewry. Unlike the Sabbatians, they did not become a secret sect, but were an accepted trend in Judaism, and within a single generation most of the divisions between them and their opponents were removed. A number of customs that characterized Hassidism became objects of scorn to their opponents the "Mittnagdim" and especially to the Haskalah writers. These customs included blind veneration of the "rebbe", faith in his magic powers, quarrels between dynasties of tzadikim, and the blessings and magic amulets distributed by the rebbes to their Hassidim. Other values, such as the stress laid upon the unity of all sections of the people,

(Above) RABBI ZVI KALISCHER, A PRECURSOR OF THE ZIONISTS.
(Below) THE FIRST CONFERENCE OF THE "LOVERS OF ZION" (HOVEVEI ZION), HELD IN KATTOWITZ IN 1884.

the contempt for soical differences, the popular faith in the approaching Redemption, became a living treasure to the people and influenced movements and trends that came after Hassidism, even those which had very little in common with it.

New social and ideological trends, whose roots were to be found in their environment, began to appear among the Jews. Not only were these unrelated to Jewish tradition, but to a large extent they were directed against it. Chief among these new movements were the Haskalah movement for enlightenment which began in the 18th Century, and Jewish socialism, which began to take shape in the second half of the 19th Century. It would be fallacious to maintain that there were no principles in previous Jewish tradition to which these two movements could trace their origins. The Jewish philosophical concepts of the Middle Ages were essentially rationalistic; they considered the intellect as the main means by which one could judge natural and social manifestations, a basis which was accepted by the 18th and 19th Century rationalists. Moral preaching against the rich and powerful and the demand for social justice had

been central themes in the concepts of Jews of all generations. But in previous periods, rationalistic ideas and critical social purpose were intertwined with tradition and strengthened its foundations. They were proof that even the extreme theories of philosophers could be complemented by the religious faith of the Jewish people and the belief in its quality as a chosen people. These new trends, however, regarded Jewish tradition as a curse imposed upon the Jewish people, a "burdensome legacy" that kept it from joining in the universal development. They therefore looked to the environment for a means of reforming the Jews or reforming the whole of society, in order to change the Jew into an emancipated person.

Revolutionary in character, these were without doubt movements of redemption. Their aim was to bring about changes in the Jewish people, in order to free them from their situation, to redeem them from being exceptions to their surroundings. If, as the result of this redemption, the very existence of the Jews as Jews were to be undermined, many of the Maskilim and the socialists were prepared to pay the price. Some even hoped for this.

The Enlightenment movement that began to take shape in Europe at the end of the 17th Century had its influence on Jewish individuals right from the outset. The signs of enlightenment were first felt in Italy and Holland, countries where contact between Jews and their surroundings was freer and closer, but even there it did not become an influential movement among the Jews.

The "Haskalah" movement really began in the

(Top left) YEHUDA LEIB PINSKER, AUTHOR OF "AUTO-EMANCIPATION", AND A LEADER OF THE "LOVERS OF ZION".
(Top right) MENAHEM USSISHKIN, A REPRESENTATIVE OF THE "LOVERS OF ZION" IN PALESTINE AND A LEADER OF THE LAND ACQUISITION MOVEMENT FOR JEWISH SETTLEMENT.
(Below) "MIGRANTS," A DRAWING BY LILIEN SYMBOLIZING JEWISH MIGRATION.

*Meiner lieben Verbindung
Ivria..!
Dezember 1896*

Theodor Herzl

DR. THEODOR HERZL, FOUNDER OF THE ZIONIST MOVE-
MENT.

MAX NORDAU AFTER HIS SPEECH ON THE CONDITION
OF THE JEWS IN THE WORLD AT THE SECOND ZIONIST
CONGRESS, SEEN WITH DR. THEODOR HERZL.

circle of Moses Mendelssohn in Berlin. He was
the first German Jew to remain faithful to the
precepts of Jewish religion and at the same time
to be accepted as an equal by enlightened Christians. Moses Mendelssohn believed that there is
a correspondence between the demands of reason
and the fundamentals of Jewish religion, which
approximate to the "natural religion" that is ingrained in every person. Because the principles of
natural religion can be explained in a rational
manner, Jewish religion does not rely on theoretical dogmatic principles but rather on "mitzvot",
laws of performance. Its precepts are a "Law
from Heaven" given to Moses and the Children of
Israel, and cannot be repealed save by a similar
act of revelation. Mendelssohn does not emphasize, however, the rational values of the laws of
the Torah but stresses their educational and
disciplining values. Everyone, according to Mendelssohn, who lives in accordance with natural
religion achieves happiness, and this emphasis led
many to conclude wrongly that this "Law from
Heaven" is more of a burden than a blessing.

Mendelssohn wished to leave the choice of religious faith to the decision of the individual,
changing the religious institutions into free associations without powers of compulsion. This
attitude caused him to oppose wholeheartedly the

internal Jewish autonomy, and strengthened similar views in enlightened Christian circles and
among the authorities. His translation of the
Bible into German and his rational commentary
to it also helped to attract Jewish youth to the
culture of their surroundings and to distract them
from tradition. The friends and admirers of Mendelssohn drew up plans for spreading general
education among Jewish youth and some cooperated with the authorities or urged them to spread
enlightenment among the Jews by compulsion if
necessary.

A short time after the death of Mendelssohn it
became apparent that his idea of compromise
between the Jewish tradition and the cultural
influence of the environment contained an inherent contradiction. Some of the young Jewish
members of this circle, Mendelssohn's family
among them, were converted to Christianity and
even those who did not take this drastic step
began to neglect Jewish tradition and culture,
identifying themselves completely with the culture and concepts of their environment. The
Hebrew-language organ of the German Maskilim,
"Hameasef", existed for only a few years.

The first attempt to combine complete immersion in the life of the surrounding society with
loyalty to Judaism had been made by German
Maskilim by way of reforms in religion and by
scholarly investigation into the history and
essence of Judaism, the "Science of Judaism".

However, the effort to discard the national element in Judaism drained off much of its positive religious uniqueness for if Judaism were to contain nothing but general moral precepts, to do good and to love one's neighbor, such as bind any intelligent person, then there would be no sense in its separate existence, certainly not enough to force a person to bear all the discrimination, the degradation and the attacks that were the fate of the German Jew during the first half of the 19th Cenury. Conversion appeared to be justified.

Faced with this, the reformers and the Jewish intellectuals tried to find a justification for the existence of Judaism and emerged with the concept of its mission. Judaism, according to this concept, has a mission to spread pure faith in God and sublime moral principles throughout the world, and by its very existence to serve as a "light to the nations". In order to do so it must lay bare the shortcomings of Christianity, and emphasize the differences between the two faiths. These scholars spoke disparagingly of the Christian doctrines of the trinity and the incarnation and contrasted them with the pure spiritual monotheism of Judaism. They stressed the serious social problems of Christian Europe, its social conflicts, the crime and corruption that mirrored its moral weakness. Hence the existence of Judaism was a universal necessity as an example of a pure, rational religion and a harmonious society.

This theory held within itself a contradiction regarding the desired end, for the very people whose object was to bring the Jews closer to the

ZIONISTEN-CONGRESS.

Vorläufige Anzeige.

Am 25., 26. und 27. August 1897 findet in München ein Weltcongress der Zionisten statt. Zweck dieses Congresses ist, eine Annäherung und Verständigung zwischen allen Zionisten herbeizuführen und dem gemeinsamen Bestreben einen einheitlichen Zug zu verleihen.

Der Congress wird die Wünsche unserer an verschiedenen Orten bedrängten Brüder entgegennehmen und die Mittel zur Abhilfe berathen.

Wer am Congress theilzunehmen gedenkt, hat sich bis spätestens 15. August anzumelden. Die Anmeldestellen in den einzelnen Ländern (Landescomités) werden demnächst bekanntgegeben. Vorläufig können Anmeldungen an das Centralbureau des Congresses (Verein „Zion", Wien II. Rembrandtstrasse 11) gerichtet werden. Die Angemeldeten werden die Eintrittskarten rechtzeitig zugestellt erhalten. Für Unterkunft der Congresstheilnehmer in München, wird auf Wunsch Vorsorge getroffen werden.

Die officielle Einladung zum Congresse wird, von sämmtlichen Einberufern unterfertigt, an Vereine und Körperschaften verschickt werden, sobald die Tagesordnung endgiltig feststeht.

Den Congress wird der Alterspräsident eröffnen. Hierauf erfolgt die Constituirung. Die Verhandlungen sollen nach den Grundsätzen einer vernünftigen und würdigen Redefreiheit geleitet werden.

Für jeden Punkt der Tagesordnung wird ein Referent aufgestellt, an den schon jetzt direct oder durch Vermittlung des Vereins „Zion" in Wien, Mittheilungen gerichtet werden können.

Die bisher bestimmten Referate sind:

a) die Lage der Juden in den einzelnen Ländern (ein Specialreferent für jedes Land), ökonomische, sociale und politische Zustände. Referent Herr Dr. **Max Nordau**, in **Paris**, (84 Avenue de Villiers)

b) die Colonisation, ihre bisherigen Ergebnisse und ferneren Aussichten. Agrarische, industrielle, commercielle, technische Fragen. Referent Herr **Willy Bambus**, in **Berlin**, (W. Bülowstrasse 80)

c) die Aufgaben der jüdischen Wohltätigkeit in Palästina. Referent Hr. Dr. **Hirsch Hildesheimer** in **Berlin**,

d) Finanzfragen, Referent Herr Dr. **Max Bodenheimer** in **Köln a. Rh.** (Hohenzollernring 18)

e) die Judenfrage und der nächste diplomatische Congress der Grossmächte. Referent Dr. **Theodor Herzl** in **Wien** (IX. Berggasse 6)

f) eine Beschickung der Pariser Weltausstellung 1900 mit jüdischen Colonialproducten.

Die weiteren Punkte der Tagesordnung sind später zu publiciren.

Die officiellen Delegirten der eingeladenen Vereine und Körperschaften werden zur Congresszeit in München eine besondere Berathung abhalten und deren Ergebniss dem Congresse mittheilen.

Viele praktische Fragen, welche den Congress beschäftigen werden, enthalten ein Element von Actualität und können desshalb nicht Monate vorher formulirt werden.

Findet es der Congress für nöthig, so wird er ein Executivcomité zur Führung der jüdischen Angelegenheiten bis zu seinem nächsten Zusammentritt einsetzen.

So erhalten die gemeinsamen Bedürfnisse ein Organ. Es wird ein Zufluchtsort für die Wünsche und Beschwerden unserer Brüder geschaffen. Die Judensache muss den Belieben vereinzelter Personen — wie gutwillig diese auch seien — entrückt sein. Es muss ein Forum entstehen, vor dem Jeder für das was er in der Judensache thut und lässt zur Rechenschaft gezogen werden kann. Dem wird sich kein redlicher Mann widersetzen.

Wir sind der Theilnahme aller Menschen gewiss, die unseren Gedanken richtig verstanden haben. Es handelt sich darum, eine dauernde, gesicherte Heimat für diejenigen Juden zu schaffen, welche sich an ihren jetzigen Wohnorten nicht assimiliren können oder wollen.

Der Congress zu München wird zeigen, was der Zionismus ist und will. Dass er etwas ist und dass er etwas will.

Dr. Theodor Herzl
Wien, IX. Berggasse 6
im Namen der vorbereitenden Commission.

(Top) PRELIMINARY ANNOUNCEMENT FOR THE FIRST ZIONIST CONGRESS OVER THE NAME OF DR. THEODOR HERZL.
(Below) THE BUILDING IN BASLE WHERE THE FIRST ZIONIST CONGRESS WAS HELD.

Christian society appeared as severe critics both of Christianity and of the society itself. They hindered the desired merging of the Jews with their surroundings and aroused criticism of "Jewish presumptuousness".

From Germany the Haskalah spread to Galicia and Russia. There the struggle of the Maskilim was fought in the very midst of a compact and united Jewish society. The vernacular of the Maskilim there was Hebrew and to a certain extent Yiddish. In addition to the demand for a general education and the need to learn the language of the state, the Maskilim in the East stressed the need to change the sources of livelihood of the Jews to make them more productive,

to change them from commerce and distribution to productive occupations such as agriculture and skilled trades. In eastern Europe, every deviation from tradition, however small, was interpreted by the majority of the community as atheism. Therefore, despite the fact that most of the Maskilim there were faithful to tradition, they were strongly persecuted by both the Jewish leaders and the masses. In desperation, the Maskilim pinned their hopes on the authorities and suggested to them that parts of their program should be forcibly imposed upon the Jewish community. This deed turned them, in the eyes of most Jews, into traitors and informers, who incited the authorities to persecute the community. Jewish hostility made the position of the Maskilim impossible and increased their dependence upon the authorities.

These desperate communal struggles provided fertile soil for the growth of a polemical literature in Hebrew. The Maskilim of Galicia published philosophical works and conducted important research and laid the foundation for a new Hebrew literature. But no sooner had a group of young Maskilim arisen in eastern Europe with the aid of the authorities, than they began to assimilate with the environment and turn to its language. The Haskalah writers, who had once striven so hard for this very goal, gradually began to understand that this was the beginning of the end for their spiritual and literary enterprise, and to fear that their struggle had been in vain.

Jewish socialism was started in the 1870's in Russian rabbinical schools and among yeshivah students. Its originator was Aaron Samuel Liberman, who decided to work, not among the Russian peasants as other revolutionaries did, but to organize revolutionary activities among the Jews in their own language. While he was in London in 1876, he organized the "Jewish Socialist Association" which was intended to "spread the ideas of socialism among the Jews wherever they lived". In 1877 in Vienna, he began to publish the first socialist periodical in the Hebrew language "Ha'emeth", Truth.

Liberman's intention was to interest Jewish

DR. HERZL OPENING THE SECOND ZIONIST CONGRESS IN BASLE IN 1898.

youth in socialist activity through criticism both of the Maskilim and of the government. He and other Jewish revolutionaries stressed that the Jews who were in the main poor and struggling, should not be regarded as the group of exploiters they were represented to be by most Russian revolutionaries. The Jewish masses must become allies of the workers of Russia in their struggle against the Czarist regime and in their struggle for social revolution. As long as the revolutionary circle of the Jews was limited, and their main preoccupations were with ideological problems, the students who were instructors of these groups could content themselves with teaching Polish or Russian to the few workers who participated, so that they could themselves read revolutionary literature. In the 1880's socialist literature began to appear in Yiddish and when, in the 1890's, the revolutionary circles decided to begin large-scale propaganda, Yiddish became its main vehicle.

The Jewish socialists did not recognize any necessity to represent specifically Jewish national demands and some of them denied the national characteristics of the Jews. It was only at the fourth conference of the "Bund" the Jewish Socialist Union in Russia, in 1901, that it was decided for the first time that "the term nation be also applied to the Jewish people". But subsequently they feared that "the national feeling . . . would befog the class-consciousness of the proletariat". It was their belief that the solution to the Jewish problem would come as a result of a change in the order of society and the victory of socialism. As late as World War I, the "Bund" maintained its neutrality in relation to the national question; that is, it was committed to striving for freedom of Jewish development through either national consolidation or assimilation, but it was not committed to a decision which of the two alternatives was the more desirable.

THE FUNERAL OF DR. HERZL, 1904.

For the "Bund", the vital issue was that it should not be considered a nationalist movement by the International or the Russian socialist democratic movements. Nevertheless, like the other Jewish parties in Russia at the beginning of the 20th Century, it too was forced to present a program for Jewish cultural and national autonomy, demanding that the government recognize the right of Jews to conduct their cultural and educational affairs independently.

Many Jewish proponents of the national idea were scornful of the spiritual creativity of Judaism in earlier generations. But modern anti-Semitism and the difficulty of integrating into their environment taught them that the denial of their past could not of itself bridge the gap separating the Jew from the various strata of European society. Hence they aspired to solve the Jewish question by modern social and political means, on the basis of ideas that had evolved in Europe during the 18th and 19th Centuries. They hoped thereby to change the Jewish People from the "peculiar people" it had been considered to be during the whole of the Middle Ages and later, into a nation "like all nations".

Those aspiring to the normalization of the Jewish People during the last quarter of the 19th Century could be divided into a number of schools of thought. The "Autonomists" maintained that it was possible to achieve normalization by guaranteeing the rights of the Jewish minority in each country and conferring on them a limited autonomy primarily in the cultural sphere. The "Territorialists" did not believe that guarantees of Jewish rights would suffice and sought a new territory for the Jewish people where they could live an independent life. The Zionists maintained that only in Palestine, the Land of Israel, could this ancient people return to an independent political and national life.

At first, the outstanding difference was between those who proposed to rebuild an autonomous Jewish life in the old countries, and those who called for emigration. The great emigration of Jews from eastern Europe in the 1880's and later, served as the realistic background for these ideological differences. The Autonomists maintained that even if the Jews migrated, they would carry the "Jewish question" with them wherever they went, and that there was no certainty that the position of the Jews would be any different in the new lands from what it was in Europe. There were many nations in Europe who did not possess an independent national framework but were partners in multi-national states like the Austro-Hungarian, Russian and the Ottoman empires. In the opinion of the Autonomists there was a need eventually to find federal forms to guarantee the rights of all nations and the function of the Jewish Autonomists would be to ensure the inclusion of the Jews in the overall arrangement.

The Autonomists argued that the Jewish community, which had been the basis for Jewish survival in many countries during previous periods of history, could serve as the kernel for the future national existence of the Jews. Their task would be to exchange the former religious content of the community for a secular one.

Assuming that multi-national states would continue to exist, because they were economically more viable than smaller states, they hoped for the further development of Yiddish as the special national language of the Jews, and for the creation of further independent national Jewish institutions, such as the National Council of Russian Jews, which would safeguard the autonomous national existence of the Jews. Some among them hoped that national affiliation would eventually take the place of state affiliation as the primary loyalty, and that the multi-national state would become an alliance of national corporations. Similar ideas were forming in Austrian social-democratic circles during the same period.

The developments that followed World War I did not fulfill the hopes of the Autonomists. The principle of self-determination brought about the fragmentation of the large multi-national states and the creation of small national states. The guarantees that had been given to national minorities, Jews included, under the guardianship of the Great Powers and the League of Nations proved to be ineffectual. Most of the new European states that arose after the Treaty of Versailles did not honor their undertakings. Even in those countries where there was special representation for the

A HASSIDIC RABBI WITH HIS FOLLOWERS IN POLAND.

Jews the privileges were cancelled after a short while. And none of the guarantees was of any value once Nazis started their massacre of the Jews.

Among the Jews of Europe in the 19th Century were some who realised that the rising wave of anti-Semitism left no solution for the Jews but to leave the countries that were permeated with hatred for them, and make their home in some land of their own. Y. L. Pinsker, one of the founding fathers of the national movement maintained: "It is not a Holy Land we need, but our own land".

During the first stages, settlement in Palestine seemed to be more feasible than settlement in other lands and there was no difference of opinion at the time between the Territorialists and the Zionists, who were, in effect, the first territorialists of the 1880's and the 1890's. The program of political Zionism for the securing of rights in Palestine from the Sultan, brought these camps even closer together. Only when the difficulties in realizing the Zionist program of Theodor Herzl became apparent and when the persecution and pogroms against the Jews of Russia caused emigration to swell to a flood, were voices raised to say that an alternative territory should be sought,

at least as a temporary measure. After the death of Dr. Herzl, the Territorialists split away from the Zionist Organization and founded the Jewish Territorialist Organization. Some even went so far to declare that by Marxist analysis "there was no connection between Zionism and Palestine".

The many attempts to seek a different territory for Jewish settlement in which to create an independent Jewish center were fruitless. Hopes that the Jews would gain the sympathy and support of the powers interested in colonization projects were dashed. The few Jews who settled in the new colonies did not create independent Jewish centers, but became just further concentrations of Jews who within a short time were urbanized within the framework of the general society of those countries.

The only one of the Jewish national movement that attained the realization of its political program, in theory as well as in practice, was Zionism. True, the dream of the extreme Zionists, to gather all the Jews to Eretz Israel, and thereby to make the Jews a nation "like all nations", was not realized. But Zionism caused the majority of

(Above) BARON HIRSCH, FOUNDER OF THE JEWISH COLONIZATION ASSOCIATION WHO ENCOURAGED JEWISH SETTLEMENT IN ARGENTINA, PARTICULARLY IN AGRICULTURE.
(Below) RUSSIAN, POLISH AND YIDDISH NEWSPAPERS PUBLISHED BY THE BUND, THE FIRST JEWISH SOCIALIST UNION IN EASTERN EUROPE.

the Jewish people, and much of world opinion, to recognize the fact that the Jews constitute a distinct people for whom the Zionists succeeded in creating an independent cultural and political center.

The initiators of the Zionist movement were the "Hovevei Zion" the "Lovers of Zion", in Russia, Rumania and a number of other countries. The Hovevei Zion believed in the possibility of a Jewish national revival through settlement, primarily agricultural, in Palestine. The activities of the early Hovevei Zion in the 1880's and 1890's, while arousing national pride among many Jews, had disappointing results in Palestine; though a few thousand agricultural workers settled there they could survive only through the financial assistance of Baron Rothschild. Ahad Haam, the philosopher of Zionism, gave a damning report on the agricultural activities of the "Hovevei Zion", maintaining that such activities could not alter the difficult economic and social position of the Jews of eastern Europe, and that the main objective of Zionism should be the moral and cultural revival of the nation, by the creation of a spiritual center in Eretz Israel to constitute the backbone of the nation in dispersion.

The establishment of the Zionist Organization by Dr. Theodor Herzl infused new spirit into zionist activity. The "political Zionism" of Herzl placed emphasis on international recognition of the movement and of its activities in Palestine. He was so adamant in his political outlook that he considered Jewish attempts at settlement in Palestine before the granting of a charter from the Sultan to be harmful and that political activity by Zionists in European countries should be forbidden, so as not to antagonize the various governments.

This attitude was criticized by many active

JEWISH SELF-DEFENSE GROUP IN RUSSIA, 1905.

Zionists. At the Fifth Zionist Congress in 1901, the "Democratic Faction" headed by Motzkin and Weizmann, was organized to oppose the policy that Zionist activity should be restricted to diplomatic methods. The group maintained that a playing down of popular participation in Zionist activity would be harmful to the democratic nature of Zionism. The meeting between Herzl and the Russian Minister of the Interior, von Plehve, who had been the chief instigator of the anti-Semitic policy of the Russian government, angered the members of the Democratic Faction, although the Jews of Russia, who were the victims of von Plehve's policies, welcomed Dr. Herzl with wild enthusiasm.

PICTURE POSTCARD PRINTED AFTER THE KISHINEV POGROM SHOWS A CRIPPLED JEWISH SOLDIER RETURNING HOME TO FIND HIS FAMILY SLAUGHTERED.

AHAD HA'AM, WHO ENVISIONED ISRAEL AS THE JEWISH
SPIRITUAL CENTER.

The death of Herzl was a severe blow to the whole Zionist Organization, particularly to its "political" trend. The revolution in Russia in 1905 had placed the Jews there in such a position that they could no longer adopt a passive attitude and many became active in the general political movements that were embracing all classes in Russia and were particularly strong among the Jews. The Zionist Assembly in Russia in 1906 authorized an ad hoc program for a National Council of representatives of all Russian Jews, for the creation of special Jewish representation in the "Duma", the Russian National Assembly, and for wider autonomy for the Jews of Russia.

Zionist activity was not confined to Europe. The revolutionary wave in Russia brought about the foundation of a Zionist-Socialist Party "Poale Zion", branches of which were organized in Austria and in the United States, that regarded the link with Palestine as fundamentally ideological. The leader of this movement was Dov-Ber Boro-

chov. In the period following the 1905 revolution, Jewish youth, particularly supporters of Poale Zion, started a new wave of immigration to Palestine, known as the "Second Aliyah" to lay the foundations of Jewish independence there. Agricultural settlement again became one of the important aspects of Zionist activity. During the years preceeding World War I, the first foundations of independent Jewish organization, of settlement and of self-defense were laid in Palestine. In the Balfour Declaration of 1917, Britain, and indirectly the Allied Powers, gave formal recognition to the idea of establishing a "National Home for the Jewish People" in Palestine, the culmination of the labors of the Zionist pioneers in the preceding decade. The Zionist, combining modern cultural and political programs with the traditional Jewish bonds with the Land of Israel, with the Hebrew language and with independent Jewish creativity, had laid the foundations for renewed national independence for the Jewish people.

ISRAEL ZANGWILL, FOUNDER OF THE TERRITORIALIST
MOVEMENT, A GROUP SEEKING A JEWISH NATIONAL
HOME, NOT NECESSARILY IN PALESTINE.

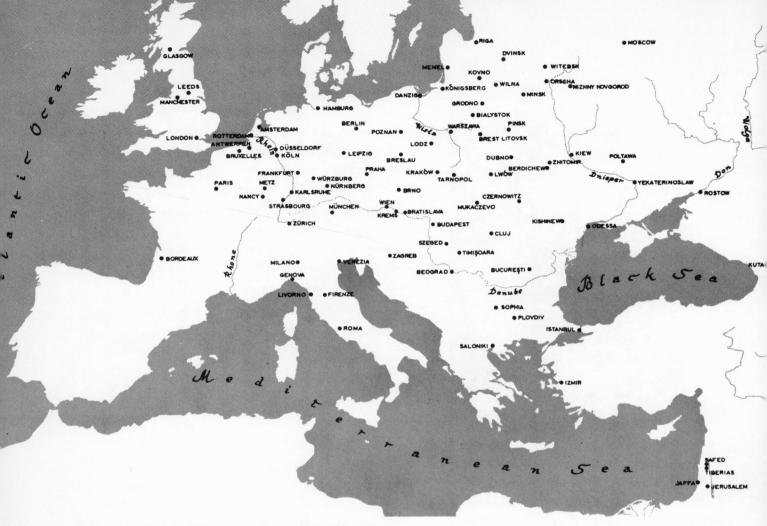

IMPORTANT JEWISH COMMUNITIES IN EUROPE AT
THE BEGINNING OF THE 20TH CENTURY.

THE JEWS IN AMERICA

THE FIRST JEWISH IMMIGRANTS TO ARRIVE IN NEW
AMSTERDAM, 1654.

THE JEWS IN AMERICA

One test of a people's ability to maintain its creative powers is the manner in which it fashions new instruments of survival or remakes old ones. In the United States, Jews have given strong evidence of their ability to foster a vital Judaism in the midst of a free and multi-cultured nation. Jewry has adapted its community structure and its religious and educational institutions to the democratic principle of voluntarism. In some cases, as in the functioning of the synagogue and the rabbi, in the work of defense against anti-Semitism and in the activities of Jewish labor unions and secular groups, some of the adapta-

tions have been of such magnitude as to be virtually new cultural creations.

To see the experience of the Jews in the United States in perspective, it is necessary to set it against the background of the stream of American life, which ever breaks out into new directions. American Jewry today is as different in quality from its Colonial ancestry as the present population of almost six million American Jews is from the first little group that came to New Amsterdam in 1654.

American civilization, says John Kouwenhoven, is open-ended. It proceeds without an apparent end-in-view, but it always manages to attain at each moment of its development a meaning and beauty that give purpose to the nation's exist-

THE ROUTE BY WHICH THE EARLY JEWISH SETTLERS REACHED NORTH AMERICA, FROM BRAZIL TO NEW AMSTERDAM.

ence. One might compare American culture as a whole to the skyscraper, complete at any height, to which nonetheless can be added many more floors without changing its essential character. Similarly, the American tradition of freedom has already produced a moral and spiritual pattern which can well be expanded indefinitely by increasing the ingredients it already contains.

Yet Kouwenhoven's analogy is not enough. American freedom and the culture founded on it continue to grow in quality as well as in quantity. Americanism, for example, is today not simply the totality of many cultures living side by side. It is the resultant of their individuality in interaction.

The interplay between freedom and culture is clearly marked in the reciprocal effect on each other of the American environment and the Judaism that has grown within it. The Jews came to the United States in their successive waves, like all other future Americans. They came with their varying vocational and economic potentials, their prejudices and their moral virtues, their religious traditions and their secular ideologies. They affected the life in their new community and were in turn affected by what they found there.

Perry Miller, an outstanding authority on the Puritans and the Colonial period, has described the emergence of religious freedom in the United States in these words: "The point is, to put it baldly, that in both education and in religion, we didn't aspire to freedom, we didn't march steadily toward it, we didn't unfold the inevitable propulsion of our hidden nature; we stumbled into it. We got a variety of sects as we got a college catalogue: the denominations and the sects multiplied until there was nothing anybody could do about them. Wherefore we gave them permission to exist and called the result freedom of the mind. Then we found, to our vast delight, that by thus

[1]) *Religion and Freedom of Thought.* Doubleday, New York, 1954.

THE FOUNDING FATHERS WERE DEEPLY INFLUENCED BY THE JUDAIC TRADITION.
(Top) THE PRELIMINARY DESIGN OF THE SEAL OF THE UNITED STATES, RECOMMENDED BY FRANKLIN, ADAMS AND JEFFERSON. THE DESIGN AT RIGHT SHOWS THE CHILDREN OF ISRAEL ESCAPING FROM THE EGYPTIAN TYRANT.
(Below) A RELIEF OF MAIMONIDES, NOW IN THE CAPITOL BUILDING, WASHINGTON, D.C.

negatively surrendering we could congratulate ourselves on a positive and heroic victory. So we stuck the feather in our cap and called it Yankee Doodle".[1])

American Jewry, beginning three centuries ago, also had to struggle for its rights. This struggle has gone on concomitantly with the struggle of America as a whole to overcome the tendency of successive generations of new settlers to perpetuate some of the European social and religious prejudices which they had brought with them.

The first Jewish colonists, from Recife in Brazil,

FACSIMILE OF THE MANUSCRIPT OF THE HEBREW
ORATION DELIVERED BY SAMPSON SIMSON AT THE
COLUMBIA COLLEGE COMMENCEMENT, 1800.

led by Asher Levy, had to fight their battle with
Peter Stuyvesant for civil and religious rights, a
battle fought patiently, persistently and triumphantly. Over a hundred years had to elapse before
the Jews of New York State were accorded complete equality before the law, in the State Constitution of 1776. But in assessing the spirit of
America in the Colonial period it is important to
realise, that the legal disabilities during these
decades were amply compensated for by the
emerging social democracy. Their fellow colonists
accorded the Jews the opportunity to worship
without harassment. Though the Jews were legally unable to engage in certain occupations,

UNIVERSITY SEALS WITH HEBRAIC INSCRIPTIONS:
DARTMOUTH COLLEGE AND COLUMBIA UNIVERSITY.

their neighbors shut an eye to the strict letter of
the law and the Jews were allowed to prosper and
in time, to secure full legal rights.

Indeed, the first century and a half of American
Jewish history was marked by the influence on
the early colonists of some of the ideas of Judaism, even before the arrival of the Jews. The
Bible, and the People of the Bible, were of absorbing interest to the founders of the Republic
and to its leading minds. The biblical influence in
early America is well-known. The Bible, after all,
gave early Americans their children's names and
the designations of many of the towns they inhabited. The Jewish Bible was the basis of Puritan
thought, in many respects more so than the New
Testament, and provided equal inspiration for
other schools of Christian thought. It remained
a text for constant study and reading, and it provided much of the moral and intellectual form
and content of the early American mind.

Also to be remembered is the great interest in
the Hebrew language: at one time it was even
suggested that Hebrew become the national language. As late as 1800, Sampson Simson, a Jewish
layman, who later was one of the founders of Mt.
Sinai Hospital in New York City, delivered a
graduation oration at Columbia University in
Hebrew.

The first Jewish colonialists, all Sephardim,
numbering between two and three thousand at the
time of the American Revolution, laid the ground-
work for the equality of status and opportunity
now enjoyed by the American Jewish community.
But the structure of American life, and Jewish
life with it, began to assume its present shape
during the second century and a half of American
Jewry's existence. During this entire period, the
Jewish group has played its unique role in American civilization and has itself been transformed.

The Western European Jews, some of whom

NAMES OF SITES IN THE UNITED STATES WITH BIBLI-
CAL ASSOCIATIONS. *(Map by Lottie and Moshe Davis)*

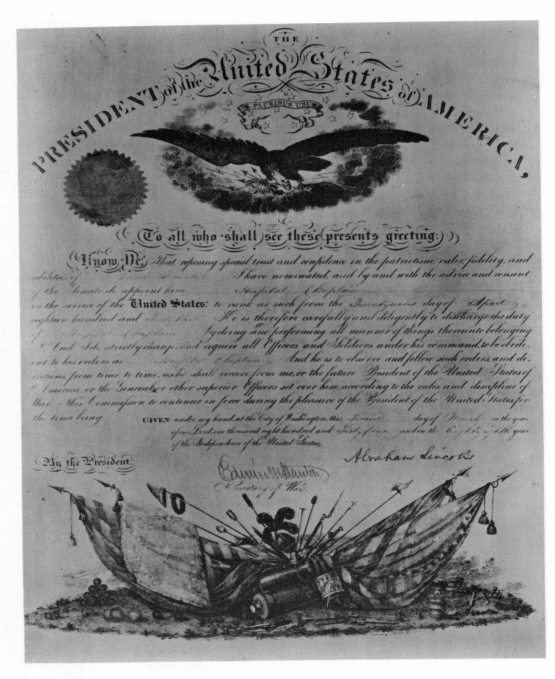

LETTER OF APPOINTMENT FROM ABRAHAM LINCOLN
TO THE FIRST JEWISH MILITAY CHAPLAIN DURING THE
CIVIL WAR.

HEROES OF JEWISH HISTORY: SCULPTURES AT THE
WEST POINT ACADEMY.

THE INTERIOR OF THE SHEARITH ISRAEL SYNAGOGUE,
NEW YORK.

had arrived even in the Colonial period but who immigrated in large numbers particularly after the European upheavals of 1848, arrived at a time of national expansion. The United States was moving rapidly toward its manifest destiny. Breaking through natural and political frontiers, America spread out. The western European Jews followed suit. Working hard to secure an economic foothold, they settled throughout the land and brought a new vision to America's mercantile interests. By the 1880's, when the mass immigration of eastern European Jewry began, the immigrants from western Europe were economically and socially prepared to welcome the newcomers and to assist them in their period of integration.

Western European Jewry had already had a history of differentiation when its large scale immigration to the United States took place. The process set in motion during the intellectual career of Moses Mendelssohn in the last half of the 18th Century had shown its results in the first half of the next century with the emergence of Reform Judaism and Historical Judaism, and had triggered the Orthodox response of later decades. It is not surprising, therefore, that Western Euopean Jews should have played a leading role during the decades of their settlement in the new country in translating the beliefs and practices they brought with them into the American idiom.

Thus western European Jews contributed heavily to the emerging patterns of religious thought, practice and organization which characterized the developments in the Reform, Orthodox and Historical trends of Judaism of the 19th Century. Western European Jews played crucial roles in the creation of Reform Judaism and Historical Judaism (which later became Conservative Judaism) and were very active in the establishment of the Union of Orthodox Jewish Congregations.

JULIUS MEYER, AN INDIAN TRADER, IN OMAHA, 1870.

MORDECAI MANUEL NOAH (1785-1851) WHO HOPED TO FOUND A JEWISH STATE IN AMERICA ON A SMALL ISLAND THAT HE NAMED ARARAT. THE INSCRIPTION MARKS THE "FOUNDATION" OF ARARAT.

NEW YORK'S LOWER EAST SIDE, WHERE THE MAJORITY
OF IMMIGRANT JEWS SETTLED ON THEIR ARRIVAL IN
THE UNITED STATES, IN 1894.

CASTLE GARDEN, THE POINT OF DISEMBARKATION FOR IMMIGRANTS IN NEW YORK.

It was western European Jews who were responsible for the formation of the Union of American Hebrew Congregations (1873), the Hebrew Union College (1875) and the Central Conference of American Rabbis (1889). Rabbi Isaac Mayer Wise, a German Jew, is the man who stands out as the leading figure in 19th Century Reform Judaism. His efforts were indicative of both the strength and weakness of American Jewry and an omen of the many problems which confront it in the second half of the 20th Century. The Reform movement, in applying freedom to the Jewish tradition, contributed importantly to the strength of American Jewry and to its capacity to meet the ever new demands of the environment. In its early years, Reform Judaism had embraced certain principles or practices which it later revised or even renounced under the force of changing circumstances. In 1885, for instance, it had rejected all aspirations for a Return to Zion yet now it is almost completely involved in the building of Zion. This flexibility testifies to the fact that Reform was and is a movement for Jewish survival, one of the first movements in modern Jewish history to recognize that freedom and change are organically related.

Wise had sought to devise a Minhag America, a specific American liturgy, which would bring all American Jews together in worship. He thus implicitly placed his hopes for Jewish unity on the common acceptance of a revised order of prayers. Wise attempted to effect a restoration of Jewish

communal solidarity on a synagogal basis. In this procedure he was followed by the other synagogue movements, each in terms of its own philosophy. In the light of the subsequent history of denominationism in Jewish life, it is at least open to challenge whether Jewish unity in a democratic environment can be achieved by trying to gain acceptance for a unified dogma or form of worship. Under freedom, it is inevitable that men should find their spiritual needs met by different ideologies, religious and secular, and by varied forms of observance and celebration.

The character of Jewish life was drastically altered by the millions of immigrants who poured

IMMIGRANT JEWS MADE THEIR LIVING CHIEFLY IN THE NEEDLE TRADES.
(Top) IN A "SWEAT SHOP" OF THE 1880's.
(Bottom) WORKING AT HOME. THE WHOLE FAMILY WAS CALLED ON TO HELP.

into the country in the decades between 1880 and 1920. Of the million Jews residing in the United States at the turn of the century, at least 600,000 had come during the closing two decades of the 19th Century. By 1910 they numbered over two million and when America entered World War I they totalled two and a half million.

It was the character of the immigration, as well as the numbers, which brought profound changes to American Jewish life. Eastern Europe had given birth to a rich Jewish culture, ranging from religious traditionalism to secularism and varieties of revolutionary social theory. By the time the Jews began their trek to America, the relative uniformity of the centuries-old Jewish community had begun to crumble. The process increased in tempo under the conditions of freedom. Interestingly, however, what occurred did not prove to be disintegration as much as a meta-

morphosis in the form and content of Jewish life. Forces of assimilation and disintegration, of course, made their appearance. Like the Sephardi and western European Jews before them, the eastern European immigrants often paid heavily in Jewish morale and cultural worth for their departures from religious and ethnic tradition and for their determination to adapt to the American scene. More importantly, however, the combination of tradition and enlightenment which they brought with them spurred them to create numerous institutions that today constitute a unique and creative Jewish community.

The religious freedom and pluralism of America stimulated new Jewish theologies, ritual departures and ethical concerns, even while they led some Jews to adopt a radical traditionalism or isolationism. American Orthodox Judaism, for instance, which at times has tried the path of geographical and cultural isolation, has now taken a new turn toward involvement in all aspects of contemporary life, and may be included today in the mainstream of American culture. Yeshiva University, which, under the leadership of Bernard Revel, became the leading educational institution of Orthodox Judaism, has been deeply affected by the American atmosphere; it is today inextricably involved with, and affected by, Jews of non-Orthodox bent and has departed from its more rigid forerunners in the nature of its curriculum, in the approach of many of its teachers

GREAT NAMES IN AMERICAN JEWRY
(Left to Right)
RABBI JUDAH L. MAGNES, (1877-1949) SCHOLAR, EDUCATOR AND FOUNDER OF THE HEBREW UNIVERSITY.
PROF. ALBERT EINSTEIN, (1879-1955) NOBEL-PRIZE WINNING PIONEER OF MATHEMATICS AND PHYSICS.
JUSTICE LOUIS D. BRANDEIS (1856-1941) FIRST JEWISH JUDGE ON THE SUPREME COURT, LIFELONG ZIONIST.
HENRIETTA SZOLD (1860-1945) EDUCATOR, SOCIAL WORKER AND FOUNDER OF HADASSAH, THE WOMEN'S ZIONIST ORGANIZATION.
ABRAHAM CAHAN, (1860-1951) TRADE UNIONIST, JOURNALIST AND HISTORIAN.
MAYER SULZBERGER (1843-1923) JURIST, HEBRAIST AND COMMUNAL LEADER.
PROF. LOUIS GINZBERG (1873-1953), TALMUDIC AND MIDRASHIC SCHOLAR AND HISTORIAN.
LOUIS MARSHALL (1856-1929) LAWYER, COMMUNAL AND CIVIL LEADER.

to the study of sacred text and the philosophy of Judaism, and in its desire to be considered part of the American academic tradition.

From its infancy, Conservative Judaism openly espoused the modernism which was accepted into Orthodoxy only much later and with reluctance. Conservative Judaism early adopted the scientific analysis of the Jewish past and of the classic texts and readily acknowledged the need for a more flexible interpretation of the Halakhic tradition than Orthodox Judaism was willing to grant.

Conservative and Orthodox scholars both cite Isaac Leeser as a forerunner of their respective movements. As one of the leading figures in the Historical School, Leeser's efforts could reasonably be cited by both modern movements as having had some influence on their thinking, but it was Leeser's pioneering efforts in establishing Maimonides College for the training of rabbis that later culminated in the creation of the Jewish Theological Seminary of America, the school of modern Conservative Judaism.

Under the influence of Leeser, a German Jew, who gave three decades of leadership until his death in 1868, the Historical School developed Jewish thought in the American idiom. Leeser translated the Bible into English and first formulated the idea of a Jewish Publication Society, thereby clearly supporting the view that Jews in America would have to wed themselves to the English word.

Later under Solomon Schechter, when the Historical School had already undergone the metamorphosis into Conservative Judaism, the new School reaffirmed its dedication to the integration of Jews and Judaism into American society and culture; but at the same time it proclaimed with equal force its loyalty to the traditional religious culture as it expressed itself in the Jewish people and rabbinic law. Conservative Jewry's departure from Orthodoxy, as we have said, has been highlighted by its adoption of the scientific study of Torah. Its opposition to Reform has been manifest in its determination to preserve the core of the rabbinic tradition even while it has sought to relate itself to the problems of the present.

In the course of its history, Conservative Judaism, more than any other movement in American Jewish life, has felt the tension between the Jewish tradition and some of the manifestations of American culture. For example, in pursuing the scientific study of the classic texts, Conservative scholars have constantly been challenged to resolve the conflicts in Jewish theology and practice suggested by such study, as, for instance, the historicity and significance of the revelation at Sinai, the authority of Jewish Law, the method of ritual change, and so forth. Some of its scholars have considered these conflicts to be of no significance or even to be non-existent. Others, however, have called attention again and again to what they claim to be inconsistencies, in meetings of

A SELECTION FROM THE MANY JEWISH PERIODICALS PUBLISHED IN THE UNITED STATES, INCLUDING "HADOAR", THE ONLY HEBREW WEEKLY.

the Rabbinical Assembly and the United Synagogue of America.

The latest contribution of American Jewry to the Jewish religious spectrum is Reconstructionism. In the brief span of less than three decades since its journal, "The Reconstructionist", made its first appearance in 1934, Reconstructionism, while lacking organizational form and strength, has provided a vocabulary for discourse on Jewish problems, on Jewish civilization, unity in diversity, the organic community, peoplehood and creativity. It has formulated the questions for consideration and has been both widely accepted and widely disputed in its demands for a naturalist approach to theology, prayer and ritual, contributing, in essence, a new and far-reaching program for the simultaneous integration of American-Jewry into American life and the preservation of its distinctiveness. The historical verdict on Reconstructionism remains to be given, but whatever the decision, the emergence of Reconstructionism is already part of the story of American-Jewish growth. Reconstructionism, by virtue of its comprehensive understanding of Jewish peoplehood, has sought to bridge the intellectual gap between religious Jewry and the important segment of secular Jewry.

Alongside the religious movements, there arose in American Jewry an inchoate secularism, which is beginning to achieve theoretical expression among some of the leaders of the Labor Zionist Organization of America, the Jewish Labor Committee, the Arbeiter Ring and other groups. Jewish secularism grew largely out of the laboring masses who, while they reflected the various socialist and democratic socialist trends in the general labor movement, were also involved in the cultivation of Yiddish culture in the United States, in some of the social welfare activities of the Jewish community and in the support of labor

Zionism. The ethical and cultural leadership supplied by Jewish labor to the general American trade union movement should also not be ignored. While much of that leadership has disappeared, as a result of the changes that have taken place in the economic structure of American Jewry, the American labor movement has benefitted from the broad conception of social welfare which east European Jews in particular introduced into its program.

Undoubtedly, the major impact of American Jewry is a religious one but it would be oversimplifying the nature of Judaism and of the American Jewish community to adopt the view that religious Jewry is that segment which is organized in synagogues and that secular Jewry is the remainder; for the synagogues abound with "secular-minded" members, while thousands of

THE SHEARITH ISRAEL SYNAGOGUE, BUILT IN 1897 IN NEW YORK.

"religious" men and women, who conceive their religion in terms which the synagogues cannot satisfy, are unaffiliated.

There is a crisis in worship, in America as else-

(*Left to right*) RABBI BERNARD REVEL, FOUNDER OF YESHIVA UNIVERSITY, RABBI ISAAC M. WISE, FOUNDER OF HEBREW UNION COLLEGE, RABBI SOLOMON SCHECHTER, FOUNDER OF THE UNITED SYNAGOGUE OF AMERICA, AND LONG-TIME HEAD OF THE JEWISH THEOLOGICAL SEMINARY.

where in the world, and Jews are among the first to experience it. Their sensitivity to changes in the universe of discourse is proverbial, and the advance of science and the naturalistic philosophies to which the modern temper has been so hospitable has had a profound impact on American Jews. American Jewry is trying to overcome the crisis by different and often by contradictory means. It sometimes seeks to restore traditions once abandoned but also to eliminate old ones or to create new ones. It tries to reassert the authority of the rabbinate but also to raise that of the laity. It tries pietism, but also rationalism. It simplifies public worship and at the same time introduces a heightened estheticism. Whatever one may say about its total effect, such a paradoxical procedure is inherent in voluntaristic societies.

The American synagogue, the synagogue center and the Jewish community center, which has now become an important arm of adult Jewish education, are all responses of the Jewish will to survive under freedom. All these institutions reflect the influence of the majority Christian and secular cultures but, far more significantly, they indicate the determination of American Jewry to resist assimilation.

The positive mood of the foregoing description must be balanced by the realization that American Jewry has many weaknesses, some of them being the counterpoints of its virtues. Its freedom sometimes sprouts anarchy and confusion. The opportunity of participating in the cultural milieu and in the affairs of the society, places a heavy burden on Jewish education which it has not always been able to meet, and American Jewry suffers from the many intellectual, moral and spiritual deficiencies of the general environment. Nonetheless, the Jews have succeeded in building a strong and vibrant Jewish life in the voluntary setting of the United States. When the so-called defense agencies, the American Jewish Committee, the American Jewish Congress, the Anti-Defamation League and others, which were once completely given over to combatting anti-Jewish manifestations, came to recognize that self-knowledge for the Jew is more important than apologetics and public relations, American Jewry could be said to have attained a high level of maturity. To this may be added the phenomenon of the flowering of adult education in synagogues, centers, Zionist and fraternal bodies (Hadassah and B'nai Brith between them number almost 750,000 members), and the potential of American Jewry is seen to be great. One of the most inter-

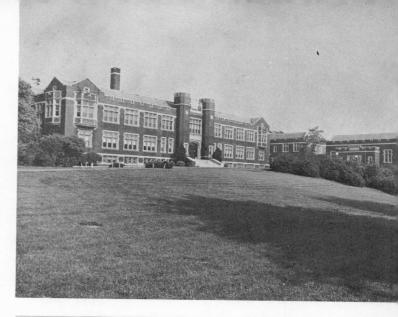

esting, and perhaps most important aspects of the growing respect for Jewish knowledge, is the intellectual respectability that has been accorded to Jewish studies on many college campuses. During recent decades, departments of Judaica have sprung up throughout the United States, and the Jewish component of civilization is being given a wider and more serious hearing in the several dsciplines of the humanities.

American Jewry, long deficient in the quality of its elementary schools, has developed a major network of diverse types of schools from the Sunday school to the all-day school, and has buttressed the classroom work with a program of Hebrew, Zionist and Jewish summer camping,

JEWISH CENTERS OF STUDY FOR THE SOUL AND FOR THE BODY.
(Top) HEBREW UNION COLLEGE, CINCINNATI.
(Center) MOUNT SINAI HOSPITAL, NEW YORK.
(Bottom left) JEWISH THEOLOGICAL SEMINARY, NEW YORK.
(Bottom right) YESHIVA UNIVERSITY, NEW YORK.

publication, supervision and teacher training. At the present writing, the community is turning its attention to secondary education.

Jewish education is entering a new phase that is, to a great extent, bound up with a struggle taking place within American Christianity. With the advance of American democracy, the Christian community, particularly the Protestant segment, finds itself in the peculiar position of having to redefine the meaning of Christianity in a modern society. By having created a society in which church and state are separated, Christian sects have found that their social strength and unity have dissipated and that they have been unable to restore the Christian community around the traditional beliefs and dogmas. Moreover, with the inroads of modern intellectualism, naturalism and internationalism, all of which have found fertile soil in American democracy, the Christian churches are handicapped in the transmission of their traditions. From this have stemmed the recent efforts to restore the study and practice of religion into the public school curriculum, the demands for federal support for church-sponsored schools and the various schemes for the teaching of moral and spiritual values in schools.

The Jewish community is alert to the posibility that some form of common-core Christianity may be sought and achieved in the American public schools, or that the growing strength of Catholic parochial education may force a similar development upon the Protestants. Many Jews themselves are no less eager that their own children shall have the opportunity to learn their Jewish heritage in the same way. The great American tradition of the common school is today threatened. The outcome of the struggle is bound to have far-reaching consequences for the role of American Jewry in American society.

The future of American Jewry depends on the way in which it handles many current problems. It must learn how to reckon with the voluntarism of American society, it must decide on the form of its organization within the democratic society of the United States, it must clarify its relationship to Israel and the Jewish communities of the rest of the world. American Jews must decide how to maintain the continuity of their theological and ritual tradition and, at the same time, enhance it by the application of their own experience so that the moral thrust of the Prophets may be employed to project American Jewry into the endless struggle for human improvement, and that their prophetic religion may be nourished by Jewish education and by the synagogue.

These problems and others have been studied by the various branches of Jewry, in more or less comprehensive fashion. While it is unlikely that one group has all the answers there is reason to hope that creative responses will be forthcoming from the impact of the various movements of thoughtful Jews one on another.

Thus, the panorama of American Jewry discloses a people once again revealing its adjustability and its capacity for metamorphosis The religious-cultural status of the Jews in America is a dynamic one, fully capable of being adjusted to further changes in the environment, as long as the environment itself continues to be a free one. There is no reason to doubt that in the foreseeable future the American principle of freedom will be preserved and that Jews will contribute to it and benefit from it. The future of American Jewry lies, therefore, essentially in its own hands.

THE ILLUSTRATED HISTORY OF THE JEWS

TWO WORLD WARS

THE REFUGEE SHIP "ELIAHU GOLOMB" DOCKED IN HAIFA HARBOR, 1947.

TWO WORLD WARS

The First World War claimed a heavy toll of Jewish lives, particularly in eastern Europe. More than half a million Jews died as war casualties or as the result of pogroms and epidemics during the war. In 1919 three and a half million Jews were living in Russia, slightly more than three million in Poland, almost one million in Rumania, half a million in Hungary, 350,000 in Czechoslovakia and 700,000 altogether in Germany and Austria. The countries of western continental Europe had a Jewish population of 300,000, Great Britain and the Empire a total of 350,000, Latin America 150,000 and the United States three

and a half million. The center of Jewry, numerically, culturally and spiritually, remained where it had been for generations, in eastern Europe.

The end of the war produced a number of changes which seemed to promise a new era for the Jews. In Russia, the Communist Revolution brought political emancipation and economic upheaval. To the Jews of Poland, Rumania, Hungary, Lithuania and Latvia, the "National Minority Rights", embodied in the peace treaty of 1919 that followed World War I, brought assurances of legally buttressed cultural and religious rights. To the Jewish people everywhere, the Balfour Declaration, issued by Britain on November 2, 1917, brought a burst of hope that Theodor Herzl's Zionist vision was now moving towards fulfilment.

It did not take long before the Jewish people became disillusioned with the Russian Revolution, the Minority Rights Treaties and the Balfour Declaration.

The overthrow of the old regime in Russia had put an end to the Pale, the area to which Jews were restricted, and the Soviet authorities ruled anti-Semitism a crime. However, hatred for the Jews continued to pervade the minds and hearts of many people in all strata of society. Embers of the Czarist past were fanned by widespread envy of the comparative wealth of the Jews and again by the publicity surrounding Stalin's purge of his rivals, some of whom were Jews. In the Ukraine, there were open pogroms.

The Revolution resulted in a far-reaching vocational redistribution of the Jewish population, that shifted the bulk of Jews from the lower middle class of petty merchants, craftsmen and white collar workers, into the working proletariat, with all the attendant hardships. The anti-religious policies adopted by the Communist Party affected the Jews more than any other religious

TRADITIONAL JEWISH LIFE CONTINUES—A "HEDER" IN POLAND.

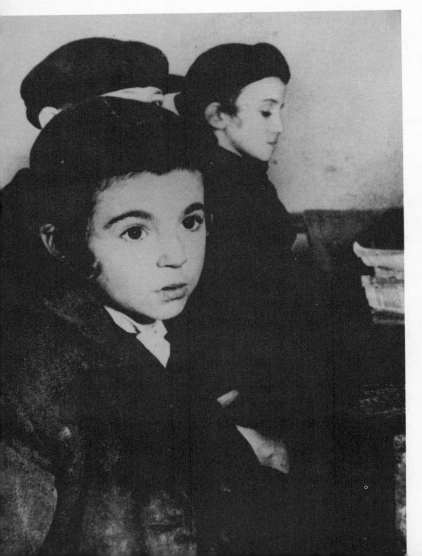

group because of the vigilance and zeal of the Yevseksia, the Jewish section of the party. Jewish religious observances were frowned upon, and public instruction in Hebrew was banned. At first Yiddish was tolerated and for a time even encouraged as part of the general policy of encouraging culture that was Communist in content, national in form. For a number of years there were Yiddish schools, newspapers and theatres, and authors were allowed to express themselves in Yiddish, but later the language fell from official grace.

Nevertheless the Soviet regime did make efforts to solve the problem of the Jewish population. With the help of the American Joint Distribution Committee, it encouraged the establishment of Jewish agricultural settlements in the Crimea. In 1926 it declared an autonomous Jewish republic in Biro-Bidjan, in Siberia, motivated by a number of reasons—to provide the Jews and their culture with a territorial base similar to that of the other ethnic minorities, to set up a buffer state bordering on Manchuria, and to offset the impact of the Balfour Declaration. However, the Jews preferred to remain in the cities, and the response to Biro-Bidjan was meager. Eventually, Zionism was banned and Jewish communal life was made virtually impossible. Russian Jewry, which had been a spiritual and cultural fountainhead for generations, began to decline. What had been the largest and most important of Jewish communities was now virtually cut off from the rest of the Jewish people.

The high hopes aroused elsewhere in eastern Europe by the Minority Rights clauses in the peace treaties were also soon dashed. Although these guarantees had been endorsed by the League of Nations, it became apparent that they were worthless in practice. The upsurge of wild nationalism in these countries was accompanied by deteriorating economic conditions to which the predominantly urban Jews were particularly vulnerable. They were envied by their non-Jewish neighbors, whose deeply rooted anti-Semitism was

EARLY PIONEERS IN AGRICULTURE:

(Above)
BETH ALPHA, A KIBBUTZ IN THE JEZREEL VALLEY, IN 1926.

(Center, left to right)
A. D. GORDON, A VISIONARY WHO PREACHED ON THE SANCTITY OF LABOR AND OF THE AGRICULTURAL LIFE, AND INSPIRED THE EARLY HALUTZIM.

GUARDING THE NEWLY FOUNDED KIBBUTZ AT EIN HAROD, A MOUNTED MEMBER OF HASHOMER, THE DEFENSE ORGANIZATION OF THE YISHUV THAT PRECEDED THE HAGANAH.

HALUTZIM AT WORK IN A QUARRY.

(Below, left to right)
THE TENTED BEGINNINGS OF KIBBUTZ TEL YOSEF AT THE FOOT OF MOUNT GILBOA.

FARMERS AT MIGDAL. A VILLAGE NEAR THE SEA OF GALILEE.

NAHALAL, THE FIRST MOSHAV, WHICH WAS PREPLANNED ON IDEALISTIC LINES.

IN DEGANIA, THE FIRST KIBBUTZ, FOUNDED IN 1909.

fomented by demagogues for whom the Jews were useful scapegoats.

The two relieving factors in this situation were the massive economic relief that was extended by American Jewry and the rising star of Zion, as seen in the growth of Jewish settlement in Palestine.

The largest east European Jewish community outside of Russia was in Poland. When that country was re-established as an independent state by the Versailles Peace Conference, more than three million Jews lived within its borders, making it one of the three largest Jewish communities in the world. Despite the legal guarantees, the Jewish population was soon faced with resurgent Polish nationalism. As Polish armies advanced and retreated in the face of the hostile

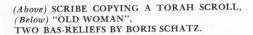

(*Above*) SCRIBE COPYING A TORAH SCROLL,
(*Below*) "OLD WOMAN",
TWO BAS-RELIEFS BY BORIS SCHATZ.

Russians, tens of thousands of Jews were killed. Economic failure led to the dismissal of many Jews from their posts, their exclusion from certain occupations and the boycotting of their businesses. Jewish students were compelled to occupy separate benches at the universities and the number of Jews allowed into any course was limited.

Many sought and found consolation in their religion; others turned to Zionism. A third group, the Bundists, clung to the principle of linking their future to that of the country in which they lived. It proved to be an ill-founded hope.

The situation in Poland was distressingly paralleled in Rumania, Hungary, Lithuania and Latvia, which between them had nearly two million Jews. Jewish communities were physically terrorized, economically impoverished and legally disfranchised. After Hitler's rise to power, anti-Semites throughout eastern Europe redoubled their efforts. When the Nazis finally overran these countries during the second World War, they found

JAFFA, PRINCIPAL PORT OF PALESTINE UNDER THE
TURKS, ARRIVAL POINT FOR THE EARLY WAVES OF
HALUTZIM.

MOUNT SCOPUS, THE ORIGINAL SITE OF THE HEBREW
UNIVERSITY, IS SEEN ON THE SKYLINE, OVERLOOKING
THE OLD CITY OF JERUSALEM (FOREGROUND).

THE CITADEL OF ACRE IN WHICH MEMBERS OF THE
UNDERGROUND WERE IMPRISONED BY THE BRITISH.
HERE TOO THE DEATH SENTENCES WERE CARRIED
OUT.

THE HOME OF THE JEWISH AGENCY, THE KEREN HAYE-
SOD AND THE JEWISH NATIONAL FUND, IN JERUSALEM.

that the soil had been well-prepared for their barbaric anti-Jewish measures.

The most disastrous changes in Jewish life between the wars, took place in Germany. The Versailles Peace Treaty, which had left Germany defeated, frustrated and embittered, provided the ground for Hitler's astounding rise to power. His own fanatical hatred of Jews, coupled with a demonic conviction of the value of the Jew as a scapegoat, was a major weapon in rallying the German people to his banner of National Socialism. It also helped him to infiltrate other countries where anti-Semitism was strong. Western political leaders did not realize until it was too late that Hitler's anti-Semitism was part of his design for world conquest. Had they seen the implications, Hitler could have been stopped at an early

stage, when he made his first declaration of war against the Jewish people.

The rapid rise of Hitler and Nazism came as a shock to the Jews of Germany, who had been the most assimilated of all Jewish communities. For two generations Jews had played an important part in science, culture, art and other professions, a part symbolized by such names as Albert Einstein, Martin Buber, Hermann Cohen and Max Reinhardt. In 1931, as Hitler was gaining power, the majority of German Jews refused to believe that he could succeed. With the support of industry, the lower middle-class and the army, Hitler dissolved all political parties other than his own and also the labor organizations. In 1933 he had decrees promulgated excluding Jews from civil, political and economic positions. Two years later, in 1935, the Nuremberg race laws were adopted, depriving Jews of their German citizen-

"THE LONGING FOR ZION," A DRAWING BY LILIEN.

TEL AVIV—A CITY GROWS IN THE SAND:
1) THE BEGINNING, 1909.
2) HERZL STREET, 1924.
3) THE HERZLIYA HIGH SCHOOL.

ship and confiscating Jewish property.

These laws were the signal for more violent anti-Semitic acts. A number of leading Jews were rounded up, maltreated and imprisoned in concentration camps. The burning of Jewish books became common-place as Nazi Germany embarked on a world-wide campaign of anti-Semitism.

In March 1938, Hitler annexed Austria and applied the Nuremberg laws to the 200,000 Jews of Austria. The occupation of Czechoslovakia in October brought a further 300,000 Jews under his control. On November 10 of the same year, following the assassination by a Jewish youth of a minor Nazi official in Paris, the mobs were turned loose for a day of officially encouraged anti-Jewish rioting. They set fire to nearly every synagogue in Germany and Austria. Tens of thousands of Jews were beaten, arrested and sent to concentration camps. A collective fine of one billion Reichsmark was levied on the Jewish community.

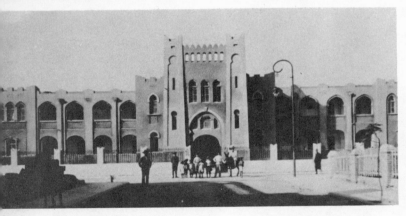

In the face of these horrors, Jewish refugees fled to every possible country. Many, however, had nowhere to go as the civilized world had placed limits on the number of refugees it would accept. At the very time when the gates of the Jewish National Home should have been wide open, the British Mandatory government was yielding to Arab pressure and tightening restrictions. Between 1933 and 1939 only just over 100,000 refugees were able to reach Palestine, and many of these had to enter illegally. In the same period 175,000 were admitted to the United States, 75,000 to Great Britain and smaller numbers to other countries.

KINGSWAY, THE MAIN THOROUGHFARE IN DOWNTOWN HAIFA, IN 1939.

The Jewish communities of the host nations helped the refugees to adjust themselves to their new environment and at the same time contributed funds which enabled others to be settled in Palestine and elsewhere. Jewish communities also joined in protests against the Nazi outrages, but to no avail. One of the most active bodies in this work was the World Jewish Congress which had been founded in Geneva in 1936 under the joint leadership of Dr. Stephen Wise and Dr. Nahum Goldmann for the purpose of defending Jewish rights. The Congress tried to promote an anti-Nazi boycott, and to press Britain to ease immigration restrictions in Palestine, a task complicated by strong Arab counter-pressure.

After issuing the Balfour Declaration, the British government had bowed to Arab opposition. By the time the League of Nations confirmed

Great Britain as the Mandatory power in Palestine in 1922, Britain was already acting on the basis of an attenuated interpretation of the Balfour Declaration. The Colonial Secretary, Winston Churchill, ruled that economic absorptive capacity was to be the guiding criterion for immigration. The entire area east of the Jordan was severed from Palestine. The high hopes aroused in 1920 by the appointment of Sir Herbert Samuel, a distinguished British Jew, as Palestine's first High Commissioner, quickly faded. The ensuing years were punctuated by a succession of restrictions on Jewish rights to immigration and to purchasing land. Jewish public opinion around the world was outraged, and the Jewish community in Palestine refused to accept these measures

INAUGURATION OF THE HEBREW UNIVERSITY, 1925.

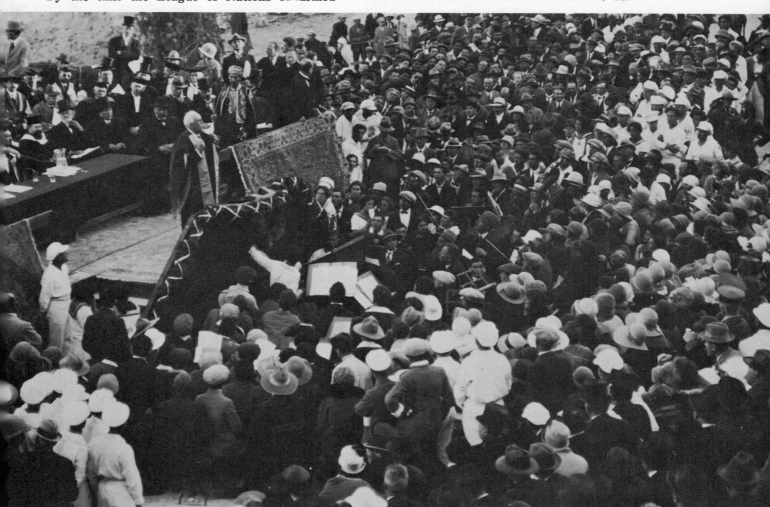

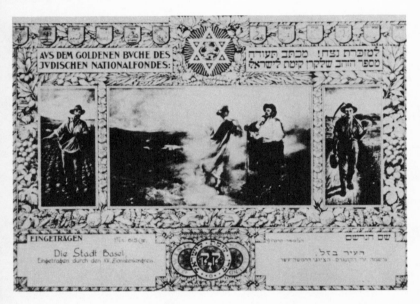

AT THE FIFTEENTH ZIONIST CONGRESS, BASLE, 1927.
(Top) DR. CHAIM WEIZMANN SPEAKING AT A CEREMONY
TO MARK THE THIRTIETH ANNIVERSARY OF THE
FIRST CONGRESS.
(Bottom) THE CITY OF BASLE IS INSCRIBED IN THE
GOLDEN BOOK OF THE JEWISH NATIONAL FUND.

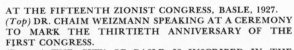

but the Mandatory government used every Arab
riot as a pretext for new restrictions.

From the beginning of the Mandate, the Jewish
community in Palestine, the "Yishuv", had realized the vital importance of organization and
communal discipline. Although Palestine had
only 52,000 Jews in 1919 — nine per cent of the
total population — they soon organized themselves under a National Council (Vaad Leumi),
which was the executive arm of an elected Assembly. Over the objections of the orthodox religious

elements, women were given the right to vote. In 1928, the Vaad Leumi was accorded official recognition by the Mandatory government and empowered to deal with matters of health, education, social welfare and religious affairs among the Jews, including the selection of the Chief Rabbi. It also had the right to impose a number of communal taxes including a defense fund to meet Arab attacks.

The Vaad Leumi was the Yishuv's recognized spokesman in relation to the Zionist bodies, to the Mandatory government and to the League of Nations. It led the struggle against the restrictions on immigration and land purchase and was looked upon by the Jewish people as "the Jewish State in the making", serving as an important training ground for Jewish self-government. From 1931 its president was Itzhak Ben Zvi.

One of the Yishuv's most important instruments was the Jewish self-defence force, the Haganah. It was established in 1921 following the Arab attacks in the Galilee in 1919 in which Joseph Trumpeldor was killed. In 1920, Arab attacks occurred in Jerusalem. In 1921, there were Arab attacks all over the country, in which 47 Jews were killed and many wounded. Casualties would have been higher had it not been for Jewish self-defense, particularly in the smaller settlements. The Haganah was developed to put the defense on a wider basis and in the course of time it was given semi-official status. The British forbade Jews to have arms except in isolated settlements, where they had to be kept in sealed stores for use in emergencies. These prohibitions were not implemented once the Arab attacks became more frequent and widespread. The year 1928-29 was a year of riots in which 132 Jews were killed and 318 wounded. Arab casualties were 116 dead

BADGES OF SEVERAL ZIONIST CONGRESSES.

and 232 wounded. The three years of Arab disturbances from 1936 to 1939 were better planned and executed. They reached their peak in 1937, when the British Government announced its proposal to partition the country into a Jewish and an Arab State. The Arabs conducted a campaign of murder, and derailed trains and punctured pipelines. To help meet this wave of violence the British brought in 20,000 troops. In this three year period there were nearly 6,000 casualties in the country. Jewish dead amounted to 450, with 2,000 wounded; 2,200 Arabs were killed and 1,500 wounded. The British suffered 140 killed.

There was world-wide admiration for the Yishuv's valor in standing up to these attacks. Thanks to Haganah training, the Jewish settlers were able to defend themselves and not one Jewish village or settlement was abandoned.

Meanwhile a split developed in the Jewish defense structure. The Haganah, obeying the instructions of the Vaad Leumi, limited itself to pure defense, and refrained from retaliatory measures. This policy was rejected by the Revisionist movement which set up, under the leader-

(*Above*) DEMONSTRATION AGAINST THE WHITE PAPER.
(*Below*) THE BRITISH WHITE PAPER OF 1939 WHICH FORBADE JEWISH IMMIGRATION AND JEWISH LAND PURCHASE IN PALESTINE.

PALESTINE
Statement of Policy

*Presented by the Secretary of State for the Colonies to Parliament
by Command of His Majesty
May, 1939*

LONDON
PRINTED AND PUBLISHED BY HIS MAJESTY'S STATIONERY OFFICE
To be purchased directly from H.M. STATIONERY OFFICE at the following addresses:
York House, Kingsway, London, W.C.2; 120 George Street, Edinburgh 2;
26 York Street, Manchester 1; 1 St. Andrew's Crescent, Cardiff;
80 Chichester Street, Belfast;
or through any bookseller
1939
Price 2d. net

Cmd. 6019

ship of Ze'ev Jabotinsky, the Irgun Zevai Leumi (National Military Organization) to follow a more aggressive policy.

This may have been one of the reasons that prompted the Mandatory government to accord recognition to the Haganah. Colonel Orde Wingate, one of the most experienced guerrilla fighters in the British Army, was allowed to train the Jews in new defense tactics. The Haganah, which began as an unpaid body, gradually developed a highly professional core. It cooperated with the Jewish Agency in its program of immigration and settlement in dangerous parts of the country. 55 new agricultural settlements were established in the dangerous and difficult years of 1936-39.

The Vaad Leumi represented the internal autonomy of the Yishuv, but the World Zionist Organization, which represented the Jewish people in the implementation of the Balfour Declaration, was recognized as the main political instrument in negotiations by the Mandatory government. Its leadership was composed of representatives of the Yishuv and of European and American Jewry. The World Zionist Organization served as the "Jewish Agency" referred to in the Mandate, which was to be representative of World Jewry, and to be recognized as a "public body for the purpose of advising and cooperating with the Administration of Palestine in such economic, social and other matters as may affect the establishment of the Jewish National Home."

The principal fund raising arm of the Zionist

Organization was the Palestine Foundation Fund (Keren Hayesod), which was established in 1921, after a sharp difference of opinion between the supporters of the American Zionist leader, Justice Louis D. Brandeis, and those led by the President of the World Zionist Organization, Dr. Chaim Weizmann. The Brandeis group believed that the Jewish National Home should be built up mainly by investments, while the followers of Dr. Weizmann emphasized the importance of contributions from the masses of the Jewish people. The latter view prevailed, and Keren Hayesod campaigns

BOOK ON JEWISH ART PUBLISHED IN YIDDISH IN THE SOVIET UNION.

"BLACK LEAVES", A VOLUME OF POEMS ON JEWISH
THEMES IN GERMAN, BY SALAMON DEMBITZER. THE
ILLUSTRATION IS BY LILIEN.

CHAIM NACHMAN BIALIK, THE GREAT HEBREW POET WHOSE WORK BRIDGED THE DIASPORA AND THE RETURN TO ZION.

were started in many countries, to provide the money for the practical program of the Jewish Agency. At the same time the Jewish National Fund, which had been established in 1901, continued with its popular, and by then already traditional, smaller-scale collections for the purpose of redeeming and rehabilitating land in Palestine to become the inalienable property of the Jewish people as a whole.

In 1939, Dr. Weizmann, with the help of Louis Marshall, a non-Zionist leader of American Jewry, succeeded in establishing an enlarged Jewish Agency. This included eminent personalities such as Felix Warburg in the United States and Leon Blum in France. When on several occasions political crises that violated the letter and spirit of the Balfour Declaration threatened the development of the Jewish National Home, it was the Zionist Organization and the enlarged Jewish Agency which mobilized the support of World Jewry and such other peoples and governments as it was possible to influence. This was the case with the British White Papers of 1929 and 1939, which would have prevented the Jews from ever becoming more than a minority in the "Jewish National Home".

Zionist Congresses provided the opportunity to review the past and to formulate policies for the future. One of the most important of these was the Zurich Congress of August 1937, which for the first time dealt with the possibility of a partition of Palestine. In the previous year, at a time of Arab riots, the British Government had sent a Royal Commission to Palestine, headed by Lord Peel that had stated that the Arab-Jewish conflict being irreconcilable and the Palestine Mandate unworkable, the recommended solution would be the partition of Palestine into separate Arab and Jewish States. Both the Jews and the Arabs were asked to consider the report.

On the Jewish side, this issue was sharply debated at the Zurich Congress. Those in favor of partition were led by Dr. Weizmann, the President of the Zionist Executive. The opposition was led by M. M. Ussischkin, Chairman of the Zionist Governing Council of the Jewish National Fund. By a narrow majority the Congress authorized Dr. Weizmann to begin negotiations with the

RABBI ABRAHAM YITZHAK HACOHEN KOOK, CHIEF RABBI OF ERETZ ISRAEL AND ONE OF THE GREATEST RELIGIOUS MINDS IN RECENT GENERATIONS.

MOSHE SHERTOK (SHARETT) ADDRESSING SOLDIERS OF THE JEWISH BRIGADE IN EGYPT, 1944.

British government, in order to ascertain the precise terms of its proposal for a Jewish State. This was the first time the Zionist Organization had received a specific offer of a Jewish State, but that offer came to naught when the Arabs demanded a complete stoppage of Jewish immigration.

In 1939 the Mandatory regime yielded to the Arabs and announced that after the permitted immigration of 75,000 Jews within the next five years, the gates of Palestine would be closed to additional Jewish settlers. Just twenty years after the end of the First World War, the Balfour Declaration appeared to have become valueless. Despite this, on August 29, 1939, less than a week before the outbreak of the Second World War, Dr. Weizmann sent a letter to Prime Minister Chamberlain in which he said: "The Jews stand by Great Britain and will fight on the side of the democracies."

In those two decades, in spite of all the difficulties, the Yishuv had made striking progress. In the decade from 1920 to 1930, the Jewish popu- lation had grown from just over 50,000 to 175,000. Most of the newcomers were from eastern Europe, principally Poland, where Jewish life was becom- ing increasingly difficult. Many of these immi- grants were pioneers, "halutzim", dedicated to a life on the soil. In the next decade the main source of immigration changed to central Europe, where the impact of Nazism was growing. From Hitler's rise to power in 1933 until the outbreak of the Second World War in 1939, more than 100,- 000 Jews arrived in Palestine. Many had to come into the country illegally, to circumvent the re- strictions imposed by the Mandatory authorities. This operation, "Aliya Bet", was an epic of Jew- ish heroism, in which the refugees shared the great risks with those who organized their im- migration and with those who took them off the ships when they reached the shores of Palestine.

By 1939, the Jewish population of Palestine totaled 550,000 and formed more than one third of the country's population. This growth of the Yishuv was reflected not only in the cities, Tel Aviv, Jerusalem and Haifa, but also in the rural areas, which largely consisted of Kibbutzim (col- lective farms) and Moshavim (cooperative villages of individual family units). It had been part of the Zionist plan that the Jewish National Home should normalize the occupational structure of the Jews by settling a substantial portion in agriculture. In 1939 farming accounted for almost a quarter of the Jewish population. Compared with 45 agricultural villages in 1919, there were now more than 250.

The General Federation of Jewish Labor, the "Histadrut", played a dominant part in the life of the Yishuv. Its network of institutions and services ranged from labor unions to the Workers' Sick Fund, "Kupat Holim", with a chain of hospitals and clinics. The pioneer in the field of health had been Hadassah, the medical organization run by the Women's Zionist Organization of America,

· THE FORMER BRITISH HEADQUARTERS IN THE KING DAVID HOTEL IN JERUSALEM AFTER IT WAS BLOWN UP BY THE IRGUN ZEVAI LEUMI IN 1946.

which was founded in 1912 by Henrietta Szold.

In 1925 the Hebrew University was founded in Jerusalem. By 1929 Hebrew language and culture were widespread, and Chaim Nachman Bialik was the outstanding literary figure. Indigenous music and art were developing at the same time. The Habimah and the Ohel theatres first performed in 1928, and the Palestine Symphony Orchestra gave its inaugural concert in 1936. The stimulus of this renaissance of the Hebrew language and culture was felt by Jewish communities in all parts of the world.

In the period between the wars a special responsibility rested on British Jewry, which valiantly stood its ground in resisting the British Government's attempts to evade the obligations imposed upon it by the Palestine Mandate. British Jews also bore their responsibilities well in welcoming and integrating the refugees from Nazi persecution. Theirs was a well-organized community with the Board of Deputies of British Jews as its representative spokesman. In their religious life, orthodoxy was dominant, synagogue affiliation was the rule, and Jewish education for the children was taken for granted. Anti-Semitism at no time presented a serious threat in Britain and the fascist leader and admirer of Hitler, Sir Oswald Mosley, found but meager support. Jews played an important part in British political life as members of Parliament and in high government posts. Rufus Isaacs, later Lord Reading, an English Jew, was successively Viceroy of India, Ambassador to the United States and Lord Chief Justice. The outstanding Jewish man of letters was Israel Zangwill and Dr. Chaim Weizmann's achievements in chemistry and his contribution to the British war effort in the First World War had helped to win him the government's ear for the Jewish people's claim to Palestine.

Jewish communities in the British Dominions, in Canada, South Africa, Australia and New Zealand, patterned their communal organizations and institutions on those of British Jewry. As in the mother country, Jews in the Dominions rose to high positions in economic and political life, and their communities took in and absorbed substantial numbers of refugees from Europe.

In western Europe before World War II, there was a growing trend toward assimilation and intermarriage, though the pattern varied from country to country. Thus in Holland and Belgium, there were solid nuclei of Orthodox Judaism which were strengthened by immigration from eastern Europe. In most west European countries Jews enjoyed economic prosperity and held important positions in cultural and intellectual life. Occasionally they even managed to rise to the highest political posts, as was the case with Leon Blum, who became Prime Minister of France in 1936.

During the same period Latin American Jewry was beginning to come of age, to find a secure economic footing and to join the mainstream of world Jewry. The largest and most active communities were in Argentina and in Mexico. Latin American Jewry consisted largely of immigrants from eastern Europe, although some of its constituents had come from the Near East; Yiddish was widely used, and Zionism was a strong force. In contrast to the Jews of Britain or North America, the Latin American communities tended to be secular in tone, interests and affiliations. During the Nazi period these communities absorbed many refugees.

It was in the period between the two World Wars that the Jewish community in the United States emerged as the unquestioned leader of Diaspora Jewry. This was due not only to its numerical and economic strength, but also the

(Top) IMMIGRANTS ARRIVE FROM YEMEN IN 1943. *(Bottom)* BRITISH SOLDIERS FORCIBLY REMOVE REFUGEES FROM THEIR SHIP AND EXPEL THEM TO CAMPS IN CYPRUS.

growing influence of the United States in world affairs.

Between 1919 and 1939 American Jewry grew from 3,500,000 to 4,500,000. It collected and spent large sums of money for the relief and reconstruction of Jewish life in Europe, the upbuilding of the Jewish National Home in Palestine and for the furtherance of American Jewish institutions. In the decade ending in 1929 the unprecedented sum of one billion dollars was raised for these purposes. Zionism flourished, and American Jews began to play an important part at World Zionist Congresses.

By 1939 the 4,500,000 Jews living in the United States (nearly half of them in Greater New York) not only represented the largest Jewish commu-

nity ever gathered in one country in the Diaspora; they were also a source of strength to the Jewish people everywhere.

Thus the twenty years between the wars witnessed radical changes in the distribution of the Jewish population. The center of Jewry shifted, and the Yishuv in Palestine became more and more important as it approached statehood.

Of the 18 million Jews in the world in 1939, nearly one half were still living in eastern Europe. Of these one third, in Russia, was virtually cut off from the rest of the Jewish world. The remainder were in precarious economic and political straits. The Nazis forced hundreds of thousands of central European Jews to find new homes in Palestine, the United States and elsewhere. It was a testing time for the Western democracies, but they failed to rise to the occasion, by vigorous, meaningful protest against Nazism or by opening their doors wide to its victims.

During these years the Jewry of the United States found itself called upon to become the

REFUGEE SHIP "EXODUS" IN HAIFA PORT. ITS BANNER IS ADDRESSED TO THE BRITISH: "THE GERMANS DESTROYED OUR FAMILIES AND HOMES. DON'T YOU DESTROY OUR HOPES."

guardian of the distressed Jews of Europe. Its sense of responsibility grew in proportion to the challenge.

The critical times and the aspirations for the Jewish National Home in Palestine, welded the scattered segments of World Jewry and imbued it with a keener and deeper sense of peoplehood and mutual responsibility, greater than had been felt at any previous period in modern Jewish history.

In Palestine, the developing Jewish community was permeated by a growing sense of national purpose. It was embattled in its resolve to keep the gates of the Jewish National Home open to all and determined in the face of formidable obstacles to fashion a way of Jewish life worthy of its great past, to reclaim the soil and soul of the Jewish people and to foster the renaissance of Hebrew culture.

THE ILLUSTRATED HISTORY OF THE JEWS

THE HOLOCAUST

THE HOLOCAUST

"The Holocaust" is a term denoting chain acts carried out during the period of Nazi regime in Germany. It commonly refers to the murder of about six million Jews in most European countries. It also included theft of property, destruction of synagogues and other public as well as private property, the deliberate fostering of systematic and venomous hatred, exploitation of man's baser instincts and the direction of them against the Jews.

When the total number of Holocaust victims is being tabulated, one should take into account not only those who were killed in the planned and mechanized programmes of mass murder, but also those who died prematurely because of the persecution. Also, many Jews committed suicide out of despair even after they had succeeded in escaping from the countries under Nazi domination.

These events ended one of the most important chapters in the history of our people. Since the time of the Nazi regime, the centre of Jewish life has moved outside of Europe.

The period called the Holocaust began on January 30, 1933, when Adolf Hitler was appointed Chancellor of the German Reich. This event gave control of one of the largest and most developed countries in Europe to a movement favoring extreme anti-Semitism. Farsighted people, particularly among the Jews, quickly perceived that the new government signified a new era for German Jewry, though its significance for Jewry as a whole was not generally understood for a number of years. A knowledge of the far-reaching changes that occurred in Europe in the wake of the First World War is necessary for an understanding of that short but decisive era in Jewish history when the Nazis were in power.

During the period following World War I the anti-Semitic movements spread simultaneously with the achievement of equal rights by Jews in all the countries of Europe. The attempts made from time to time to circumscribe the rights of

(Top) SIGN IN OCCUPIED HOLLAND FORBIDDING JEWS ENTRY TO A PARK.
(Bottom) PLACARD CARRIED BY NAZI PARTY-MEMBER READS: "IN ANSWER TO ATROCITY PROPAGANDA, NO GERMAN WILL BUY FROM THE JEWS IN THE FUTURE."

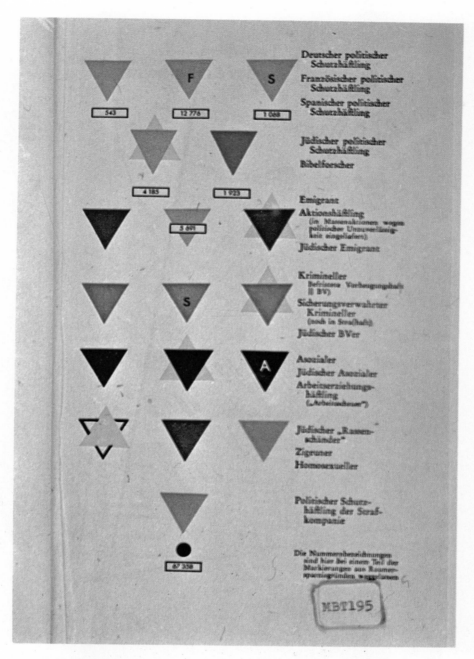

IDENTIFICATION BADGES WORN BY CONCENTRATION CAMP INMATES.

(Row 1, left to right) POLITICAL DETAINEES: GERMAN, FRENCH, SPANISH.

(Row 2, left to right) JEWISH POLITICAL DETAINEE, JEHOVAH'S WITNESS.

(Row 3, left to right) EMIGRANT, POLITICALLY UNRELIABLE, JEWISH EMIGRANT.

(Row 4, left to right) CRIMINAL, CRIMINAL IN PROTECTIVE CUSTODY, POLITICALLY UNRELIABLE JEW.

(Row 5, left to right) ANTI-SOCIAL, ANTI-SOCIAL JEW, WORK-SHY.

(Row 6, left to right) JEWISH "RACE-DEFILER," GYPSY, HOMOSEXUAL.

(Row 7) POLITICAL DETAINEE IN PENAL DETACHMENT.

IN THE OCCUPIED COUNTRIES, AS IN GERMANY ITSELF,
JEWS WERE FORCED TO WEAR YELLOW STARS.

THE GHETTO BAKER'S CART, PRESSED INTO SERVICE AS A HEARSE *(contemporary drawing by a ghetto inmate).*

MEMORIALS IN REMEMBRANCE OF THE VICTIMS OF THE HOLOCAUST.

(Top) "OHEL YIZKOR" MEMORIAL SHRINE OF YAD VA-SHEM ON HAR HAZIKARON, JERUSALEM.

(Bottom) CHAMBER OF THE MARTYRS ON MOUNT ZION, JERUSALEM. THE INSCRIPTIONS PERPETUATE THE NAMES OF DESTROYED COMMUNITIES AND OF THE DEATH CAMPS.

OFFICES OF SHIPPING LINES AND CONSULATES, BE-
SIEGED BY JEWS TRYING TO FLEE TO SAFETY.

Jewish citizens were carried out indirectly, with every effort being made to avoid explicitly mentioning Jews in edicts that were primarily or completely directed against them. The fundamental innovation in the Germany of 1933 was that, for the first time in the modern era, a party came to power that called for the abolition of equal rights. It included this goal in its program and publications, and promised to carry it out when it came to power.

The Jews of Germany had set the pattern for the modern Jew of the West. The great majority of German Jews were divided into two groups: those who considered themselves to be mainly Germans, and Jews only to a limited extent; and those who considered themselves to be Germans and Jews to exactly the same degree. The anti-Semites, on the other hand, considered the Jews a foreign element among the German people.

"None but members of the nation, 'Volksgenossen' may be citizens of the State. None but those of German blood, whatever their creed may be members of the nation. No Jew, therefore may be a member of the nation."

This doctrine was proclaimed by the Nazi party from its very foundation. Its "legal" formulation came only two and a half years after the establishment of the Nazi regime in Germany, with the promulgation of the Nuremberg Laws in September 1935. In these two and a half years various edicts were proclaimed against the German Jews though officially they still remained citizens. The strong reaction in the free press of the Western countries angered the new rulers. The extreme anti-Semites in the party were responsible for the imposition of a comprehensive boycott against Jewish businesses in Germany, which, at the last moment, was limited to a single day. On Saturday, April 1, 1933, Nazi guards were stationed in front of all Jewis-owned businesses; anti-Semitic slogans as well as boycott stickers were put on display windows and on the signs of Jewish businesses and name-plates of Jewish professional men.

The Nazi learned that the Jews could not be easily removed from German society. There were economic considerations (Germany's poor condition during the Depression) as well as political ones (Nazi rule was not firmly established). After the first outbursts, a multitude of "laws," ordinances and regulations intended to conceal discrimination and violence, theft and murder were guide-posts along the path of repression. On April 7, 1933, some days after the boycott, the "Civil Service Restoration Acts" was published. This was the first law which mentioned the term Aryan, and which brought in its wake discrimination against non-Aryans not only in laws, but also in the regulations of all the companies and associations in Germany. This process, which was called Gleichschaltung (unification) was directed against all the declared enemies of the Nazis, without regard for their individual deeds or views, but the Jews were the only ones affected as a group in the first year of the Nazi regime.

The exclusion of the Jews from the economy meant their isolation and later, their emigration. Tens of thousands of Jews fled in the first months of the Nazi regime, and emigration continued slowly. A world that was in the throes of a depression and in which security was lacking, was not prepared to open its gates to refugees from Germany.

The consolidation of the Nazi regime and its domination of all spheres of life allowed for the enforcement of its policies towards the Jews. There came, in the wake of social isolation and legal discrimination, a lower form of civil status specifically for Jews. They were no longer to be citizens, but only nationals: on Sept. 15, 1935, emancipation came to an end in the country where the struggle for equal rights for Jews had begun. Two laws concerning Jews were promulgated that same day in Nuremberg, the Reich Citizenship Law and the Law to Defend German Blood and Honor. This latter law made intimate relations between Jew and non-Jew, whether married or not, a grave crime — "race defilement." On the other hand, the Nuremberg laws involved certain relaxations for the offspring of mixed marriages. "Quarter-Jews," who had previously been considered "non-Aryan," were regarded as equal to Germans if they were not Jewish by religion.

Nazi Germany enjoyed success after success: the government cast off the last restrictions imposed on Germany under the Versailles Treaty; a large and modern army was established; mass unemployment ended; and the country appeared to flourish. But as far as the Jewish problem was concerned, the Nazi regime was unable to achieve the goal that it had set for itself. The pace of emigration did not increase and, therefore, the number of Jews in Germany declined by only some 20 per cent after twenty months of Nazi rule (and this included the excess of deaths over births that was characteristic of German Jewry for several generations). The character of Nazi Germany forced it to an unavoidable conclusion: the repressions must be intensified to the extent necessary to force all Jews to leave Germany. During the year 1938 they were confronted with a flood of new edicts removing them from German economic life and subjecting them to abuse and ridicule. The Jews of Austria felt the effects of the new policy from the very first day that Austria was annexed to Germany (March 13, 1938). The goal of this policy—emigration, —began to appear more and more like expulsion and expropriation. The Jews were forced to steal across closed frontiers and, because of British policies there, had to enter even Palestine illegally. The Jews of Germany itself, needed a rude shock in order to realize the significance of the new policy. The flames that rose up from the synagogues all over Germany on November 10, 1938, made the entire world aware of their abject situation.

Despite the internal dissension that had been characteristic of German Jewry, the policies of discrimination and repression that began in 1933 served to strengthen it from within. A "return to Judaism" and a "proud stand" were not empty slogans for the greater part of the Jewish community. Vocational training and a program of studies prepared the Jews for emigration. The ever-hardening line of policy against the Jews could not accept their internal independence. The institutions created by the Jews

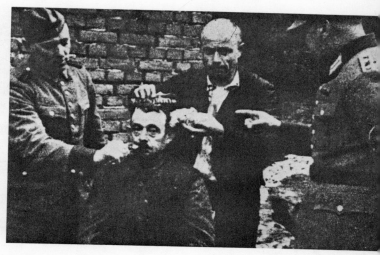

(Top row, left) GERMAN WOMAN WHO HAD BEEN INTI-MATE WITH A JEW IS MARCHED THROUGH THE STREETS CARRYING A SIGN, "I AM THE BIGGEST PIG IN THE PLACE."
(Top row, center) JEW IS FORCED TO WEAR PHYLAC-TERIES AND PRAYER SHAWL FOR THE AMUSEMENT OF GERMAN SOLDIERS.
(Top row, right) JEWS BRANDED WITH THE STAR OF DAVID.
(Bottom row, left) A "ROUND UP" IN THE WARSAW GHETTO.
(Bottom row, right) ONE JEW BEING FORCED TO CUT AN-OTHER'S HAIR. A SCRUBBING BRUSH IS IN HIS HAND.

themselves during that period, as well as the communities that had enjoyed legal status for generations, were both changed beyond recognition after the riots of November 1938. The National Representation of German Jews, which was composed of representatives of the public, was transformed by a law promulgated on July 4, 1939, to the National Association of Jews in Germany. The latter body was imposed upon the Jews from above and was under the control of the infamous Jewish section of the Gestapo and of its head, Adolf Eichmann. This event was an important milestone on the path to the subjugation of the Jews and to transforming them into a kind of chattel to be handled by their rulers as they saw fit, and to be allowed to live or be killed at will.

The outbreak of the World War II brought additional edicts for the Jews of "greater Germany" and severe repressions for those in conquered areas. Not only did the victories and successes of the war fail to alleviate "the Jewish problem," which the Nazi fanatics considered as perhaps the most crucial one facing them, but actually made it more severe. Every additional German conquest automatically increased the number of Jews under Nazi control. Until September 1939 it might have been thought possible to get rid of all the Jews (of Germany, Austria and Czechoslovakia) by a program of forced emigration, under which the Nazis (in their opinion) generously allowed the Jews to leave. Afterwards, however, it was clear that even the methods of forced emigration, developed under the direct supervision of Eichmann, were insufficient. Even before Warsaw had fallen to the Germans, Heydrich, the head of the Reich Security Police and of the SS Security Service, called together a group of SS officers and presented them with his plan for the solution of the Jewish problem. Its major point was that the Jews should first of all

CONCENTRATION CAMP NUMBER BRANDED ON THE ARM OF A BABY.

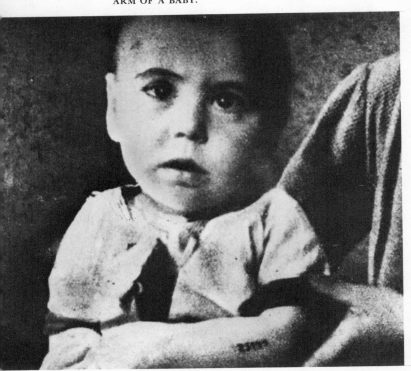

be gathered together in the Polish ghettos and sent afterwards to the "East," to an area that had not yet been defined. While this plan was not carried out in the few weeks or months originally considered necessary, its basic lines guided the policies against the Jews. The existing organizational frameworks of the Jewish communities were destroyed in the conquered regions as well, and replaced by Jewish Councils, the only purpose of which was to serve the authorities. Regulations imposing discrimination, degradation, forced labor and seizure of property rained down upon the Jews one after another and were accompanied by innumerable "unofficial" atrocities. Most Jews were forced to live under conditions that imperiled their existence, and this was just what the Germans wanted. All the "actions" carried out against the Jews — including the mass expulsions from the territories annexed by the Reich to the area of the General Government (Central Poland), and the expulsion from German to Soviet territory—taken together constituted a policy of "indirect extermination," i.e. the masses of Jews were placed in a situation that would cause a maximum death rate, whether by hunger, sickness or torture.

The high point of this policy was the "territorial solution of the Jewish problem," as the Nazis called it. An area in Eastern Poland, initially in the vicinity of the townlet of Nisko and afterwards to include the entire Lublin

OPPOSITE PAGE:

(Top row, left) JEWISH PRISONER BEING SUBJECTED TO SCIENTIFIC EXPERIMENT.
(Top row, center) WORK IN THE QUARRIES.
(Top row, right) PRISONER WHO TRIED TO ESCAPE.
(Center row, left) ROWS OF ELECTRIFIED FENCES SURROUNDING THE CAMPS.
(Center row, right) THE END OF THE LINES—AUSCHWITZ.
(Bottom left) STUDIES IN BESTIALITY — A GROUP OF DEATH CAMP WARDRESSES.
(Bottom right) S.S. GENERAL ALERTED TO STOP THE JEWISH UPRISING IN THE WARSAW GHETTO.

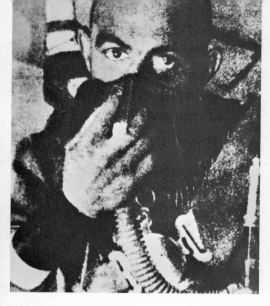

district, was to be set aside as a reservation for the Jews. In October 1939 Jews were deported there from Czechoslovakia and Vienna. In the beginning of 1940 Jews from Stettin and Pomerania were deported to this vicinity. In both cases the deportations were carried out without any preparation and the people were abandoned to their fate. With the fall of France, the Nazis took up the idea of settling the Jews in Madagascar and developed a plan which meant, in fact, the establishment of a giant concentration camp for millions of Jews, who would be subject to the arbitrary rule of a German governor appointed by the SS.

Several factors were apparently responsible for the cancellation of the earlier plans formulated in 1939. One factor was the significant economic activities of the Jews in the conquered Eastern European territories. It was not convenient for the Germans to forego their services. The Jewish public reshaped its character as a community in all spheres of life, and even had to be on a semi-legal or on an underground basis. The Halutz movements continued with their training (Hakhsharah and educational activities) for a number of years. Large numbers of religious Jews continued to fulfill the religious precepts, including those calling for study of the Torah, despite the strict prohibitions imposed upon them. The Jews, organized on an improvised basis, did their utmost to outwit the merciless oppressor and to thwart the verdict calling for their slow but certain death.

The decisive change in European Jewry's fate came with the Nazi invasion of the Soviet Union. The tremendous expansion of German rule over the vast stretches of the Soviet Union, from the Baltic Sea to the Black Sea, added millions of Jews to those masses already under the Nazi yoke, and the "territorial solution" no longer

appeared realistic. In the wake of the conquering armies there came Action Groups (Einzatzgruppen), which were in reality bands of uniformed murderers, set up, first and foremost, to kill, the Jews. In a few months they shot hundreds of thousands of Jews in the conquered areas of the Soviet Union. The time of direct extermination had begun. However, it quickly became clear to the architects of the "final solution" that they would be unable to carry out their plan in this way; there were even complaints from members of the execution squads and from the non-Jewish population. The public became aware of the shootings and the difficulty of burying hundreds of thousands of corpses was also causing problems. All these factors prompted the Nazis to seek a more efficient method of killing Jews than that used by the Einsatzgruppen. They were concerned only with technical and administrative difficulties. The mass murders had become a task to be carried out in a routine manner, and a "clean" way of doing it was found. Mass killings of German mental patients in Germany itself, had been carried out in gas chambers from the very beginning of the war. Pressure from the public and from the ecclesiastical authorities forced the Nazis to greatly reduce the scope of this program, but the experience gained was afterwards used in carrying out the "final solution." After preparations had been completed, mobile gas vans constructed, and the first extermination camp established at Chelmno (December 1941), Heydrich called together the leading officials from the government to officially decide on the means to carry out the great task. He was put in charge of this program by Goering in a letter dated July 31, 1941.

OPPOSITE PAGE:

(Top) JEWISH MOTHER AND CHILD ABOUT TO BE SHOT.
(Bottom) GERMAN SOLDIERS LOOK ON APPROVINGLY AS LITHUANIANS BEAT JEWS TO DEATH WITH IRON BARS.

At this conference (which after the war came to be called the Wannsee Conference, after the street in a Berlin suburb where it was held), the general plan for the extermination of European Jewry was officially presented for the first time. It encompassed eleven million people, including Jews living in countries that were still free. No objections were made except in regard to the offspring of mixed marriages, namely half-Jews and quarter Jews, who had been granted a special status under the Nuremberg laws.

Of course, these things were not definitely known until after the defeat of Nazi Germany. While these events were taking place, people, including even the Jews under Nazi rule, did not believe that the Germans had decided to kill every last Jew they could. Jews trapped in the countries controlled by the Nazis and their satellites therefore continued to hope for at least partial salvation. It was only this feeling, this

refusal to deny any ray of hope even on the threshold of death, which can explain the conduct of most of the Jews. Life continued "normally"—while the Nazis began their "combing-out operation," as they called the gathering of the millions who were sent to slaughter. Transports with about a thousand Jews in each were despatched from all the countries of Nazi-controlled Europe. The Jews were crowded into freight trains or cattle wagons, the conditions in which ensured that some of them would die during the prolonged journey. The last stop for the death train was the "camp," whose major or sole mission was mass murder with poison gas. These camps were established on Polish soil and their names — **Auschwitz-Birkenau, Belzec, Treblinka, Majdanek and Sobibor**—together with the aforementioned **Chelmno,** will forever be remembered in the annals of man's infamy. Even there the murderers still continued to foster illusions among their victims, as they had done previously. The ghettos, work camps and internment camps, in various

PILED BODIES OF THE DEAD.

(Left) SOME OF THE PRIMITIVE WEAPONS IN THE GHETTO FIGHTERS' ARMORY.
(Right) EMERGING FROM A DUG-OUT IN THE WARSAW GHETTO.

countries were gradually emptied; the death factories worked at full speed. Many people, and particularly Jewish youth, resolved to oppose the frequent "actions," as the rounding up of people for the "transports" were called. After much heart-searching, and difficulties within the Jewish sector as well as with the outside world, groups of underground fighters, were organized. There is evidence of dozens of uprisings in the ghettos and in the camps. The most famous of them was the revolt that broke out on the eve of Passover (April 19, 1943) in the Warsaw Ghetto, in which only an eighth of the previous population still remained, after the large-scale "actions" of the summer of 1942. For about a month German army, police and SS units fought the defenders of the Ghetto and did not subdue them until it was burned to the ground. This uprising served as an example and an inspiration for all those fighting a war of despair against the Nazis.

Another type of struggle was carried on by the thousands who succeeded in escaping from the ghettos and camps and reaching the forests, where they set up or joined existing partisan units. Like the soldiers in the regular armies they fought to achieve victory over Nazism everywhere.

There were also fighters who carried out rescue operations and sabotage in the underground, with or without "Aryan papers." Even those thousands of Jews who hid from the enemy with the assistance of Christian friends or acquaintances were well aware that their very existence was part of the struggle against the murderous plans of the Nazis.

The liberation of Europe from the yoke of Nazi Germany, which continued for many months, revealed the whole truth — every place the victors reached they found evidence of the methods of terror and murder by which the Nazis had ruled. Very few Jews were found alive. The survivors, who slowly gathered together after Germany's defeat (mainly in Germany, Austria and Italy), had a single goal before them: to leave Europe, which had become a cemetery for the Jewish people. The great majority of them went to Israel. In the Jewish State they found some measure of consolation for their suffering. In this way the ancient Jewish prayer, "from slavery to redemption," was fulfilled.

(Top) THE BREAD LINE. *(Bottom)* INTIMIDATION
THROUGH A PUBLIC EXECUTION. CONTEMPORARY
SKETCH OF GHETTO LIFE BY INMATES.

THE WAR OF INDEPENDENCE

SHELL-MARKED BUILDING AT KIBBUTZ RAMAT RAHEL
NEAR JERUSALEM.

THE WAR OF INDEPENDENCE

On November 29, 1947, the General Assembly of the United Nations resolved, by a majority of 33 to 13 that Palestine be partitioned into three parts: a Jewish State, an Arab State and an International Zone consisting of Jerusalem and its surroundings. The Jewish community of Palestine was filled with joy at the impending creation of a Jewish State.

The following day Arab bands ambushed a Jewish bus in the vicinity of Lydda Airport, on its way from Nataniah to Jerusalem. There were five dead and seven wounded.

It became clear that resolutions alone could not create a state. It was to take twenty months of bitter fighing to crush the terrorism of the Palestinian Arabs and repel the subsequent invasion by the Arab armies before the State of Israel could be firmly established.

At the outset of the conflict, the Jews faced the Arabs of Palestine who were assisted by volunteers, arms and supplies from across the borders.

(Left) REJOICING IN THE STREETS AS NEWS OF THE UNITED NATIONS DECISION TO SET UP A JEWISH STATE, REACHES PALESTINE.
(Right) WITHIN HOURS OF THE UNITED NATIONS DECISION, ARAB MOBS INTENSIFIED THEIR TERRORIST ATTACKS, FORCING THE JEWS INTO DEFENSIVE POSITIONS.

The Mandatory Government had given notice of its unwillingness to assist in the implementation of the UN partition, and withdrew its armed forces by stages. The gradual withdrawal of these forces enhanced the power of the attackers, and there were many cases of intervention on behalf of the Arabs, at times on local initiative, at times on orders from above. The Arab Legion, commanded by British officers, was stationed in part inside Palestine. While the Mandatory Government continued to prevent the arrival of Jewish immigrants and of all military supplies from abroad, the land borders of the country were wide-open to the flow of Arab volunteers and arms. There were isolated instances of British assistance to the Jews, but the hostile attitude of the British Government to the partition plan, and the conduct of its local representatives, manifested itself in a friendly neutrality toward the Arab aggressor.

In December 1947 when the conflict began, Jewish strength was at low ebb. The total mobilized force of the Haganah consisted of only 4,000 men who belonged mainly to Palmach, a special striking force. They were equipped with

small arms, light machine guns and several dozen mortars. Part of this armament was manufactured by the Haganah and the rest secretly purchased within the country or abroad. There was a serious shortage of ammunition; the Haganah had neither tanks, nor aircraft nor artillery.

The Jewish settlements were concentrated mostly over five zones: along the coast, in the valley of Jezreel, in eastern Galilee, in western Galilee and in the south. The other settlements were distributed singly or in groups, from Hanita in the extreme north to Gvulot, Beit Arava and Gush Etzion in the south. Some military experts advised the Haganah to concentrate its strength in the coastal strip, the center of the Jewish population, thereby abandoning countless settlements and surrendering in advance large areas of the country.

The decision was taken to defend every settlement whether it was within the borders assigned to the Jewish State or not, regardless of all difficulties of supply and communications. The lines of communication between the main centers of the Yishuv, all the roads linking Jerusalem to the areas of Jewish settlement, and all the roads to the Negev and to Galilee, ran through hostile territory. In the five cities with a mixed population, Jerusalem, Haifa, Jaffa-Tel Aviv, Safed and Tiberias, Jewish and Arab quarters were actually intermixed.

The Palestine Arabs did not have organized fighting units at the beginning of the war. The Jews, on the other hand, had volunteered to the British Army in the thousands during World War II, and their training and experience far surpassed that of the Arabs. The leaders of the Arab

(Top) BEN YEHUDA STREET IN CENTRAL JERUSALEM AFTER TWO TRUCKLOADS OF HIGH EXPLOSIVES HAD BEEN DETONATED BY BRITISH SOLDIERS.
(Center) FOOD CONVOY ENTERING JERUSALEM.
(Bottom) "DRAGONS TEETH" (ANTI-TANK OBSTACLES) ARE SET UP IN THE MAIN STREET OF JERUSALEM.

bands who had taken part in the earlier riots returned and organized their separate groups without the benefit of mutual cooperation, and occasionally even in hostile competition.

The Arabs of Palestine outnumbered the Jews, but few of them were trained for modern war. The exceptions were the Transjordan Frontier Force which numbered close to 2,000 and which was disbanded soon after the resolution on par-

(Top) THE LEADER OF THE ARAB TERROR-GANGS, ABD EL KADR HUSSEINI (center bareheaded) WITH HIS STAFF. (Bottom) AN ARAB GANG RETURNING AFTER AN AT-TACK ON A JEWISH SETTLEMENT.

tition, and the Transjordan Arab Legion of ap-proximately 10,000 men, trained and commanded by British officers who were unable to restrain their men from sporadic attacks against the Jew-ish community.

On the first day after the United Nations reso-lution on partition, Arab rioters looted and burned the commercial center in Jerusalem and followed this by sniping and indiscriminate firing on the Jewish areas in Tel Aviv bordering on Arab Jaffa, and in the lower town of Haifa. On Decem-ber 9th, the first Jewish casualty occurred in the Negev. The Haganah proclaimed mobilization and henceforward Jewish vehicles travelled only in guarded convoys. As yet the actions of the Ha-ganah were confined to retaliation against those Arabs who had in some way participated in the attacks. It was hoped in this way to limit the spiralling wave of provocation and retaliation. Later, however, in retaliation for the murder of thirty-nine Jewish workers in the oil refineries of Haifa, the Haganah attacked also two villages which had seved as a base for the killers.

At the end of March a large Jewish convoy, re-turning to Jerusalem from Gush Etzion drove into an ambush. The passengers were released at the intervention of the Red Cross, but their arms and vehicles, which included most of the armoured trucks used on the road from Tel Aviv to Jeru-salem, were handed over to the Arabs. A few days after this event a Jerusalem-bound convoy was attacked in the vicinity of Har Tuv and com-pelled to turn back and a convoy to western Galilee was attacked and wiped out near Yehiam. The road to Jerusalem, the last stretch of which runs between mountains that cannot be by-passed, was closed by the Arabs with mines and road blocks. Jerusalem was cut off from the plains, Gush Etzion from Jerusalem, western Galilee from Haifa, the Negev from the center of the country.

THE POLICE FORTRESS AT NEBI YUSHA, WHOSE CAPTURE BY THE HAGANAH OPENED THE WAY TO THE CONQUEST OF UPPER GALILEE.

The situation of Jerusalem was especially precarious: the fate of one hundred thousand Jewish inhabitants hung in the balance, and with them the political future of the city and possibly that of the future State. The road to Jerusalem had to be reopened at all costs by the occupation of a corridor on either side.

To ensure the success of this operation, codenamed "Nachshon", a force of brigade strength was thrown into the attack, the largest force so far deployed. The troops were equipped with arms which had arrived from Czechoslovakia only the previous night. The road was reopened, and reinforcements reached Jerusalem. The storming of the Castel, which had dominated the last stretch of the road to Jerusalem, marked a turning point in the struggle for the city.

In those first days of April, the "Arab Liberation Army", composed largely of Syrian and Iraqui volunteers under the command of Fauzi el Kaukji, launched an attack against Mishmar Haemek. Its fall would have endangered the val-

SURRENDER AGREEMENT SIGNED BY THE ARAB LEADERS IN JAFFA (Left) AND NAZARETH (Right).

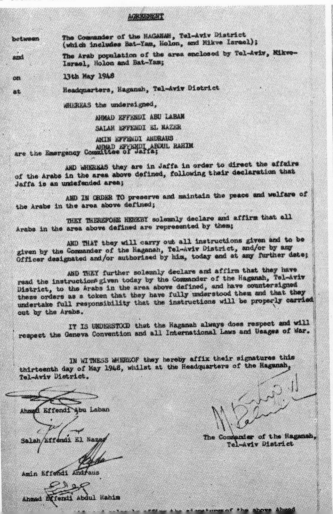

SOLDIERS PRAYING IN A BUNKER.

ley of Jezreel and all communications between Tel Aviv and Haifa. After three days of battle the Arabs were forced to retreat.

The Haganah assumed the initiative from that day forward. Retaliatory actions against Arab aggressors or the destruction of their bases were no longer sufficient. The aim of the Haganah now was control of all areas allotted to the Jewish State and territorial continuity with all settlements beyond those limits.

On April 18th, the Arabs abandoned their quarters in Tiberias, and a few days later the Arabs of Haifa were defeated and most of them left the city. At the beginning of May the Arab districts of Safad were captured by a daring attack of the

Palmach, and western Galilee was wholly cleared of Arab forces. By May 14th, when the Mandate came to an end, the Jews, though still inadequately armed, had succeeded in crushing the military force of the local Arabs and of the foreign volunteers who had come to their aid.

At this point the governments of the neighboring Arab states, realizing that without their active support the Palestine Arabs would be defeated, decided to intervene with their armies and their air forces. The invasion began the day after Israel declared its Independence and initiated the decisive phase of the struggle.

The Arab plan had basic simplicity. The Egyptians were to advance upon Tel Aviv from the south by way of the Negev and simultaneously dispatch a force toward Jerusalem. The Arab Legion would at the same time concentrate its main attacks against Jerusalem and the center of the country. The Syrians would enter from the northeast, reinforced by Iraqi troops, while the Lebanese army would march south into Galilee. By the reckoning of British and Arab commanders, the Jews, smaller in size and armed with inferior military equipment were expected to surrender within a fortnight. But the Arab invaders

(Left to right) ALUF (GENERAL) YITZHAK SADEH, THE OUTSTANDING PRE-STATE MILITARY LEADER.
GENERAL YAAKOV DORI, FIRST CHIEF OF STAFF OF THE ISRAEL DEFENSE FORCES.
GENERAL DAVID MARCUS, FORMER COLONEL IN THE U.S. ARMED FORCES WHO WAS KILLED IN COMBAT WHILE SERVING AS A VOLUNTEER FIGHTER FOR ISRAEL.
GENERAL YIGAEL YADIN, CHIEF OF OPERATIONS DURING THE WAR OF INDEPENDENCE AND LATER CHIEF OF STAFF.

THE ROAD TO JERUSALEM. AT THE SIDE LIES THE
BURNT OUT WRECKAGE OF JEWISH VEHICLES AM-
BUSHED BY THE ARABS.

JERUSALEM UNDER BOMBARDMENT.

THE WALLED CITY OF OLD JERUSALEM SEEN FROM
JEWISH HELD NEW JERUSALEM WITH THE MINED
AREA OF NO-MANS-LAND IN BETWEEN.

THE MONASTERY AT LATRUN (BACKGROUND, RIGHT)
AROUND WHICH BITTER FIGHTING RANGED IN AT-
TEMPTS TO OPEN THE ROAD TO JERUSALEM.

THE SUMMIT OF MOUNT CASTEL FROM WHICH THE
ARABS CONTROLLED THE APPROACHES TO JERUSALEM
TILL ITS CAPTURE BY THE HAGANAH.

SAFED.

NAZARETH

RIDDLED BY SHELL AND MORTAR FIRE, THE WATER
TOWER BEARS MUTE WITNESS TO THE PROLONGED
SIEGE SUFFERED BY KIBBUTZ NEGBAH IN THE NEGEV.

THE POLICE FORTRESS AT IRAQ SWEIDAN, THE MAIN
STRONGPOINT OF A POCKET IN WHICH A LARGE
EGYPTIAN FORCE WAS ENCIRCLED.

A SYRIAN TANK DESTROYED BY THE JEWISH DEFEND-
ERS OF KIBBUTZ DEGANIAH.

A MEMORIAL TO THE ISRAELI SOLDIERS WHO FELL DE-
FENDING KIBUTZ NEGBA.

WAR CEMETERY IN JERUSALEM.

could not achieve their objectives. Their leadership was disorganized, their troops imperfectly trained and devoid of fighting spirit and they were confronted by an aggressive, even desperate opponent who, though poorly equipped, was well led and prepared for any effort. As the war continued, the Jews received increasing supplies of arms and ammunition. Part of the equipment had been readied in Europe before the end of the Mandate and merely awaited the lifting of the blockade along the coast of Palestine. By the first cease-fire, on June 11th, the army of Israel had acquired its first tanks, guns and military aircraft.

The main battles of the Arab Legion took place in and around Jerusalem. After a bitter struggle the Jewish quarter of the Old City was forced to surrender at the end of May 1948 and earlier, on the eve of the end of the British Mandate, the Arab Legion had captured the settlements of Gush Etzion. Jerusalem was surrounded and under siege with large units of the Legion dug in around the police fortress of Latrun and the villages of the area. In the besieged city, water had to be rationed and was doled out from horse-drawn carts which continued to circulate despite continuous artillery barrages. At the end of May the daily ration of the soldiers had to be cut to two slices of bread per man.

On May 25th an attack was launched against the positions of the Arab Legion in Latrun by a new brigade composed mainly of recent immigrants. Although it did not capture the fortress itself, it managed to break the siege by opening up an alternative route, a dirt track that skirted Latrun and over which supplies were carried into

(Top to bottom) CAMP IN THE FIELD; CAPTURE OF AN ARAB VILLAGE; BRIEFING BEFORE AN ATTACK (BY MOSHE DAYAN, LATER TO BE CHIEF OF STAFF); MORTAR TEAM IN ACTION.

EGYPTIAN SOLDIERS SURRENDERING.

the besieged city by mule and on the backs of men and, after improvements, by jeep and by truck. It was named the "Burma Road", after a great predecessor.

In the south the Egyptians advanced along the Negev roads, through the Arab city of Beersheba and moved to within thirty kilometers of Tel Aviv. Four settlements, Kfar Darom, Nirim, Beerot Yitzhak and Negba, which were located on roads vital to the Egyptians, were exposed to Egypt's most determined attacks. None of these was captured, but two other settlements, Yad Mordechai and Nitzanim, fell. But the momentum of the Egyptian advance had been diminished and it was brought to a halt when the first planes of Israel's new air force appeared in the sky.

The Syrians had expected to move along the eastern shore of Lake Tiberias, to capture the Jordan Valley, to unite with the Arabs in Nazareth, and from there advance towards Haifa. They were stopped at Degania in one of the major battles of the war. They succeeded in capturing Mishmar Hayarden in the north, but were unable to advance further to cut off even part of upper

Galilee. The Iraquis, repelled when they attacked in the Jordan Valley on the left flank of the Syrians, subsequently moved south, occupying the central part of Arab inhabited Palestine and the area known as the Arab Triangle. The Israel army failed to eject them from these areas but it succeeded in stopping their advance and in depriving them of all future initiative.

The Lebanese launched several attacks on the north, in the Malkieh area. At the time of the first cease-fire it was clear to all that the State of Israel was firmly established and that the military threat no longer endangered its existence. The cease-fire lasted twenty-eight days, and both sides exploited the breathing space for reorganization,

(Below) "SAMSON'S FOXES," THE ISRAELI COMMANDO FORCES WHICH HARASSSED THE ENEMY IN THE NEGEV.

training and re-equipment. The truce conditions precluded the entry of men of fighting age thus depriving Israel of reinforcements.

With the renewal of war on July 8th, the superiority of Israel's army, which had been officially sworn in during the truce, came into prominence. The Israelis attacked simultaneously on two fronts. In the center, Lydda and Ramle were captured, thereby reducing the pressure on Tel Aviv and gaining the largest airfield in the country, while the threat from Latrun was diminished though Latrun itself remained in the hands of the Arab Legion. In the north, Arab forces were forced out of additional areas in Galilee. On July 18th, the Security Council called for a further truce without specifying an expiration date.

In the south and in the Negev the front line of the second truce was virtually unchanged from that of the first truce.

The Egyptians limited their operations to the area surrounding the Negev settlements but the Israeli army did not succeed in breaking this stranglehold. Though Negba did not fall, Iraq Sweidan remained in Egyptian hands. In this situation an agreement was reached through the United Nations by which, for the duration of the second truce, Israeli forces were to be permitted free movement from north to south through Egyptian controlled territory during certain hours, and the Egyptians were to move from east to west through Israeli controlled territory at other hours of the day. The Egyptians did not abide by this agreement, and in October the Israel army launched another campaign to create a wide corridor to the Negev. After a week of fighting the road was open, Beersheba captured and most of the northern Negev cleared of enemy forces. An Egyptian force of brigade strength, with Col. Abdel Nasser as one of its senior officers, was surrounded in a pocket in the Faluja region. A number of attacks

on this pocket met with failure and the surrounded force was eventually allowed to retreat to Egypt under the armistice agreement.

The "Arab Liberation Army" in the north was determined to achieve some small success by capturing at least one Jewish settlement. Manara, overlooking the valley of the Huleh was attacked. In a lightning counter-move the Israeli forces launched an offensive that drove out the Arab forces from all of Upper Galilee in a mere fifty hours and pursued them into Lebanon. All of Galilee was freed from the enemy.

HOISTING THE ISRAEL FLAG IN NEWLY LIBERATED ELATH ON THE RED SEA.

The future of the Negev was still undecided, and the Egyptians continued to reject a United Nations resolution of November calling for armistice negotiations. Major fighting flared up once more in the Negev in December. This was "Operation Horev" which led to the fall of Asluj and Auja (Nitzana) with Israeli forces thrusting to Rafiah and deep into Egypt near El Arish on the coast. Pressure from the major powers compelled Israel to withdraw its forces to the old International frontier, without completing an attack that would have cut off from the south the Egyptian forces occupying the coastal region of Palestine, in what is now known as the Gaza Strip. The defeat of its army finally persuaded the government of Egypt to enter negotiations for an armistice, and the agreement was signed in February, on the Island of Rhodes. An armistice agreement with Lebanon followed shortly thereafter.

One further and important area that had been allocated to the State of Israel still remained beyond its jurisdiction: the southern Negev. In March, Israeli forces moved southward and with practically no resistance occupied the entire region up to Elath. With the raising of the Israel flag at the State's most southern point, the war came to an end. An armistice agreement was later signed with the Hashemite Kingdom of Jordan, and on July 20th, 1949, a fourth agreement, with Syria.

MAP OF THE WAR OF INDEPENDENCE.

 AREAS UNDER JEWISH CONTROL AT DECLARATION OF STATE, MAY 14, 1948.

 AREAS TAKEN BETWEEN MAY 14, 1948 AND JAN. 8. 1949.

AREAS ADDED TO ISRAEL BETWEEN JAN. 8, 1949 AND JULY 20, 1949 (DATE OF FINAL ARMISTICE AGREEMENT.).

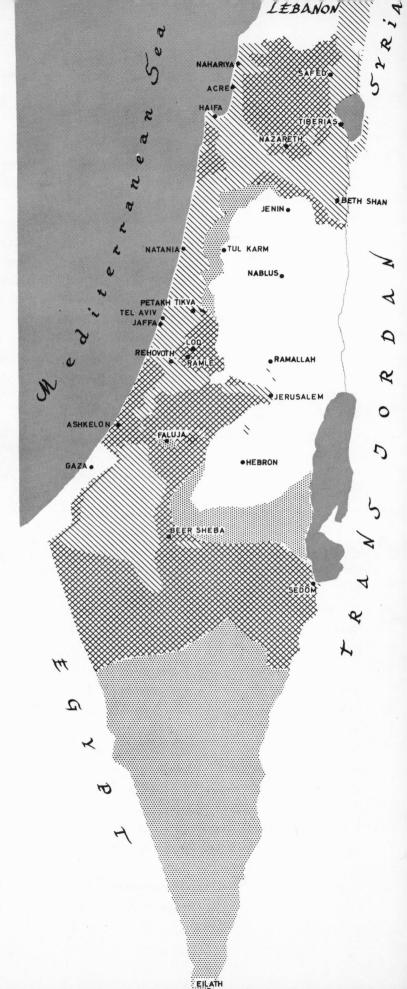

THE ILLUSTRATED HISTORY OF THE JEWS

THE RISE OF ISRAEL

FIFTEEN YEARS OF STATEHOOD

THE RISE OF ISRAEL

On Friday, May 14, 1948, at four o'clock in the afternoon at a modest but momentous ceremony in the Museum of Tel Aviv, David Ben Gurion rose to read the "Declaration of the Establishment of the State", formally declaring Israel's independence. It was to go into effect at midnight, the hour set for the termination of the British Mandate.

As Ben Gurion spoke, the armies of the neighboring Arab countries stood poised along the borders awaiting the order to invade and destroy the new State. They were to attack the following day, although some bombs from Egyptian planes were dropped during that night.

On the day of independence, at the United Nations' temporary headquarters in New York's Flushing Meadows, voices droned in unreal debate. Few in the General Assembly chamber realized that they had been overtaken by history until a Washington newsflash reached them, interrupting their deliberations. The news reported a statement by President Truman that "This Government has been informed that a Jewish State has been proclaimed in Palestine.... The United States recognizes the Provisional Government as the de facto authority of the new State of Israel."

The President issued his recognition declaration at 6.11 p.m. Washington time—eleven minutes after midnight Israel time—a bare eleven minutes after independence had gone into operation. From the Soviet Union recognition came three days later. The existence of Israel was a fact—albeit a precarious one.

With the proclamation of statehood, a Provisional Government and a Provisional Council of State were established. They were in fact the interim Cabinet and Parliament of Israel until the general election took place on January 25, 1949, and gave way to the popularly elected Knesset,

(Right) THE DECLARATION OF INDEPENDENCE, SIGNED IN TEL AVIV ON MAY 14, 1948.

comprising 120 members, and the Government, constituted on the basis of its command of a Knesset majority.

Israel, like Great Britain, has no "written constitution", but its democratic forms are guaranteed by a series of Fundamental Laws. Supreme authority is vested in the Knesset. Executive power resides with the Prime Minister and Cabinet who are answerable to the Knesset; they remain in office only so long as they command the confidence of the Knesset. The President, head of State, stands above politics. He is elected for a five years' term by a majority of the Knesset. One of the most popular early acts of the Provisional Council of State was to vote Dr. Chaim Weizmann, the renowned Zionist leader and scientist, as first President of the new State of Israel.

Following the January 1949 elections, many countries which had not yet done so rushed to extend diplomatic recognition to Israel. They were

(*Above*) DR. CHAIM WEIZMANN TAKING THE OATH AS FIRST PRESIDENT OF THE STATE OF ISRAEL.
(*Below*) IMMIGRANTS MOVING INTO THEIR NEW HOMES IN ISRAEL.

undoubtedly also encouraged to do so by the fact that, though hostilities were not yet over, it was clear that the Arab invasion had failed and that Israel had won its war of independence. On February 24, an armistice agreement was signed with Egypt. On that very day, Israel submitted a request to the Security Council for membership of the United Nations. By then, of the 58 countries who were members of the UN, 45 had recognized Israel. A week later, the Council recommended approval, and on May 11, the General Assembly formally accepted the recommendation and admitted Israel as a member of the UN. It was a year, almost to the day, since independence had been proclaimed.

Much had happened in that year. Born and cradled on the battlefield, the new State was confronted by unique burdens, all of which had to be shouldered immediately and simultaneously. No

newly emergent State had ever had to face such problems. In the midst of fighting for her life along all her frontiers, and having to train, arm, feed, clothe and transport her troops, Israel also had to cope with the anarchy left by the Mandatory authority; create the machinery of government and staff a State administration in its entirety; develop her resources and secure additional funds to meet the enormous expenditures, swollen by military needs; and fling open her gates to Jewish immigrants, notably the hundreds of thousands languishing in the Displaced Persons camps in Europe and the internment camps of Cyprus.

Perhaps the most expressive act which symbolized the true meaning of Israel's independence was the abolition of the Mandatory restrictions on Jewish immigration and the welcoming of all Jews seeking to enter the new State. Statutory sanction to this "open door" policy was given in the "Law of the Return" entitling any Jew the inherent right to enter Israel and become a citizen. Streams of newcomers poured in. No one was daunted by the fact that there was a war. Indeed, many arrived eager to participate in Israel's defense. The numbers mounted month after month. The figures were staggering. By 1961, the immigration total exceeded a million.

The immigrants were of course to prove a massive factor in the development of the country. But in the early months and years they were a heavy charge on an already overburdened national ex-

(Above) LEARNING THE LANGUAGE; ONE OF THE MANY INTENSIVE HEBREW COURSES FOR NEWCOMERS. (Below) IMMIGRANTS ARRIVE BY AIR FROM YEMEN, AND BY SEA FROM EUROPE.

HAIFA PORT, MARITIME GATEWAY TO ISRAEL.

MODERN TRANSPORT IN ISRAEL.

HOUSING FOR NEW IMMIGRANTS.
(Above) THE TALPIOT QUARTER IN
JERUSALEM. *(Left, top)* THE NEW
TOWN OF KIRYAT SHMONE. *(Left, bottom)* A NEW SUBURB OF BEER-SHEBA.

THREE VIEWS OF ELATH, ISRAEL'S GATEWAY TO EAST
AFRICA AND ASIA. *(Above)* THE AIRPORT. *(Top right)*
THE HARBOUR. *(Bottom right)* RESIDENTIAL QUARTERS.

HEAVY INDUSTRY.
(Opposite, top) **CEMENT WORKS NEAR HAIFA.** *(Above and opposite, bottom)* **DEAD SEA WORKS CHEMICALS PLANT.**

SOLAR ENERGY COLLECTOR DEVELOPED BY THE
NEGEV RESEARCH INSTITUTE.

EXPERIMENTAL NUCLEAR REACTOR AT NAHAL RUBIN.

TWO KIBBUTZIM: TEL YOSEF *(Top)* AND BET HASHITTA.

INDEPENDENCE DAY PARADE IN JERUSALEM.

THE TOMB OF THEODOR HERZL IN JERUSALEM.

THE SINAI CAMPAIGN, 1956.
(Left to right, top to bottom) TANKS IN ACTION; EGYPTIAN PRISONERS; CAPTURED EGYPTIAN GUN POSITION OVERLOOKING THE ENTRANCE TO THE GULF OF ELATH; ISRAELI SOLDIERS IN THEIR FOXHOLES; THE SPOILS OF WAR; EGYPTIAN SOLDIERS SURRENDERING; WAITING TO GO INTO ACTION; THE ISRAELI FLAG OVER MOUNT SINAI; ENTERING ENEMY TERRITORY.

chequer. Almost all were without means, having come from countries of poverty and persecution. They had to be fed, clothed, sheltered and cared for until they could start earning a living. Their supplies limited, the people of Israel shared equally with the newcomers, accepting a rigid system of rationing. With the immigration rate rapidly overtaking the pace of house-building, scores of thousands were given shelter in tented or hutted transit centres. In time, however, with financial help from overseas Jews, notably the Jews of America, and with international loans, and the taxation of Israel's population, a national housing program

was launched to ensure permanent shelter for immigrants.

In time, too, a large number of immigrants settled on the land and industrial projects were built, offering productive employment. Immigrants who had been a "financial liability" on their arrival were now a vital asset, assisting newer immigrants and contributing to the wealth of the nation. The successful integration of the newcomers into the economy of the country—social and cultural integration would be a longer process—was a spectacular vindication of a visionary policy by the architects of Israel's independence.

Israel signed an armistice agreement with her fourth warring neighbor, Syria, on July 20, 1949. (The February armistice with Egypt had been followed by similar agreements with Lebanon in March and with Jordan in April.)

However, hostility, sporadic attack and the open threat of another invasion by the Arab States have provided the dangerous background against which Israel's remarkably varied and revolutionary development has been carried out. The years that followed the 1949 armistice were years of brittle truce, shattered every so often by Arab marauding assaults across the borders, reprisal raids by Israel forces, and an Arab military build-up for a "second round". Matters came to a head in 1956. In that year, strengthened and made confident by a massive arms deal with the Soviet bloc in September 1955, Egypt stepped up her incursions into Israel from bases in the Gaza Strip and the Sinai peninsula, and closed the Suez Canal to Israel shipping and to all ships trading with Israel. Egyptian coastal guns at the southern end of the Gulf of Aqaba blockaded Israel's port of Elath, cutting Israel's maritime lines to the East.

On October 29, 1956, Israel struck back. In a lightning six days' campaign, she routed the Egyp-

DAVID BEN GURION, PRIME MINISTER OF ISRAEL FOR MOST OF ITS FIRST FIFTEEN YEARS, ADDRESSING THE NATION.

tian forces, drove them from Sinai and Gaza, smashed the fedayun strongholds there, destroyed a good part of their newly acquired Soviet armaments, and broke the blockade of Elath.

Emergency resolutions of the United Nations called upon Israel to withdraw from Sinai and the Gaza Strip. Israel insisted on remaining until Egypt would offer appropriate guarantees backed up by a UN Emergency Force stationed on the Gulf of Aqaba, along the Israel-Sinai frontier and in the Gaza Strip. When this action was accomplished, Israel withdrew, the last Israel soldier retiring on March 8, 1957. The UN Force is still posted in the former trouble spots and Israel has enjoyed comparative peace ever since.

In the international sphere, Israel has developed a reputation out of all proportion to her size. The addition of newly independent states since Israel herself became free has enabled her to establish an impressive network of relationships. Her friendship with the newly independent states of Asia and Africa, despite persistent Arab efforts to undermine that friendship, is particularly notable. Many of these governments were deeply impressed not only by her development but also by the spirit of pioneering in the country. They requested technical aid which Israel was glad to extend, sending hundreds of experts, allowing an increasing number af Africans and Asians to come to Israel for study and training and establishing joint enterprises. In a basic way, the aid extended

PRESIDENT BEN ZVI TAKING THE OATH OF OFFICE FOR HIS SECOND TERM.

by Israel to these young states only a few years after she herself acquired statehood is in itself expressive testimony to the remarkable development of her land, her resources and her people.

Celebrating fifteen years of statehood, Israel could look back on a period of immense effort and sacrifice as well as immense achievement. Her enemies had been routed and swept from the soil of Israel. Her Declaration of Independence stood the test of battle. It had been given immediate meaning by the welcoming of Jewish immigrants. A State administration was established and runs smoothly. Democratic elections had been held and a constitutional parliament and stable government are going about their business. Israel had been formally admitted into the family of nations as an equal and sovereign member, and her prestige in

THE EICHMANN TRIAL IN JERUSALEM. THE ACCUSED IS SEEN IN THE SPECIAL BULLET-PROOF DOCK.

the world is high. Economically it achieved goals nobody dared to dream about, and it is rapidly developing and advancing the welfare of her people, both those already there and the masses who would be coming. The years ahead could be dangerous and difficult. But with her experience of the grim struggles she had just encountered and successfully overcome, she can look to the future with quiet confidence.

THE THIRD PRESIDENT OF ISRAEL, MR. ZALMAN SHAZAR, TAKES OATH OF OFFICE AT A SPECIAL SESSION OF THE KNESSET (ISRAEL'S PARLIAMENT), SUCCEEDING THE LATE PRESIDENT ITZHAK BEN-ZVI, MAY 1963.

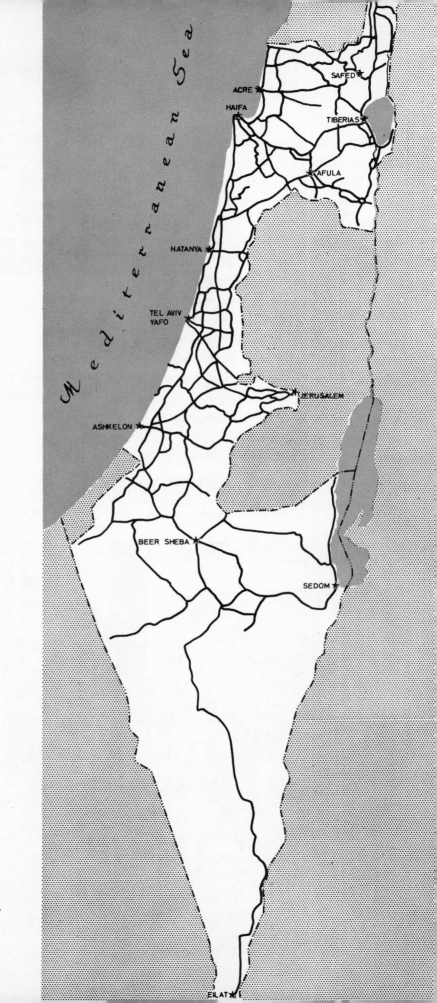

ROAD MAP OF ISRAEL.

THE ILLUSTRATED HISTORY OF THE JEWS

THE RISE OF ISRAEL

THE NEW ANCIENT LAND

THE EMBLEM OF THE STATE OF ISRAEL.

THE RISE OF ISRAEL

The overall task of developing Israel was nothing less than the rapid and revolutionary conversion of a backward colonial territory into a modern sovereign State, able to sustain a vastly expanding population at 20th Century standards.

While the fighting was on, the economic and social planners were busy, charged with devising a master plan to build and defend the State. They had to create a system which would enable the nation to work yet be prepared at any moment of the day and night to meet and beat an attack. It is not surprising, in the Land of the Bible, that they proposed a modern version of the "one hand on the plough, the other on the sword" principle, broadly envisioning a citizen army.

Israel's system of defense, which went into effect early in 1950 and which is still used, is based on a comparatively small Regular Army; on National service conscripts, mobilized at the age of 18, young men for 2½ years, women for 2 years; on frontier settlements; and on the reserves which include every able-bodied male up to the age of 49 and most childless women up to the age of 34. The key feature of this system is the speed and efficiency with which the reserves can be called into action. The mobilization procedure is probably the fastest in the world. An entire division can be assembled, equipped, transported and flung against the enemy in 24 hours. This means that the bulk of the population can proceed with their productive labors right up to the moment of attack, the first

THE ENTRANCE TO THE CITY OF JERUSALEM. THE NATIONAL CONVENTION CENTER, SITE OF ZIONIST CONGRESSES, IS ON THE RIGHT.

shock being held by the regular and conscript forces and the border villages.

Behind this protective shield, Israel could proceed with the development of the country. A major priority was the enlargement of agricultural settlement in order to raise food for the growing population and raw materials for local industry; to cut down imports and speed progress towards self-sufficiency. The results have been remarkable by any standards, particularly so when it is recalled that Jews had been divorced from the soil for centuries and that most of Israel's farmers today are newcomers who had never worked on the land.

The special types of agricultural society fashioned by Israel's pioneers before the birth of the State have continued. The kibbutz, that idealistic pattern of living whose members share their material wealth and respect the principle of human brotherhood, grows apace, and new kibbutzim are established each year. More popular among the immigrants is the moshav type of settlement, the cooperative smallholders' villages, an offshoot of the kibbutz, where members live with their families in their own houses, work their own plots, but cooperate with each other on marketing and purchasing and tend the fields of fellow-members when they are sick. These two forms of agricultural organization account for the bulk of the country's farming. Private farms and plantations account for the rest.

The key to agriculture is water. Since Biblical times, when the Patriarchs wandered with their

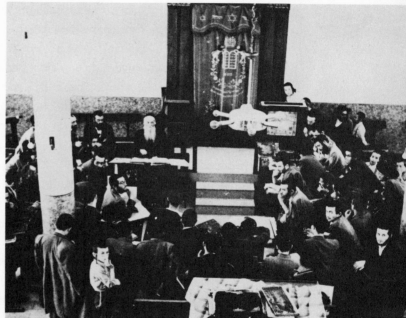

STUDYING THE TORAH: *(Top)* YEMENITES; *(Bottom)* HASSIDIM.

flocks from well to well, Israel has been a thirsty land. The rains fall only in winter and only the north is well-watered. Major irrigation projects were started according to particular needs of the time. The most spectacular scheme, soon to be completed, is the National Water Carrier, which will bring water from the River Jordan in the north to the Negev in the south, and link up with

(Below) THE LATE RABBI MAIMON ADDRESSING A RABBINICAL CONVENTION.

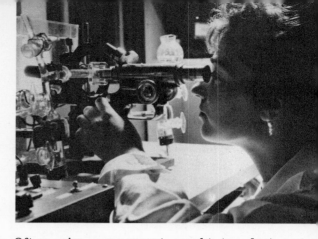

regional projects already functioning. Israel scientists are also engaged in exciting research on methods to turn salt and brackish water into fresh water.

Before 1948, the emphasis in the country's economy was on agriculture, and the impact of this "back to the land" movement on the new Israel was impressive and permanent. With statehood, however, and the need for fast development similar pioneer efforts turned towards industrialization. As a result, Israel's industrial development has also been outstanding, covering a volume and variety of manufactured goods and basic materials which previously had all to be imported. Here, too, the aim has been to reduce imports and boost exports.

Understandably, Israel is interested in the prospect of cheap atomic power in the next decade and maintains two atomic reactors. Local scientists are world renowned for their successful research in the harnessing of solar energy.

The creation of a working population with a variety of skills drawn from an immigration from lands where such skills were largely unknown was as important a factor in the moulding of a people as it was in the economic development of the coun-

(Above) A YOUNG RESEARCHER AT WORK IN THE HEBREW UNIVERSITY'S LABORATORIES.
(Below) ONE OF THE READING ROOMS OF THE NATIONAL AND UNIVERSITY LIBRARY.

try. Often, wise management sought to adapt native skills to modern needs. A plant making the giant irrigation pipes, for example, used Yemenite immigrants as welders. It was found that these men, expert craftsmen in silver filigree work back in the Yemen, possessed the concentration, accuracy and manual dexterity required for welding. To witness one of these men lifting the modern visor of his light-shield, revealing the gentle beard and curls of a medieval face, is to recognize that he jumped from the Middle Ages to the 20th Century. This leap was taken by countless immigrants to Israel, with the goodwill and help of the veteran settlers.

To serve the new farms and factories with a modern communications system, hundreds of miles of new highways and access roads were laid and old tracks paved; the railway network was extended and completely modernized and two new communications branches were created—air and sea. Israel took to the air and its National Airline, ElAl, which began in 1948 with two small planes, has grown into a large concern serving international routes. Equally, the merchant fleet has grown twentyfold and now sails to all the continents in the world. The international airport at Lod has been rebuilt; Haifa port has been greatly enlarged; a second deep water harbour is under construction at Ashdod, south of Tel Aviv; and Elath is being developed as the gateway to East Africa and Asia.

Funds to finance these enormous development projects come from local taxation; gifts from Jewish communities overseas, with American Jews very much in the lead, who consider themselves jointly responsible, with Israelis, for the welfare

THE ROAD TO JERUSALEM WINDING THROUGH THE
JUDEAN HILLS.

THE SYNAGOGUE AT THE HEBREW UNIVERSITY'S HA-
DASSAH HOSPITAL IN EIN-KEREM, NEAR JERUSALEM. THE
STAINED GLASS WINDOWS ARE THE WORK OF THE RE-
NOWNED ARTIST, MARC CHAGALL.

JERUSALEM, HEICHAL SHLOMO.
THREE OF THE SYNAGOGUE WINDOWS DEPICT PESACH,
SHAVUOT AND SUCCOT.

A BOKHARAN JEW READING FROM THE TORAH.

WORSHIPPERS OUTSIDE THE TOMB OF SHIMON BAR YOKHAI AT MERON.

KIBBUTZ YOUNGSTERS.

SELECTING WILLOW BRANCHES FOR THE SUKKOT
FESTIVAL.

HIKING IN THE NEGEV.

THE NEGEV MOUNTAIN RANGE.

MARKET DAY IN BEERSHEBA, CAPITAL OF THE NEGEV.

THE BARAK CANYON IN THE NEGEV.

(Top) THE VALLEY OF JEZREEL SEEN FROM THE BAL-
FOUR FOREST. *(Bottom)* THE NEGEV MOUNTAINS WITH
THE GULF OF ELATH IN THE BACKGROUND.

THE ANCIENT CITY OF ACRE.

THE ROMAN AMPHITHEATRE IN CAESAREA.

VIEW OF TEL-AVIV FROM ANCIENT JAFFA.

OCEAN FRONT OF TEL-AVIV.

GENERAL VIEW OF HAIFA

NEW SUBURB IN BEERSHEBA.

THE CAMPUS OF THE HEBREW UNIVERSITY OF JERUSA-
LEM AS SEEN FROM THE ARCHAEOLOGICAL INSTITUTE.

OLD AND NEW IN JERUSALEM. THE MODERN HEAD-
QUARTERS OF THE LABOR FEDERATION ADJOINS THE
MINARET OF AN ANCIENT MOSQUE AND A DOMED ARAB
TOMB.

of Jewish immigrants; loans from such bodies as the World Bank; grants-in-aid and loans from the United States Government; reparations from West Germany; and private investment. Israel has a high reputation with international financial institutions as a country which utilizes its development funds strictly for new projects and which repays its loans in installments. Foreign investors have been inspired by the presence in Israel of a skilled and hardworking people and by the Law for the Encouragement of Capital Investment which offers inducements, like tax relief, to enterprises which increase the country's economy.

Economic progress has been accompanied by matching advances in the social services. One of the first bills passed by the Knesset established free, universal, compulsory, primary education, from the age of 5 to 14. For the "People of The Book", education is considered a cardinal right. Many proceed from primary schools to vocational schools where they receive special training in technical skills. The three most renowned centers of higher learning are the internationally famed Hebrew University of Jerusalem, the Weizmann Institute of Science at Rehovoth and the Haifa Technion.

One of the unique features of Israel's adult education program is the Ulpan, specially designed to give new immigrants a rapid and intensive course in Hebrew, the principal language of the country. This special and successful teaching system has been evolved by the leading pedagogic experts. Hebrew is a difficult tongue. Children have no problem. They learn it quickly at school and at play with their friends. Adult immigrants, however, who are unfamiliar with it on arrival, find it more difficult. But they need to know it if they are to find their place in the social and economic life of the country.

Israel—a land of wonder, continually changing before one's eyes, filled with color and vigor—is the same land as in Biblical days, yet barely recognizable with her new face and new facets. Israel is a

AN AERIAL VIEW OF TEL AVIV. THE DOMED BUILDING AT LOWER LEFT IS THE GREAT SYNAGOGUE.

(Left) THE "HABIMAH" NATIONAL THEATRE PER-
FORMING ITS CLASSIC PLAY "THE DYBBUK".
(Right) A PLAY PERFORMED BY THE CHAMBER
THEATRE.

land where yesterday and tomorrow combine to
form an exciting today.

Traditional Jewish values flourish in new ways
in modern Israel. The inherited emphasis on education and scholarship is reflected in the educational system which provides schooling from
kindergarten to university. Rapid progress is
being made in such fields as nuclear physics, de-
salination of water, exploitation of solar energy,
medicine and agriculture, and in Israel's institutes
of higher learning and scientific research. Metero-
logical rockets have been fired to aid in the study
of advancement in space, and a new atomic reactor
in the Negev is considered a pioneer station for
atomic power development.

The Jewish appreciation of culture is evident in
the increasing activities in music, art, drama and
literature. Both residents and tourists value a visit
to Bezalel, the world-renowned Museum and Institute of Arts in Jerusalem. The sight of old and
new Jerusalem seen from the modern, beautiful
campus of the Hebrew University is also gratify-
ing. There is no greater way to determine the
dynamism of the country than to contrast the
ancient architecture with the quantity of new
constructions.

The announcement "We build" is heard throughout Israel: in the cities and in the settlements; in
the industrial and commercial centers of the
coastal region on the Mediterranean shore; in the
new port of Ashdod, an indication of future sea-
faring commerce; and in the Negev, whose resources are only now being discovered.

The differences of geography, climate and people stand side by side in contrast. The past has
provided a basis for the surging changes. The old-
timers and the sabras, the old and new immigrants,
create new patterns of relationships among each
other and integrate with those who have lived
there previously. The population is comprised of
people from over a hundred different countries.
Jews from every community throughout all of
Europe live side by side with Jews from Asia,
Africa, the Middle East, and North and South
America. The Jews of Israel, sabra and immigrant,
work together in their daily lives to create a new
life and a new destiny.

Israel has a place for everyone. The coolness of
Jerusalem's stone houses in the stark and wooded
hills of Judea; the deep green Galilee whose forests contain springs in their depths; the views
from Nazareth, especially the view of the Emek
spreading its rusty brown earth; the calm Mediterranean at dawn and its surly noise at night;
the sweet smell of orange blossoms as one
drives down the coast to Tel Aviv on a modern
highway; the jewel-like lights on the Haifa hills
at night; the desert winds and mists in the southern Negev under a full moon appeal to all people.

Every phase of life has changed in modern Israel. The holidays have a new significance reflected in new forms. New holidays, such as Independence Day and Memorial Day, have been created. Passover, the holiday signifying freedom, is now celebrated with an actual feeling of freedom. And the Eternal Prayer of the House of Israel, the wish for "Next year in Jerusalem...", has become living reality.

The ancient and the new stand together. Some Israeli citizens—Moslem and Christian Arabs, Druze and other minority groups—are still inclined to cling to the ways of life of their ancestors. Yet the ancient traditions change slowly to give way to the burdens and bounties of modern culture.

Israel is a place for activity. Hiking through the Negev wastelands to the wells of Ein Gedi; exploring the Barak Canyon; swimming at the Sachneh; standing on the top of Mitzpe Ramon; buying in supermarkets; visiting the artists in Safed; enjoying the baths of Tiberias; relaxing in luxurious resorts and nightclubs; walking through beautiful Jerusalem at night; working and playing and simple good living from day to day—all of these are found in Israel.

Israel is known to all ages of man. Throughout the annals of history, Israel has been The Land. Here are the remnants of world conquerors who

(Top) PRESIDENT BEN ZVI ADDRESSING A CONGRESS DEVOTED TO CONTEMPORARY JUDAISM IN JERUSALEM. *(Below)* OLD AND NEW IN HAIFA: A RECENTLY CONSTRUCTED GRAIN SILO CONTRASTS WITH THE OLD HOUSES IN THE LOWER TOWN.

came, built, destroyed, and left with the feeling of the mystery and grandeur of everything they touched. Here are Roman remains and Crusader castles. Here is a desolate barrenness and a trove of rich treasures recording the history of mankind. All of these things can be found everywhere. This is the land whose names, people and places reflect the holy words that even today means the essence of human aspiration. This is home.

APPENDIX

WORLD JEWISH POPULATION

A statistical appraisal of the numbers, structure, natural and migratory movements of the Jewish people throughout the world, is difficult to estimate, because of inadequate data and the coordination of the existing fragmentary material. In fact, official demographic censuses in the past decade, have covered less than half of the Jewish world population, by means of questions on religion or ethnic origin or other characteristics. In other countries, approximate estimates or guesses can be gathered, due to the initiative of Jewish institutions and other bodies. Differences of opinion regarding the proper definition of "Jew", for the purpose of the collection of statistical data, add to the difficulties in collecting Jewish statistics. Differences of definition arise in the face of secession or estrangement from Judaism or organised Jewry, issues of mixed marriages, etc.

Despite this, some knowledge on the order of magnitude of the present world Jewish population is available. It may be roughly estimated that world Jewry comprises today about 12,900,000 people. Maps B and C in this book display the geographic distribution in 1960, i.e., before the mass

*according to figures based on the official USSR census of 1959; however that census probably

exodus from former French North Africa. The latest available data for the beginning of 1963 would indicate the following breakdown by continents:

WORLD JEWISH POPULATION
(rough estimates)

	Absolute numbers (in thousands)	Percentage
World Total	12,900	100.0
Africa	310	2.4
Asia (incl. Asian parts of USSR and Turkey)	2,600	20.2
Americas	6,470	50.2
Europe	3,450	26.7
Oceania	70	0.5

The Jews are widely scattered; some 70 countries have a Jewish population of 500 people or more. Among them, the United States (with some 5,500,000) USSR (with some 2,300,000*) and Israel (with 2,070,000) include about 76% of world Jewry. Map C in which the Jewry of each country is indicated

gave an under-representation of the number of Jews in USSR.

by a circle, the area of which is proportional to the number represented, gives a geographical picture of this distribution. While the circles corresponding to the three principal centers of Jewish residence appear dominant, in the map, the Jewish populations of France, Great Britain, Argentina and Canada also count each between a quarter and half a million.

The geographical distribution of Jews today is the result of a series of transformations and events which have deeply affected the demography of the Jewish people during the past 100 years. Among the major events were:

1) During the period between the middle of the 19th century and the First World War, the Jews took an active part in the vast migratory movement from Europe to the New World. As shown by map A, millions of Jews left antisemitic Czarist Russia and Rumania, poverty-stricken Galicia etc. and sought asylum in the USA, Argentina, South Africa and other overseas countries. Search of freedom, personal safety and economic security were at the roots of this mass movement. Demographic pressure, exerted because of high fertility coupled with reduced mortality, also contributed.

2) Increasing obstacles blocking the way of international migration were set up by certain immigration countries (i.e., the USA), as well as some former emigration countries (i.e., the USSR.) The streams of Jewish emigration from Europe were rechannelled between the First World War and the establishment of the State of Israel. During this period Argentina, Brazil and Canada grew in importance as absorption countries for Jewish migrants. (In map A, which shows the intake of Jewish overseas migrants by major immigration countries over three periods, the area of the bars is proportional to the respective number of immigrants; the width of the bars corresponds to the relative length of the period.)

3) In this second period too, tiny Eretz Israel emerges for the first time in the modern era as a country able to absorb substantial numbers of Jewish immigrants. In fact, during 1915-1947, about 30% of Jewish intercontinental migrants entered this country as compared to 3% in the period 1880-1914.

4) During the Second World War, the mass extermination perpetrated by the Nazis destroyed about one third of the Jewish people and gravely impaired the age and sex distribution of the surviving remnants of the Jewish communities throughout Europe and brought about further displacement of the Jews.

5) The establishment of the State of Israel in May 1948 precipitated the "Ingathering of the Exiles"—the influx of Jews to Israel. This is indicated in map A, which shows that in 1948 Israel became the main country of Jewish immigration. The recent mass immigration has reached Israel in successive ways, the largest of which occurred between 1948 and 1951 and included about 335,000 persons from Europe, largely survivors of Nazi oppression, and 330,000 from Asia and Africa, among the latter almost the entire Jewish communities of Yemen, Libya and Iraq.

6) Recently another focus of emigration has arisen in the formerly French-dominated countries of North Africa, due to the upheavals resulting from the attainment of independence by Tunis, Morocco and Algiers. This emigration has been directed partly towards Israel and partly towards France.

As shown by map B, in the middle of the 19th Century, i.e. at the start of the migration movement mentioned in paragraph 1) above, the Jewish people was largely European—with some 65% of its population in Eastern Europe and the Balkans, 22% in other parts of Europe and only 13% in other continents.

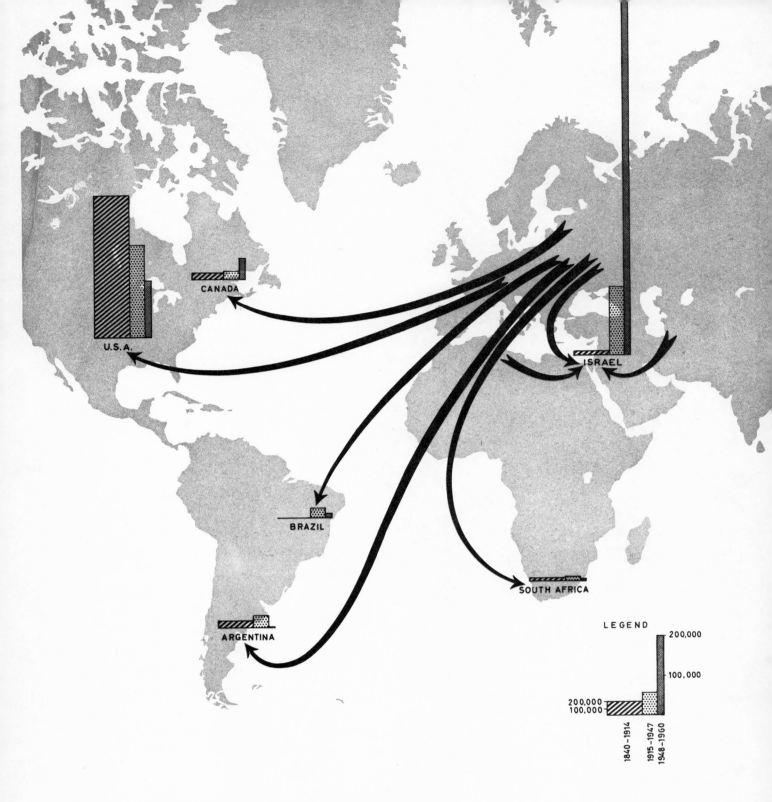

CANADA

U.S.A.

ISRAEL

BRAZIL

SOUTH AFRICA

ARGENTINA

LEGEND

200,000

100,000

200,000
100,000

1840–1914

1915–1947

1948–1960

A   JEWISH INTERCONTINENTAL MIGRATION MOVES TO
    COUNTRIES HAVING JEWISH POPULATION OF 100,000
    AND OVER. 1840 TO 1960.

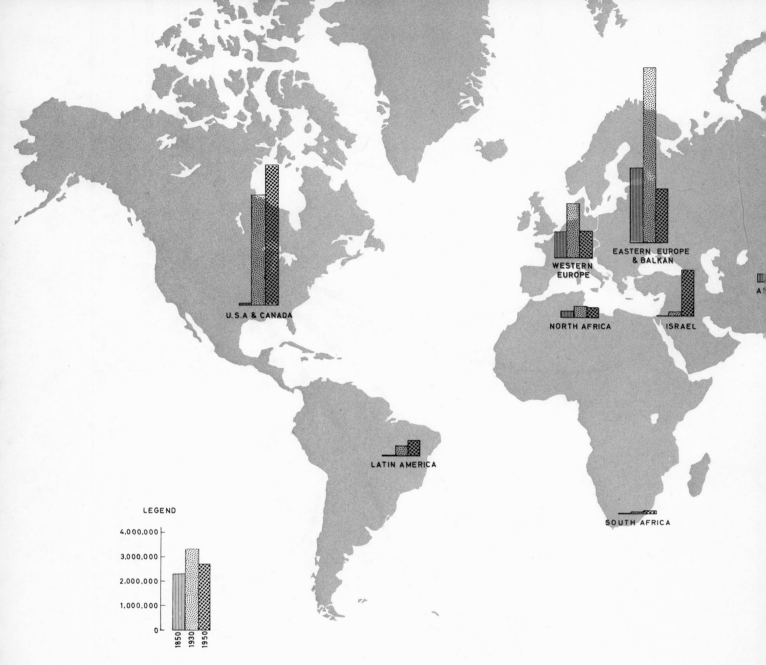

LEGEND

4,000,000

3,000,000

2,000,000

1,000,000

0

1850 1930 1950

U.S.A & CANADA

LATIN AMERICA

WESTERN EUROPE

EASTERN EUROPE & BALKAN

NORTH AFRICA

ISRAEL

SOUTH AFRICA

B REGIONAL DISTRIBUTION OF WORLD JEWISH POPU-
LATION—1850, 1930, 1960.

AUSTRALIA &
NEW ZEALAND

The mass emigration mentioned under 1) and 2), created the vast modern Jewry of the USA and Canada as well as the Jewish communities of Latin America, South Africa and Oceania. This again can be seen in map B, where the situation in 1930 is compared with that of 1850. The considerable natural increase which characterized Eastern European Jewry during most of the period from 1850 to 1930 enabled the Jews to increase in numbers while sending millions of its children overseas. In relative numbers, European Jewry decreased from 87% in 1850 to 61% in 1930, whereas the percentage of Jews in both North and Latin America increased from 1% to 32%.

The Holocaust and recent migratory movements, as set out in paragraphs 4), 5), and 6) above, have strengthened both the relative and the absolute weight of the Jewries outside Europe, as pointed out in the comparison of data for 1930 and 1960 in map B. The increase in the share of Israel is particularly striking.

Map D shows the detailed distribution of the Jewish population in the three major countries of Jewish residence:

The big concentrations in towns, in the USA mainly those along the Atlantic coast: the huge community of Greater New York (about 2,300,000 Jews) constitutes the biggest Jewish center in any locality in the world. The Jews have also been moving toward the west. On the whole, the proportion of USA Jews living in "urbanized areas" over quarter of a million inhabitants is 87%. The Jews, usually town-dwellers, have become inhabitants of the big cities and agglomerations that have sprung up (including their suburbs) in the USA.

Map D shows the distribution of the Jews by republics according to the 1959 census in the USSR (some Soviet Republics in Asia with comparatively small Jewish communities are indicated collectively in the map). The great majority of Jews

JEWISH POPULATION

500-2,500 ○

2,500-7,500 ◖

7,500-12,500 ●

50,000 ●

100,000 ●

1,000,000 ●

C WORLD JEWISH POPULATION BY COUNTRIES (COUN-
TRIES WITH JEWISH COMMUNITIES OF MORE THAN
500). 1960.

appear to be located in the Western part of the USSR territory.

Regarding Israel, Map D shows the location of places with 10,000 Jews or more: Tel-Aviv and its satellite towns, Haifa and Jerusalem, stand out as major urban centers. Aside from the larger urban localities indicated in the map, comprising 76% of the Jewish population, there are in Israel 30 other urban places and 708 rural settlements predominently inhabited by Jews (according to the 1961 population census).

While it is not possible today to determine properly the natural increase of the entire Jewish population throughout the world, it is sufficiently clear that considerable differences exist and that various Jewish communities of Central and Western Europe are heading for a decline—because the death rate exceeds the birthrate, which, in turn, is due to low fertility, distorted age structure, mixed marriages, etc. On the other hand, Israel has a considerable natural increase, due mainly to the generally low mortality in relation to the still high (though lowering) fertility of those parts of its Jewish population which hail from Asia and Africa.

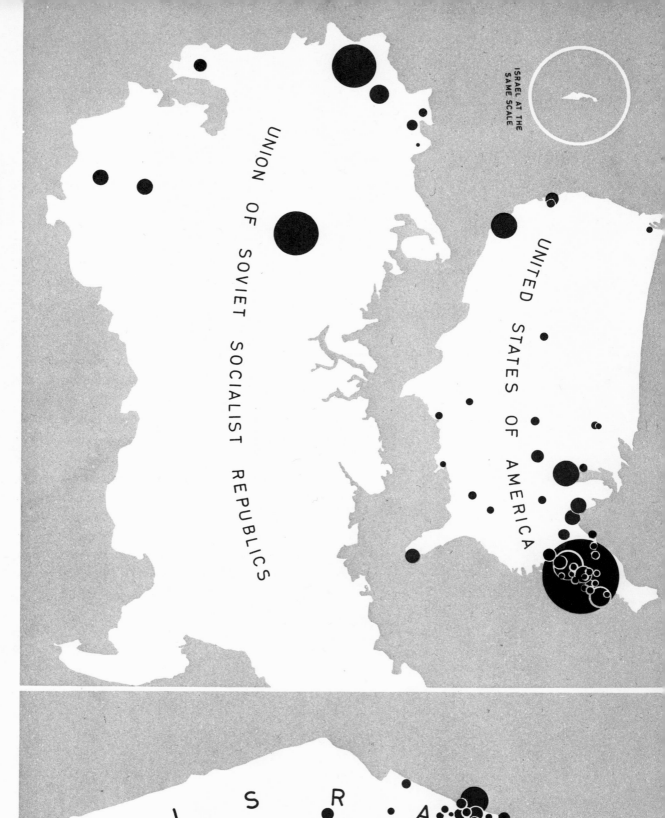

ISRAEL AT THE
SAME SCALE

UNION OF SOVIET SOCIALIST REPUBLICS

UNITED STATES OF AMERICA

I S R A E L

JEWISH POPULATION

1,000,000

500,000

100,000

50,000

25,000

10,000

D MAJOR JEWISH CENTERS IN U.S.A., U.S.S.R., AND ISRAEL
(LOCALITIES WITH MORE THAN 10,000 JEWS IN U.S.A.
AND ISRAEL; REPUBLICS IN U.S.S.R.), 1960.

INDEX

ויקח מאבני המקום

כם במקום ההוא ויחלם

וראשו מגיע השמימה

לים ויירדים בו והנה

ני יהוה אלהי אברהם

רץ אשר אתה שכב

ר והיה זרעך כעפר

ה וצפנה ונגבה

האר צה ונבר שך